MW01679474

The Magical Link:

Love, Mystery and Other Secrets About the Bond Between People and Animals

By

Barbara Meyers

www.holisticanimalconsulting.com

Guardian Press

www.themagicallink.com

Although the information and recommendations set forth herein (hereinafter "Information") are presented in good faith and believed by the author, Barbara Meyers, to be correct as of the date hereof, Barbara Meyers makes no representations or warranties as to the completeness or accuracy thereof. Information is supplied upon the condition that the persons receiving same will make their own determination as to its suitability for their purposes prior to use and will be solely responsible for any and all consequences of any nature whatsoever resulting from the use of or reliance upon Information.

Internet addresses and business contact information given in this book were accurate at the time of publication.

ISBN 978-0-615-70822-5

This book may be purchased for business or promotional use, or for special sales. For information, please write to secrets@themagicallink.com

Printed in the United States of America

www.themagicallink.com

For Jonah

Giving Back

"There are those who give with joy, and that joy is their reward." ... Kahlil Gibran (1833 – 1931).

An unsparingly generous portion of the proceeds of this book will be given to animal advocacy organizations. This gift will help to further the advancement of the struggle to end animal cruelty, abuse, neglect and exploitation, and protect wildlife and their habitats. Through the promotion of kindness and compassion, humane education, legislation, the investigation and exposure of crimes against animals, the chains of injustice will be broken one link at a time... until they are no more.

This book has been reviewed for veterinary medical accuracy
by John G. Hynes, DVM

Photo provided by John G. Hynes, DVM

John G. Hynes, DVM, is a 1991 Graduate of The College of Veterinary Medicine at Mississippi State University.

Licensed to practice in New York, New Jersey, Pennsylvania and Vermont, he is also USDA accredited in New York.

Dr. Hynes practices small animal medicine with the rare combination of competence and the art of compassionate care. Some are competent, some are caring but few are both! Among his many contributions to the profession and to those in his care, he serves on the Board of Directors for PATH – People Protecting Animals and their Habitats. www.path.org

John G Hynes, DVM

Veterinarian, friend and champion of all animals.

Contents

Intro-knowledgements

Your author's version of the introduction to and acknowledgements of *The Magical Link: Love Mystery and Other Secrets About the Bond Between People and Animals.*

Where does one begin and how much do I dare burden you, my dear reader, with an Academy Award-style of endless thanks and babbling? As said by the King to Anna in *Anna and the King of Siam,* "Tis a puzzlement." I think myself a solver of problems and *puzzlements* so this is my attempt. *You* will decide if I have been successful.

Every good attorney knows you never ask a question you do not already know the answer to. As it is no secret that I am always willing to be a *rule breaker*, I will ask questions I am not sure I know the answers to.

Shall I begin my acknowledgements and offer my thanks to my parents, who supported and defended their six-year-old in her choice to be a vegetarian and later graduate to vegan? ... And for their sterling example of the *best thing you can do for your children is to have a loving and respectful relationship with each other*?

Queenie, my canine cribmate and animal *sister* who revealed the magic to me? The bull elephant I photographed in Samburu, Kenya? Surely he deserves my thanks for his choice not to charge at me but, instead, posed for me in my impassioned and reckless decision to be much too close to him. He stayed a while and *trumpeted* off as though to say, "Good-bye."

What of all those who have taken me into their sacred circle and allowed me to touch and change their lives, the lives of their beloved animal companions, and their relationships with them? Without them, the landscape of my life and work would hold vast areas of barren desert.

All the dogs, cats, birds, goldfish and wildlife who have been part of and graced my entire life, given me their love, wisdom, trust, and the privilege of loving and caring for them? No amount of thanks or acknowledgement can equal the gifts with which they have endowed me. So many have *changed worlds* but, before doing so, changed me. The living and those now beyond this life continue to be my greatest inspiration, source of courage, joy, teachers, muses, and sages.

To an unnamed, erstwhile colleague who asked me to *co-author* a book on loss and grief for children, my debt is considerable. To my stunned dismay, she refused to even entertain the only requirement I had, which was to make no reference to the terms *pets* and *owners*. This requirement I imposed with a view to improving the lexicon of professionals and others. By refusing, she stirred in me an anger that demanded *The Magical Link* be written. When properly channeled, healthy anger can be a productive emotion. It is only unhealthy anger turned inward or out of control that is damaging.

My Editors, John Hurley and Justin Braun, deserve the literary equivalent of the Medal of Honor for both their professional service above and beyond the call of duty as well as for their friendship and support.

Equally deserving of thanks and acknowledgement is AutoExec Computer Systems, Inc. of Staten Island. Vincent E. Vetere Sr. and Vincent Vetere Jr. twice rescued my computer from the jaws of *the blue screen of death.* Without their expertise and unending patience, *The Magical Link* might have been lost in cyberspace along with my sanity.

To those friends, colleagues, and others I have not mentioned by name, you know who you are and what you mean to me. For the legions of individuals and legitimate organizations who work tirelessly to educate, inform, propose legislation to protect animals, investigate and uncover abuse and neglect, instill kindness in others and make change, I remain in their debt.

Of *this* there is no question: I offer my heartfelt and tear-stained tribute to the billions of nameless, faceless, voiceless animals who have been sacrificed on the altars of greed, avarice, arrogance, blood sport, circuses, hunting, factory farms, rodeos, road-side zoos, destruction of habitat, cruelty and abuse of every imaginable and unimaginable kind. Some have been sacrificed in the name of science for unnecessary medical testing of the most unspeakable and hideous kinds and others to the insatiable desire of humans to eat, wear and use them for vanity, convenience, fashion and entertainment. They are *not* heroes who willingly gave their lives. They are victims who had their lives taken from them in the most brutal ways.

"*Humaniac*" is an ugly slang used to describe individuals and groups of people who advocate for a more kind and gentle treatment of animals, animal welfare, and animal rights. At present, animals have few if any rights and are essentially considered property.

Fear not. *The Magical Link* is not another book written by a *humaniac* intended to fill you with nothing but horror and leave you guilt-ridden and imposed upon. While these issues are important and are badly in need of improvement, they represent only the malignant aspects of the human-animal bond.

You will also journey to that which is tender, precious, and filled with joy. It is a journey that will enhance the magic of loving, respectful and mutually beneficial relationships with companion animals and all of Mother Nature's children.

In Greek mythology, Pandora was the first woman on earth. Zeus ordered Hephaestus (the god of craftsmanship) to create her. He did so, using water and earth. The gods endowed her with many gifts: beauty from Aphrodite, music from Apollo, persuasion from Hermes and more from others. Thus, Pandora got her name which means *all-gifted* or *all-endowed*. Pandora was given a jar (*Pithos*) that she was instructed not to open under any circumstance. The jar is best known as *Pandora's Box*. It contained all the evils of the earth that included plagues, diseases and other things. Spurred by her curiosity and with no malicious intent, Pandora opened the jar and all the evil escaped and spread over the world. She tried, but could not close the lid. The entire contents of the jar escaped but for one thing, which lay at the bottom; hope.

Like Pandora, I also have a rather feline-like curiosity, particularly as regards hope. With respect to the myth, I add that it is only *false* hope that is evil. I believe *false* hope was among the evils that escaped from Pandora's jar while true hope remained at the bottom. It is only *false* hope that has the power to do harm. True hope does not. Let us keep true hope alive and not be misled or blinded by false hope.

With that in mind, it is my wish that *The Magical Link* will touch your heart and give you both hope and the practical tools that will enable you to better understand and care for your own animal family, encourage you to raise your voice for the voiceless, and inspire you to be among those who make a difference. When you do, it will help those who desperately need and deserve your advocacy, beginning with your own animal family. At the same time, the greatest difference it will make will surely be to you, personally. You will attain the certain knowledge that you have made a difference, you matter and you have left this planet better than it was when you got here.

The Native Americans
by Heléne Burrow

Heléne Burrow is an award-winning wildlife artist in England. Her lifelong fascination with wildlife and love of Native American culture is reflected in her art. A skilled photographer, she has traveled extensively to capture the images and personal experiences of her subjects. Burrow has been to the Crow and Wind River Native American reservations, Yellowstone National Park, and many other places in the United States and throughout the world.

Her works in acrylic, oil, watercolor, and graphite are interpreted through her natural talent, formal art education, careful research and photography. She has walked and howled with wolves at the United Kingdom Wolf Conservation Center and captured the essence of the wolf and each of her other subjects with respect and authenticity.

www.heleneburrow.co.uk

Chapter One

The Magical Link: The Mysterious Thread That Binds Us to Animals

"If all the beasts were gone, man would die from a great loneliness of the spirit. For whatever happens or is done to the beasts also happens to mankind. All things are connected. Whatever befalls the earth and its beasts befalls the sons and daughters of the earth."...adapted from the address to President Franklin Pierce by Chief Seathl of the Suquamish Tribe – 1855.

The *magical link* is the beauty and mystery of the human-animal bond. It is a slender, often invisible, yet powerful thread that binds paw to hand, claw to core, wing and fin to foot, whisper to whisker and heart to heart.

A bond is defined as a uniting force or influence that draws and holds together, often permanently. And so it is with the bond between and among people and animals. The bond includes not just the animals with whom we closely share our home and lives. It extends to wildlife and all the fauna of the natural world.

Early History of the Human-Animal Bond

Canine

"Dogs are not our whole lives; they make our lives whole." ... Roger Caras (1928-2001).

Bill
Photo by Barbara Meyers

Our relationship with animals can be traced back to ancient times and archaeologists have proven it time and again. Much of the historical record left for scientists to unearth includes evidence of humankind's special interaction with and love of dogs.

A particularly significant example is that of a dog cemetery found in the ancient city of Askelon in Israel. It was uncovered by Harvard University archaeologist, Lawrence Stager. The burial grounds hold several hundred mummified skeletons of adult dogs and puppies. All appear to be of a similar breed, which today would be called either Greyhound or Whippet. Each skeleton has an individual grave indicative that these dogs were prized and highly likely to have been beloved companions and members of the family.

While dogs may be thought of as unclean or undesirable in some modern cultures, historical evidence suggests an older, far different relationship with dogs. The evidence gives strong reason to believe that dogs have always been beloved animals. Some will argue that the dog is the *most* beloved. But no matter where one is on the scale of unclean or undesirable to most beloved, it is clear that dogs have a powerful place in history, the world and our lives from the beginning of recorded time.

Feline

"There are two means of refuge from the miseries of life: music and cats."... Albert Schweitzer (1875-1965).

Cats also occupy an important place in our historical development. The early Egyptians so loved and revered their cats that they would shave their eyebrows upon the death of a family cat. Out of profound love and respect they mummified their deceased cats and placed them in the tombs of their human companions or in specially dedicated cat cemeteries.

The iconography of ancient Egypt also reveals the intrinsic cultural bond to cats. Bast, (Bastet) an Egyptian Goddess and daughter of the Sun God Re, was usually depicted as a woman with the head of a cat. Until 1000 BC, she was portrayed as a lioness but the modern day Bast is in full feline form.

Modern Day Bast

It is thought that her feline characteristics derived from her father because when Re destroyed his enemies, he took the form of a cat. Significantly, Bast is the Goddess of cats, fire and fertility. Her likeness was often found in the homes of pregnant women to protect and guard over them.

Perhaps similar to domestic cats of present time, she was said to have two sides to her personality. She could be docile and gentle but could also be an aggressive and a fierce adversary. Whichever her temperament, her existence in the mythological panoply, once more, underscores the importance of the bond we share with cats.

Equine

"Where in this world can man find nobility without pride, friendship without envy or beauty without vanity? Here, grace is laced with muscle and strength by gentleness. All history is in his industry. We are his heirs, he is our inheritance. Ladies and gentlemen, "The Horse!"... Excerpt from introduction to The Horse of the Year Show... Ronald Duncan 1954.

Evidence that horses have been instrumental in our development was found in caves in France. This evidence shows that the horse was a presence in our lives as far back as the Stone Age. There can be little doubt that without horses, human civilization would not have progressed with the rapidity it has.

We have depended on horses to provide everything from transportation and companionship to partners in law enforcement endeavors and other work. They have shaped and enriched society and our individual lives in ways too numerous to count and often without choice.

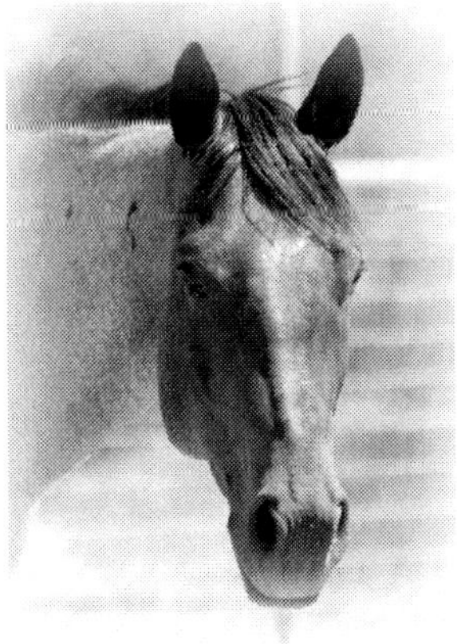

Blueper, Blue Roan American Quarter Horse

Photo by Laura Cowen

On this continent, horses were native to North America until the end of the last Ice Age (about ten thousand years ago) at which point they disappeared. On his second voyage in 1493, Christopher Columbus brought horses across the sea. Hernando Cortez followed Columbus in 1519 during his expedition from Spain. We have these early explorers to thank for re-introducing the horse to us.

Present Day

At present, the most common relationship between animals and people is our home-based interaction with companion cats and dogs but there are many more. People regularly invite birds, horses, small mammals such as gerbils, ferrets, hamsters and rats, freshwater fish, saltwater fish and reptiles of all kinds into their lives.

According to the industry's leading not-for-profit trade association survey there are approximately 15 million birds, 93.6 million cats, 77.5 dogs, 13.3 million horses, 171.7 million freshwater fish, 11.2 million salt water fish, 13.6 million reptiles and 15.9 million small mammals (gerbils, hamsters, rats, etc.) living as companions in the United States.

Spending on animal companions has risen from $21 billion dollars in 1996 to an estimated $50 billion today. Guardians often travel with their companion animals, surprise them with something new on special occasions and lavish them with holiday presents. For many of us, every day we spend with our animal families is a special occasion and a holiday.

Recognizing these trends, more companies that specialize in products for people are now doing the same for dogs, cats, reptiles and other animals. Paul Mitchell, Origins, Harley Davidson and Old Navy are among those now offering extensive lines of products for companion animals. They range from shampoos, attire and name-brand toys to gourmet treats and food. Many hotels and vacation destinations are similarly adopting animal-friendly policies. There are also vacation spots and specialty camps exclusively devoted to both people and their companion animals. It is not uncommon for many families to enjoy the company of more than one cat, dog, horse or other animal friend. These households are referred to as multi-animal or *blended* families. Generally, cats and dogs make up the greatest percentage of animals with whom people share their homes and lives. Many others find rewarding, loving and long-lasting relationships with other species. Their treasured experiences are just as worthy as those more frequently found.

It simply indicates that the human-canine and the human-feline relationships are the most common. This is explained by the vast populations who live in urban areas where living with and caring for horses or other large animals is simply not possible.

Many urban dwellers contend with smaller living spaces, demanding personal schedules, landlord-tenant regulations and a host of other factors that prevent them from living with *any* animal companions. It is, therefore, the wise and loving who recognize that while they may sincerely desire the company of animal friends, they are not in a social or financial position to responsibly care for and give enough time, love, energy or attention to any companion animal.

Acting in the best interest of animals by *not* having them as part of the family is an act of true, selfless love and, for those who make this decision, their lives need not be isolated from animals.

We can experience interaction with the immediate surrounding wildlife in our environment and, in this way, can acquaint ourselves with the distant but powerful bonds we share with the entire natural world.

Chapter Two

Paws for Thought

"In the bad old days, references to blacks, women, Jews and others were in a negative language that perpetuated poor treatment, abuse and exploitation of these people. Animals have suffered more from negative language stereotyping than all the others. It demeans them so consistently that it has created an environment that allows all sorts of cruelties, many too horrendous to describe! An animal is "it" instead of "he" or "she." This perpetuates our view of them as "things" rather than individuals and is a major first step towards cutting them up for meat and leather, testing drugs, cosmetics and household products on their bodies and tearing off their coats for furs! Those who have animals are referred to as "owners" rather than guardians, care-givers or companions; reinforcing the idea that they are property as much as slaves were considered property. Let's avoid references such as dirty rat, filthy pig, dirty dog, she's a bitch, ugly duckling, more than one way to skin a cat, killing two birds with one stone and many more."... Supreme Court Justice Arthur J .Goldberg (1908-1990).

Our animal friends have long been and are still referred to as *pets* in most of society. This includes animal professionals, associated business people, educators, physicians, therapists of all kinds, and grief therapists claiming sensitivity in the most delicate matters. Among those who continue to use the antiquated term, *pet*, though they may be aware of its underlying connotations, they simply refuse to update or improve their vocabulary. This stubbornness persists despite the fact that, for at least two decades, more acceptable terms (companion animal, animal friend, animal family) have emerged and are deemed more appropriate. At this point you may be asking, "Why the fuss?" Why is this author so adamant about the use of the word *pet*? After all, it appears to be a common word that is well understood, but is it? Does the word itself imply or support a host of meanings of which most people remain unaware?

Pet

Pet is generally defined as a domesticated animal kept for pleasure. On the surface, this definition may not seem offensive or inaccurate. But at the very least, it suggests that the purpose of domesticated animals is to amuse us and serve without any intrinsic value of their own. This is not so.

Those who have walked another path and know the love of a dog, cat, horse, bird or the mischievous chipmunk who awaits them every morning understand that the bonds of love and trust we share with *all* of Mother Nature's children are intertwined with our very being. They need no convincing except to lead the way for others by setting a higher standard.

Companion animals are far more than mere *pets* and the implications built into the word. They are our animal friends and family; the ones we choose and are not assigned by biological accident or social happenstance. Reports and news of the *magical* events that take place between companion animals and their *guardians* are matched only by similar occurrences marking heroic, altruistic and life-saving intervention by companion animals with complete strangers. Think of a world where you are the *other,* where someone you love is *it,* or a *thing* - a *number.* A world where only a few see and experience your unique qualities, call you by name and celebrate and honor your wonder.

If this strikes you as something of a conundrum, it is. However, it can be unraveled with ease by a simple shift in word use. Just as *pet* reduces companion animals to the lowest common denominator, thereby devaluing them, the intentional choice of other words will hold the same power to elevate them and the people who love them to the higher level deserved. Though we are not always conscious of it, this *mindfulness* can and will lead to the gradual crumbling of the pillars of cavalier behavior that have served as a barrier to demonstrating true caring and kinship.

If you are among the conscious and convinced, do not resort to the use of *pet* with the justification that it is what others will understand and, therefore, continue to use it and perpetuate a recurring cycle of status quo. Be strong of heart and say aloud, "this is my friend, my companion, my ....*fill in the word that works for you* and dispense with *pet* once and for all.

Owner

Owner is commonly defined as a party that possesses the exclusive right to control, hold, use, benefit-from, enjoy, convey, transfer, and otherwise dispose of an asset or property. The repeated use of this word as regards species other than our own fosters attitudes that fail to recognize and promote a responsibility far beyond that which is owed to *things.* When people begin to think of themselves as *guardians* rather than *owners,* a natural progression of sensitivity, caring and compassion can blossom in its fertile soil. To *own* also admits being in accordance with fact or to acknowledge something such as *owning* our mistakes, decisions and choices. The time has come for all of us to *own* our poor choice of words and, thereby, control and direct the change we seek in a positive and beneficial way.

As we recall the words and admirable philosophy of the late Supreme Court Justice Arthur J. Goldberg, we are also reminded that animals are still considered property by law. The most brilliant and dedicated legal scholars are working toward changing their status to *personhood* which would create dramatic progress. But even before that goal is reached, we have the power to change the way we think and speak of them. Doing so will reshape attitudes and, ultimately, lead to a kinder and more realistic understanding of who and what we really are to each other.

Beyond some of the archaic and misguided laws that currently govern the land, we should no longer take the position that we *own* animals as we do furniture, cars, shoes and other *things*. They are not insignificant property. Accordingly, we have no conscionable right to speak of or treat them as if they are.

Get Rid of

To "get rid of" means to discard, remove, or cast out or dispose of an unwanted object. Animals are not garbage, trash, or worthless, used-up junk. Too often, people quite literally *get rid* of their animals when they become inconvenient and do so in the most cruel, thoughtless and unacceptable ways. There are valid reasons and circumstances to *re-home*, which does not *get rid* of an animal companion. In these cases, the re-homing is in the best interest of everyone.

Even those who are not lacking in caring or an educated vocabulary speak of "getting rid" of a companion animal. As they re-tell their story, one can readily discern that the use of the phrase "get rid of" does not convey the depth of feeling involved. In these instances, your author suggests that *re-homing* is a better and more accurate way to think of and describe the situation. During the more than twenty-five years I have been in practice, there have been numerous individuals and families who, for all the *right*, unselfish and appropriate reasons, have had to re-home a beloved animal friend. They were not relinquished to a pound or shelter, nor were they given away casually. Despite all the care given to vetting and securing the best permanent home, the resulting guilt, regret and remorse were often unbearable and lingered for extended periods of time. Afterwards, they sought professional help, which is how I came to know them.

Using the power of words to properly describe an act or deed is not a trick to make people feel better about something they have truly done wrong. True wrong-doing presents an entirely separate set of circumstances requiring a very different approach. Careful and loving re-homing is *not* wrong-doing.

The right words are the key to undoing a self-imposed, harsh untruth and reframing thoughts and feelings in a way that is both honest and comforting. The suggested vocabulary change is not the only management tool. It is, however, the centerpiece for healing and the reduction of the distress associated with an unwarranted, self-imposed guilt.

If we all learn to similarly adapt a better and more updated lexicon and take humane education for adults and children more seriously, we will lay a lasting and important foundation for enlightenment about animals. The law will eventually catch up. It is useful to recall the words of many of our elders who have offered wisdom as we strive to communicate effectively with one another and ourselves. These great figures have offered a similar message in different ways and in different languages. Perhaps no one has said it better than Mark Twain.

"*The difference between the right word and the almost right word is really a large matter. It's the difference between the lightning and the lightning bug.*" – From his letter to George Bainton, October 15th 1888. ... Mark Twain (1835-1910).

Sentiency and Altruism in Animals

Animals are sentient beings who have value and purpose far beyond that which is related to us. They are members of their own families, troops, prides, flocks, packs, schools, etc. and play vital roles in the ecosystems of the world. Like us, they exhibit a wide range of emotions and they also experience intense pain (physical, emotional, psychic and spiritual,) trauma and suffering.

Animals are also capable of and enjoy extraordinary relationships with one another. They have the ability to love, nurture, play, and protect. Additionally, they display the need and capacity to grieve, mourn and even experience anticipatory mourning when one of their own is injured, ill or dying. These behaviors are readily observed in elephants, gorillas, dolphins, whales, cats, dogs and horses but they exist in other species as well.

We are all creatures of this earth; beings of different species. Lamentably, some of us remain committed to the idea that only a special few (ourselves) are aware of their own mortality and death. The anticipatory mourning and after-death grief displayed by species other than our own proves otherwise.

Animals are often observed gathering around their sick, injured, frail and dying to emotionally and physically support and protect them. Dolphins and other cetaceans will repeatedly bring a member of their pod up to the surface of the water enabling respiration and prevent drowning when the injured individual is in distress. When a calf dies, a mother dolphin will support the body on her head at the surface of the water for many days. This action is understood *not* as a failure to comprehend that her calf is dead, but instead suggests a strong similarity with human custom and ritual (i.e. preparation of the body, wake, shiva, etc). Notably, marine biologists have also observed female beluga whales supporting logs and driftwood with their heads. It is widely believed that in performing the ritual with its obvious correlations to that of the dolphin, whale mothers are also mourning a calf who has recently died.

One of the more striking examples of altruistic behavior occurred on Mahia Beach on the east coast of the North Island in New Zealand in March 2008.

Moko, a bottlenose dolphin well known to the people of the area, led a mother pygmy sperm whale and her calf to the safety of the open sea after they were hopelessly stranded on a sandbar.

Conservation Officer Malcolm Smith arrived on the scene at the point where, despite all efforts, the whales' demise appeared imminent. Stranded whales are under great stress and this stress, combined with their body weight, can prove lethal. Experts called to assist often have no recourse but to bring stranded whales to a swift, less painful death.

Officer Smith reported that Moko appeared in the waters off the beach and she and the stranded whales began intensely calling to one another. After communicating, Moko escorted the whales about two hundred yards parallel with the beach to the edge of the sandbar. Then she traveled along a right-angle through a very narrow channel safely leading the whales out to sea.

This account was confirmed by volunteers assisting Officer Smith. Additionally, Anton van Helden, a marine mammal expert at New Zealand's National Museum, Te Papa Tongarewa, concluded that it was "fantastic" but nonetheless believable because dolphins have "a great capacity for altruistic activities."

Bottlenose Dolphin

Along similar lines, Washoe, the first chimpanzee to successfully master sign language, stopped signing upon the death of her baby and remained silent until she was presented with an orphan to foster and adopt (Masson & McCarthy, 1995). Many species bring food to those among them who need it and also place mud and leaves over wounds when their group members are injured. Later, their burial grounds are clearly defined, and the dead are watched over, often for many days.

Are these actions merely pre-programmed mechanistic survival methods? On the contrary, the behaviors strongly validate that animals exhibiting them are sentimental, intelligent, compassionate, altruistic and loving beings.

As with humans, not all pre-death mourning in the animal world is displayed in such admirable fashion. Animals are also known to avoid ailing members of their own clan and some are moved to actively facilitate the demise of the dying.

The Words We Choose

Given the true value of animals as much more than *pets* or other tools for our entertainment or indulgences, it is crucial to establish a linguistic paradigm that reflects this reality. The words we choose are not simply a method of communication. Word-choice itself influences behavior by creating images and shaping attitudes. Adults have the responsibility and moral imperative to provide the young with a vocabulary that fosters sensitivity, kindness, empathy and a compassion that, ultimately, produces a richer life and a better living environment.

There was a time when the use of terms now considered unacceptable and politically incorrect were freely and openly employed. Today, however, one caught uttering inappropriate words faces sanction and grave risk to their reputation. As a society, the language may have been publicly cleansed but much more discourse continues unabated among those who resist changing their offensive language. Even for those who do not resist change, outbursts of offensive language are often spoken during times of trial and intensity as one's ability to filter inappropriate language is overcome by anger, distress or other volatile emotions of the moment.

Everyone can participate towards meaningful change in our use of animal-related language, thereby having a broad and easily implemented immediate impact. It should be notcd that people tend to be more open with their negative attitudes towards animals than they are about other subjects. Thus, a change in language would be a signal of shifting societal morals. At the present time, there are no social prohibitions against speaking freely, albeit inappropriately and unkindly, about animals. This is evidenced by the frequency and uncensored candor of those who admit they hate cats or any other animal. Those who openly announce that they hate Jews, Mexicans or any individual or group face censure. Regardless of the target, haters often contain their attitude only as a result of feeling constrained by circumstance but revert to unacceptable expressions in safe company. This behavior exhibits how language changes depending on audience.

For those less aware, when it comes to animals, language choice may not accurately reflect their feelings or attitude and may, in fact, be exaggerated out of habit or a host of other things that do not reflect true hate. While it remains undeniable that there will always be those who really *do* hate animals or a specific species of animal, others who *say* they hate animals are not really familiar with them or have not learned to express themselves accurately.

One need only question such statements to learn that these offenders do not really hate cats but, instead, are fearful and hold false beliefs that cats are sneaky and aloof. These people are usually quick to say that they would never hurt or want to see a cat injured but just do not want to be near one. When given the opportunity to explore their word-choice in a safe atmosphere with a non-judgmental more sensitive person, they may discover truths about their language that they themselves did not previously understand.

Hence, it is important to establish and model good word-choice to foster more meaningful dialogue. It is especially important to do so with children. This is not only true of our own children but also those we encounter in all situations. Educators and other adults have both a powerful influence over their students and the opportunity to instill improved language by using it themselves. Poor choice of words may signal reduced sensitivity and sophistication in the speaker or that she or he has not yet learned better methods of communicating. When they maintain consistent use of words like *pet* rather than *companion animal, owner* instead of *guardian* and also refer to animals as *it,* immediate reprimand or sanctions are not the best method to inspire meaningful and lasting change.

More can be accomplished by carefully guiding people to understand what words like *pet* and *owner* imply and convey. One's own repeated use of an alternate term coupled with the omission of words and phrases that do not do justice to animals or the human-animal bond may be enough to spark friendly discussion. If such actions remain unnoticed, it can be useful to find the opportunity to inaugurate a conversation on the subject. To do this, one can ask the listener if she or he has noticed that they never use the words *pet* or *owner*. The ensuing conversation can focus on why *pet* and *owner* should be phased out and what replacement terms are available. In this kind of discussion, it is counterproductive to create an atmosphere of discomfort where people may react defensively or end the conversation altogether. For many, it may be enough to set a good example of better communication, plant the seeds and allow them to take in the information without feeling either disapproval or an unspoken demand for them to change. Others will require a more extensive re-education and, sadly, some will never rise above their primitive vocabulary.

In all likelihood, seismic shift in vocabulary will not be realized in this decade. However, it remains crucial that the more aware be willing to continue to lead the way and leave footprints along the path for others to explore and follow. Strong inroads have taken hold but there remains a great need for the expansion and improvement of our communication norms in the crafting of a more consistent and reliable way for people to think and talk about animals and our relationships with them.

There are many examples of improvements to be found in veterinary teaching institutions where entire departments of *companion animal* medicine and centers for focusing on the human-animal bond are plentiful. Humane societies throughout the world have also adopted the term *companion animals* instead of the previously used *pets*. With a view toward eliminating the word *owner*, many are finding more acceptable terms such as guardian or human family, making better word-choice more widespread than ever before.

Interestingly, many of the institutions that have adopted more appropriate language still exhibit glaring inconsistencies in its use. In fact, you will find them in abundance as you visit the websites of even the superior professional and allied animal care services featured in this book. Inconstancies take the form of mission statements, general information, product names, websites, etc. An example of this is the inclusion of *some* version of the following: “Our goal is to enhance the quality of life for people and companion animals by promoting the human-animal bond.” Continued reading, however, may reveal that the same service or product provider also offers a *pet* therapy program, *pet owner's* guide to puppy-raising, *pet* bereavement support program or refers to *pet* guardians. The last example is perhaps the most confounding of all. It illustrates that consciousness has been raised to a level eliminating the use of *owner* but still refers to companion animals as *pets.*

Thus, it is necessary to encourage both the initial change in word-choice among those who have not yet made the leap into the 21st century lexicon and also inspire and support additional and consistent changes among others who have taken the first steps. When this is achieved, substantive attitudes towards animals will change far beyond the mere politically correct and become the standard of truth.

“All truth passes through three stages. First, it is ridiculed. Second, it is violently opposed. Third, it is accepted as self-evident.”
... Arthur Schopenhauer (1788-1860).

Proof Positive

In July of 2012, thanks to the efforts of their signature *Guardian Campaign,* In Defense of Animals (www.idausa.org) announced another of their significant victories. The Richmond, California City Council voted to replace *owner* with *guardian* everywhere the term appears in ordinances concerning companion animals. Richmond also recommended that the entire county of Contra Costa make the same changes! Richmond has now become an officially recognized IDA “Guardian City.”

In Defense of Animals was founded in 1983 by its President Emeritus, Elliot M. Katz, DVM. Their mission is: *“To end animal exploitation, cruelty, and abuse by protecting and advocating for the rights, welfare, and habitats of animals, as well as to raise their status beyond mere property, commodities or things.”*

For more than fifty years, Dr. Katz has *made a difference* through his profession as a veterinarian, his personal cruelty-free lifestyle, and the founding of IDA and its programs of protection throughout the world. Dr. Katz shares his life with his very special friend Charlie, his daughters Raquel and Dannielle, and his former wife, Gloria.

Dr. Katz and Charlie
Photo by Linda Fisher

The Human-Animal Bond: Exactly What it is and What it is Not

"*We need a wiser and perhaps more mystical concept of animals. In a world older and more complete than ours, animals move finished and complete, gifted with extensions of the senses we have never attained, living by voices we shall never hear. They are not brethren and they are not underlings. They are other nations, caught with ourselves in the net of life and time, fellow prisoners of the splendor and travail of the earth.*"... Henry Beston (1888–1968).

Perhaps the most important thing to understand about the human-animal bond is, first, what it is *not*. Contrary to widespread and mistaken belief, the human-animal bond is not a substitute or replacement for human companionship. It is just one example of the many relationships each of us is capable of enjoying. The human-animal relationship stands on its own, possessing unique properties that distinguish it from others. This is not to imply it is more or less important than any another relationship. Simply stated, it is valuable and worthy of its own affirmation, validation and respect.

An odd modern stereotype categorizes those with strong animal relationships as social misfits incapable of finding mates or friends. Another misconception suggests animal friends are poor substitutes for children. Unfortunately, one all too often hears statements like "If they had a *real* child, they could get rid of that stupid cat!"

Even some professionals cannot seem to refrain from placing human-animal relationships in competition with human-human relationships.

For example, both human charity workers and donors alike sometimes view the bond, care and concern for animals and animal charities as competing with human progress. They believe that the time, love, money and attention given to animals would be better spent only on human causes. These individuals fail to recognize that people have the right to decide as to their generosity in how, where and on whom they spend their emotional and economic resources. Moreover, the total resources available for human charitable causes far surpass those for animals. It is also true that often the people who build animal sanctuaries or otherwise contribute to animal causes also give of themselves to human causes like building libraries and specialty wings on children's and other hospitals. In the context of professionals, it is particularly damaging when therapists, physicians, psychiatrists, nurses, lawyers, educators and others hold fast to their limited understanding of human-animal relations and accuse people of transference and projection when they encounter someone with strong animal relations.

The human-animal bond is not, for the most part, an unhealthy or undesirable relationship. Nonetheless, there are extreme examples of this relationship gone wrong. Fringe examples do not constitute a worthy barometer of the whole. Examples of aberrant behaviors include the *collectors* or hoarders who covet unreasonable quantities of animals they are unable to care for at any acceptable level. Often kind-hearted, their initial good intentions spiral out of control creating havoc and deplorable living conditions. They may also have an overabundance of inanimate objects. While inanimate objects do not suffer from the collector's disorder, the animal hoarder can and *does* inflict harm on her innocent captives.

With the advent of hospice care for animals came an even more dangerous group of monsters; the *death-hoarders*, a phrase recently coined by Alice Villalobos, DVM. Devoid of the basic intent and construct of hospice care, they *collect* the dying behind the guise of providing so-called hospice care in free-standing facilities that are frequently nothing more than the comfortless basement of their own home or a distant site where they are less likely to be observed. These make-shift sites are without the benefit of veterinary oversight to provide proper care, pain control and the gift of a compassionate close of life when needed. *Death-hoarders* frequently hold greedy, self-serving financial and narcissistic goals that are easily accomplished at the unforgivable expense of extending suffering and misery of animal companions turned over to them by the naïve, hopeless, and desperate who entrust them with the terminally ill. They actively seek and obtain donations from those who, baselessly, are deluded into believing they are a worthy cause. Many of these despicable people are self-proclaimed *angels of mercy* who are nothing more than vicious charlatans, intent on separating the gullible and unsuspecting from the contents of their wallets and credit cards by any means possible. We, as a society, would do well to address this crime of animal abuse and neglect with legal remedies that include a vigorous program of investigation, arrest and criminal prosecution of *death-hoarders* and their hideous criminal behavior.

Hospice care that is neither profit-based nor driven by self-serving motives is a responsibility, privilege and final gift to those who have enriched and given added meaning to our lives. You will read more about it in chapter twelve.

What the Bond is

The human-animal relationship is best described as a social and emotional tapestry woven of fine thread. Many of the threads are simultaneously woven into other relationships. Some are seen in a few special relationships between and among people and others exist nowhere but in the remarkable friendships and kinships between animals and people.

In the human-animal friendship, each participant enjoys many roles that can be interchanged with great ease and adaptability. The significance and complexity of these roles may not be obvious to the casual observer but they exist nonetheless. The roles are those of friend, guardian, family member, caregiver, companion, confidant, teacher, student, healer, muse and more.

Our animal families offer unconditional love, something for which humans long but rarely, if ever, find. Every day, companion animals greet their families with the love, respect and honor afforded a returning hero and they will repeat their affections as often as their guardians leave and re-enter the family home.

Animals also welcome with more subtle but equally special salutations. These gestures of greeting may include the gentle rub of an ankle, the wag of a tail, a soft purr, the flutter of tiny wings or a tank with sleepy inhabitants who suddenly swim forward.

Unconditional love does not come without responsibility. If one views responsibility as a condition, that is a matter of personal interpretation. It seems, however, not the sort of condition we are more likely and reasonably to associate with this subject. There is no "I'll love you *if*," "I'll love you *until*," I'll love you *unless*."

While behaviors generally associated with love may be somewhat conditionally offered by animals with special needs, the love itself remains unconditional, for no paw has ever been jerked away from a disfigured hand. No whisker has ever been withdrawn from the cheek of the aged, unattractive or the dying.

Among dogs, in particular, it is not unusual to find many who will tolerate less than ideal treatment and even some abuse or neglect without retaliation and with what appears to be forgiveness.

The Extended Bond

It should be recognized that the bond between people and animals extends beyond companion animals with whom we share our homes. Equally powerful connections exist between people and the wildlife in our gardens, local communities, national preserves and in other countries. People from all walks of life are deeply connected to and concerned about animals used and exploited for food, clothing, entertainment, sport, experiment and consumption of all kinds.

Many are also touched by the plight of lost or abandoned animals as well as colonies of feral cats, packs of homeless dogs, and wildlife made homeless by wanton and selfish destruction of their habitat for generalized overbuilding and the construction of *McMansions*. These kind people stand in contrast with those who find such animals an inconvenience at best or a nuisance to be eliminated by any means necessary.

Feral Cats

The average life of a feral cat is about two years. During that time, a single pair of cats can produce dramatic numbers of offspring. Alley Cat Allies (www.alleycat.org) is a national advocacy organization devoted to the humane treatment and care of feral cats. They educate the public to successfully trap, neuter and return (TNR) cats who cannot be socialized and re-homed and offer extensive information on how to establish a healthy and stable feral cat colony.

Roger, Feral Cat with Tipped Left Ear
Photo by Barbara Meyers

A *tipped* left ear is the universal sign of a neutered feral cat. Approximately ¼ inch of the tip is surgically removed while under anesthesia during the spay/neuter surgery. It is an uncomplicated procedure and healing is rapid. Feral cats usually have more than one caregiver. The *tipped* ear allows for ease of identification and prevents an unnecessary second trapping and surgery.

The life of outdoor cats does not have to be a cycle of never-ending, uncontrolled populations of cats and kittens who live short lives of desperation under the harshest conditions.

Lucy, Teddy and Juan

The relationship we share with animals in zoos can be intense, too. One such example is that of Lucy and Teddy; two polar bears who lived at the Prospect Park Zoo in Brooklyn, New York.

On May 20th 1987, three boys under the age of twelve scaled a fence and entered into the enclave of the bears. One boy, Juan Perez, paid for the misadventure with his life. Lucy and Teddy were executed by the local police but not until they had suffered twenty blasts from four twelve-gauge shotguns firing rifled bullets and six bullets from a .38-caliber revolver.

In the aftermath, the tragedy gripped the heart of the entire community and the city at large as people experienced two very distinct but equally important losses of life: the death of the boy, Juan Perez, and the death of the bears, Lucy and Teddy. Many people were deprived of the freedom to express the tragedy of the bears' deaths except in select circles. Those who dared to speak of it openly were bombarded with a brutal array of criticism and accusations.

Lucy and Teddy lived most (thirty years) of their pathetic lives as captives in an unnatural, barren environment.

At the time of their execution, Lucy was thirty-two years old and Teddy was thirty-three. Managed for more than fifty years by the New York City Department of Parks and Recreation, the Prospect Park Zoo was finally closed for massive renovation in 1988. In 1993, it was rededicated as the Prospect Park Wildlife Conservation Center and managed by the Wildlife Conservation Society. It was too late for Lucy and Teddy.

Lucy, 1974

Photo by Barbara Meyers

Despite their own private misery, Lucy and Teddy delighted many children and adults who were unaware of the cost of their pleasure. They were the childhood friends of hundreds of visitors who came to see them regularly, calling on them immediately upon arrival and then going back to say "good-bye" before leaving. I was one of those children and I can attest to this. We knew and will always remember their names, we could distinguish between the bears and we knew what and when they ate. A special treat would be to visit them during their lunchtime. It was always a wonderful day when I would have lunch with Lucy and Teddy!

The world is a different and diminished place because Juan Perez did not get to grow up. It is also a different and diminished place without Lucy and Teddy. Each loss is great, everlasting, and deserves to be mourned.

Lucy and Teddy were two among millions of animals who continue to be exploited in zoos throughout the world where they are nothing more than prisoners. Despite some good intentions and claims of conservation, too many zoos regularly deprive their captives of natural breeding, predatory and other normal behaviors, and kill unwanted or "excess" offspring that have been propagated and *managed* by means of unnatural breeding practices. In my view, zoos are unacceptable substitutes for the protection of animals in their wild, native habitats.

Aware of the conditions in zoos, I had not seen Lucy and Teddy since childhood. Still holding them dear to me and, armed with the knowledge gained over the passing years, I returned to the zoo in 1974 to see them. It was at that time the photo of Lucy was taken. Heartbroken at the sight of my old friends who were visibly depressed and unhappy, I left promising them I would do everything I could to effect change, though it would never be adequate or timely enough for them.

The loss of Lucy and Teddy is personal to me. To this day, it is with deep pain and fresh tears that I am riveted back to the misery of their lives, the added heartbreak of their brutal deaths, and the legacy of wisdom that came to me because of them. Lucy and Teddy were my friends. Juan Perez *could* have been my friend.

On May 23rd 1987, I quietly returned to the scene of the tragedy. I left a nosegay of forget-me-nots, the symbol of love and remembrance, at the site and never went back again.

Chapter Three

Our Relationships With Animals in the Natural World

"One touch of nature makes the world kin."
... William Shakespeare (1564–1616).

The Backyard Buddies: Our Fascination With and the Pleasure Brought to Us by Mother Nature's Wild Children

Millions of people have close relationships with animals outside their homes. Backyard bird and squirrel feeders abound and we delight in the visitors they bring.

Our backyard visitors offer beauty to the eye, song to the ear and wonder to the imagination. They signal the changing of the seasons and grace every activity with symbolism and special meaning. Birds, in particular, traditionally symbolize hope, grief, despair, joy and the meaning of life itself.

Wildlife-Friendly Gardens

"Hope is the thing with feathers that perches in the soul and sings the tune without the words and never stops at all."
... excerpted from *Hope is the Thing with Feathers*
by Emily Dickinson (1830-1886).

Squirrel in Duncraft feeder
Photo by Barbara Meyers

Wildlife friendly gardens are not difficult to create or maintain. When established, they naturally invite butterflies and birds otherwise unseen into the backyard. Every state and region fosters plants, shrubs, trees and flowers that are suitable for attracting desired wildlife. To learn more, one need only look to the website of the Audubon Society (www.audubon.org). Public libraries are also filled with books, DVDs and CDs on the subject.

Rose-breasted Grosbeak
Photo Provided by Duncraft, Inc.

As an earth-friendly method of responsible gardening, I recommend using *only* native plants and other flora. Native plants, shrubs, trees and wildflowers are those that are indigenous to a particular area. While many species can grow and thrive in almost any given environment, invasive species may dominate over fragile native species, causing permanent damage to the ecosystem.

Creating a wildlife-friendly garden does not necessarily have to be expensive. It can be as simple or elegant as you like. Regardless of cost, properly administered wildlife-friendly gardens will provide shelter, food, water (an essential ingredient) and harmony to Mother Nature's flora and fauna. Being part of this symbiosis is a truly joyful experience.

My Garden Pond

Photo by Barbara Meyers

Where to Begin?

First, be sure not to casually toss bread, seed or nuts on the ground. It is neither safe nor healthy for birds or the environment. You will need bird feeders that hold the type of seed, worms or suet for the birds you want to attract. Where there is seed, there are squirrels. To avoid competition and still enjoy the beauty of the birds while being endlessly amused by the antics of squirrels, I recommend that you also have a squirrel feeder. The best resource and my personal favorite for feeders is Duncraft.

Table and Chair Corn Squirrel Feeder

Photo by John C. Gill

Founded in 1952 by Gil Dunn, Duncraft, Inc. became a pioneer in developing and producing products for what is now the second largest pastime in America – backyard bird and squirrel feeding.

Still family operated, Duncraft (www.duncraft.com) is the "go to" source for innovative solutions for backyard bird feeding, education and support about bird-housing, water features, proper habitat, and hard-to-find seed blends. A visit to the Duncraft website will take you to *all things bird and backyard-beautiful!*

Goldfinches, Chickadee and Downy Woodpecker
Dining From Sunflower Metal Haven Feeder
Photo by Marie Read

Eastern Bluebirds in Eco-Strong Bluebird House
Photo by Steve Byland

Robins in All Season Kozy Spa Bird Bath
Photo by Richard Day – Daybreak Images

The Birds Who Came For Christmas

According to the Audubon Society, more than 50,000 people participate annually in an all-day census of early-winter bird populations. The results are compiled into the longest running database in ornithology that represents over a century of unbroken data on trends of early-winter bird populations across the Americas. It is known as the Christmas Bird Count.

Prior to the turn of the century, people engaged in a holiday tradition known as the *Christmas Side Hunt*. They would choose sides and go into the fields with their guns. Whoever brought in the biggest pile of feathered quarry was the winner.

Around the turn of the twentieth century, conservationism emerged as a way to address a declining bird population. Beginning on Christmas Day in 1900, ornithologist Frank Chapman, an officer in the budding Audubon Society, proposed a new holiday tradition. Instead of killing, there would be a bloodless census of birds. Thanks to the inspiration of Chapman and the enthusiasm of twenty-seven dedicated birders, twenty-five Christmas Bird Counts were held that day.

In North America, the counting begins on December 14th and runs through January 5th. This time period, referred to as early-winter, features many birds in the late stages of their southward migration. Therefore, it cannot be considered true winter. The early-winter data is combined with other surveys such as the Breeding Bird Survey to paint a more complete picture of how bird populations change over time.

The information gathered is vital for conservation. The census monitors local trends in bird populations and serves as a warning when habitat destruction is imminent or groundwater contamination and poisoning from pesticides may be evident.

Everyone who takes part in the Christmas Bird Count, from feeder-watchers and field observers to count-compilers and regional editors, finds an outlet for their love of birds and the excitement of the count.

This tradition, started by a man who thought it was better to count than kill, demonstrates how one person can make an enormous difference. So long as birds remain, the Christmas Bird Count will go on being the most popular and rewarding bird census the world over!

The Christmas Bird Count is not the only way to observe and enjoy birds. Project Feeder Watch at the Cornell Lab of Ornithology (www.birds.cornell.edu/pfw/) provides a complete guide to watching and counting the birds in one's own backyard. It allows people to enjoy and count birds at their backyard feeders and transmit the data to scientists.

Project Feeder Watch is also a wonderful way to introduce children to nature without doing harm to birds, other animals or the environment. Many children are encouraged to hunt birds and other small animals. This misguided instruction teaches killing and disregard. While heartily defended by proponents, it is not the best way to teach anything! When children participate in non-violent activities, they learn to develop important qualities such as patience, observation and reflection, curiosity, intelligence and compassion. These habits are critical in enhancing child development.

Project Feeder Watch is an activity that can be enjoyed alone or with friends and family. It is available all year long to everyone including those who have limited access or ability to leave their homes.

The program provides detailed information on how and where to place feeders, proper landscape, what to feed birds, how to create a safe feeding environment, how to identify unusual birds, avian diseases, and much more.

Many people are under the impression that, if they feed birds all year long, they will interfere with or delay the birds' migration. This is not so. In fact, during the spring migration, a bird feeder is a most welcome and often badly needed oasis for a winged friend that that has traveled far from wintering grounds and must go still farther to reach the breeding grounds. Even when natural food sources are plentiful in summer, birds require increased fuel and energy after feeding their young. Bird feeders supply the extra nourishment they need.

Myths about birds are plentiful. A good example is the widespread belief if rice is thrown at a wedding and birds eat the rice, they will become ill and die. This belief is unfounded. Many wild birds including House Sparrows will eat rice in farmers' fields and remain quite healthy.

A better reason not to throw rice at weddings is that the practice can create slippery sidewalks that are dangerous for pedestrians. Some facilities ban rice throwing solely for that reason. If you are having a lawn wedding ceremony, there is no impediment to throwing rice, be it from concern for guests or birds.

Same Gender Animal Relationships

People are often fascinated by the rare or most unusual relationships shared by a small number of animals. Although not common, same gender relationships have been observed in birds.

Perhaps the most famous example is a pair of male, Chinstrap Penguins at the Central Park Zoo in New York City.

Roy and Silo behaved as any male and female mating pair of birds might. They would vocalize and engage in courting and mating rituals. At one time, they even began to incubate a rock, diligently keeping it warm in the folds of their abdomens. The zoo provided them with *real* egg that was obtained from a male-female penguin couple who had previously been unable to successfully hatch two eggs at the same time. Roy and Silo hatched and raised a healthy young, female chick named Tango.

Some have suggested that their bond arose because the penguins were deprived of their natural environment. While concerns about all captive animals are warranted, same gender relationships are also found in birds in the wild. These include some gulls, terns, geese, swans, parakeets and ostriches. Many of these pairs have also adopted and raised broods as well. Scientists still do not know all the reasons behind this. Love knows no boundaries!

The Legend of the Pussywillows

Myths die hard and some legends live long to delight without harm. Such is true of a Polish legend about cats. In this legend, a mother cat and her kittens were at the bank of a river. As kittens will, the youngsters amused themselves by watching and chasing butterflies.

Distracted by their play, the kittens got too close to the river's edge, fell into the rushing waters and began drowning. The mother cat became frantic and seeing this, the willows swept their branches into the water. The kittens gripped tightly to the willows and were safely brought to shore. Every spring since then, willow branches sprout tiny fur-like buds where the kittens once clung. The willow without flower, as it is often called, decks itself out in these velvety buds that feel like the silky coat of a kitten. The buds are called catkins and remarkably, in every country, these trees are named for their feline qualities. As the legend teaches, there is much in the natural world to delight and inspire. As we grow to appreciate the flora and fauna around us, our lives are immeasurably enriched.

Chapter Four

Children and Animals

"Much of the indifference, apathy and even cruelty we see has its origin in the false education given the young concerning the right of animals and their duty towards them."
... J Todd Ferrier (1855 - 1943).

Children and animals call upon our deepest emotional reserves. Oftentimes, they come to us in images that are most appealing - a dirty-faced boy with his dog or a little girl with a sleepy, calico cat in her arms. Children can have healthy and important relationships with animals long before they can establish similar relationships with adults and their peers.

Animals are often our first or only friends, siblings and significant others. Children retain the ability to maintain relationships with animals long after other relationships have changed due the demands of development and increasing maturity. Children can, in fact, maintain the human-animal bond for a lifetime. Unconditional love of animals persists in the midst of every other change and transition. As sociocultural demands increase, the secure and unchanging human-animal bond becomes even more precious. Although no empirical data exists to support the notion, it seems clear that volumes would be filled on the subject of thought processes, behavior and the deep, unspoken (even pre-verbal) emotional lives of children if all the kittens, dogs, goldfish, ponies and parakeets that befriended them would reveal the secrets told to them by children!

When the Bough Breaks

Children experience death, loss and transition in unique ways. Among the saddest experiences for children is the loss of their childhood and innocence. Sadder still is the premature loss of childhood due to an event that could have been prevented or softened by the awareness and understanding of parents and other adults.

A child's first loss is often the death of an animal. This loss comes in many forms: the death of a member of their own animal family, the death of a friend's companion animal or a school mascot, news of animals who are in peril or have died in disasters, traumatic events in zoos, stable fires or the squirrel seen dead on the side of the road.

Each situation calls for a different but sensitive response from adults. The dead squirrel (or other animal) on the side of the road presents the opportunity to display recognition, sadness and compassion through action of word and deed.

It is important to avoid knee-jerk responses such as, "It's *only* a squirrel - don't worry about it." Some children will protest and struggle against this idea but will often be overruled with disregard, admonishment or even the promise of punishment if they do not "Hush up" or "Stop nagging" about it. Other children will say nothing and retreat into their own interpretation, sadness, anger, frustration and disappointment. They often conclude that their feelings are *wrong* and take on the callous attitude modeled by the adults involved. The consequences of this can be destructive and lifelong. At the very least, these children have learned not to trust their own feelings or express their needs and wishes for fear of being dismissed or rejected.

If it is not possible to safely stop and find a way to very concretely acknowledge the death of the particular roadside animal, a caring adult would be wise to acknowledge the death on the roadway and discuss what it means to the child or children. This recognition begins by first becoming an adult who is sensitive to the death of a squirrel or any other animal.

It is not possible to fully mirror (reflect the feelings of others) or model (teach by example) empathy, respect and sensitivity without possessing at least some level of it internally. For those adults who have yet to develop a robust sense of empathy and do not possess these attributes themselves, they must still find a way to behave in a realized manner for the sake of the children. What adults teach children in relating to animals will cascade over and permeate every aspect of a child's emotional development and be carried into future life. While there are no guaranteed outcomes, it is highly likely that children who live with insensitivity or outright cruelty towards animals will, themselves, take on this behavior and not just perpetuate it with animals but with other people, as well.

In some rare and extraordinary instances, the cruel or insensitive behaviors will not be duplicated. Some children who grow up with insensitivity and cruelty are so strongly affected that they *never* repeat the offense. They make great conscious and unconscious efforts to be and do nothing like what they have been exposed to and taught by example.

Then there are those few children who come into the world as *naturals*. Absent of any modeling of a particularly strong nature in any direction, they are filled with their own innate sense of what is right, wrong, acceptable and unacceptable. Their connection with and love for animals is as visceral as their very bone, blood and DNA. Without teaching, coaching or example, they *know* that it is wrong to eat, use, harm, mistreat or even speak to or of animals unkindly. They object to this behavior in others, take strong stands against it and appear to have come equipped with the Jain principle of *Ahisma* or non-violence: "*Do not cause harm to any living being by deed, thought or words through one's self or through others by approving of (directly or indirectly) such an act by somebody else.*"

These special children benefit greatly when their parents support and nurture their innate qualities in an active way. It is equally important that even when parents do not deeply hold these qualities themselves, they do not crush, dismiss or disregard them in their children.

The Boy Who Saved Tigers

More than a half century ago, a boy was born in Brooklyn, New York. The boy had disfluency, which is more commonly known as stuttering and grew up in an era in which he was viewed as damaged, defective and even “retarded.”

Isolated, lonely and made speechless in order to protect himself from ridicule, the boy spoke little or nothing except to animals. He had turtles, a chameleon, garter snakes and other animals. He would take his friends with him into a closet and talk to them. It was there that he could communicate without judgment, criticism or ridicule.

He found that he could feel them and feel their consciousness. He also became aware that these animal friends could be disposed of, flushed away or discarded by others. The animals, like him, had no words or voice with which to protest or call for help. The boy did not have the gift of fluent speech but he had a natural empathy. With it, he made the animals his friends, his only friends.

In that small, private and sacred space, he promised them that if he ever took control of his voice, he would speak for them. This he would do in gratitude and kinship. Though no human heard the promise, his pledge to help them was deep and profound. After much struggle and hard work, the day came when the boy *did* achieve control over his speech. Since that time, he has been helping and speaking for those who cannot speak. The boy grew up to be the renowned, Dr. Alan Rabinowitz!

Alan Rabinowitz earned a Ph.D in wildlife ecology and was the Director of Science and Exploration for the Wildlife Conversation Society. Since May 2008, he has served as CEO and president of the Panthera Foundation (www.panthera.org). Panthera, founded in 2006, is the world’s leading organization devoted exclusively to the conservation of wild cats and their ecosystems. Utilizing the expertise of the world’s premier cat biologists, Panthera develops and implements global conservation strategies for the largest, most imperiled cats – tigers, lions, jaguars, and snow leopards. Representing the most comprehensive effort of its kind, Panthera works in partnership with local and international non-governmental organizations, scientific institutions, local communities and governments around the globe.

Dr. Rabinowitz has written innumerable scientific papers and books that include but are not limited to, *Jaguar: One Man's Struggle to Establish the World's First Jaguar Preserve*. All of Rabinowitz' books can be found at booksellers and libraries everywhere.

Rabinowitz has traveled to the darkest and most dangerous parts of the world to immerse himself in the study of jaguars, clouded leopards, tigers, Sumatran rhinos and other wildlife in peril. He has seen the most unusual and rare of Mother Nature's children and even discovered the Leaf Deer - a species of primitive deer previously unknown to science. He has trekked the roadless lands of Belize, Borneo, Taiwan, Thailand, Laos and Myanmar. His work in Belize resulted in the world's first Jaguar sanctuary.

Alan Rabinowitz examining jaguar paw-print in Belize
Photo by Steve Winter, National Geographic

In Taiwan, he conducted the first field work resulting in the establishment of the world's largest Nature Reserve. In Thailand, he performed the first field research on Indo-Chinese tigers in what was to become the region's first World Heritage Site. His work in Myanmar led to the creation of five new protected areas and the first Marine National Park. Included in his accomplishments is Thailand's first and largest Himalayan National Park, the country's largest wildlife Sanctuary and the world's largest tiger reserve.

Affectionately known to his many admirers as *The Indiana Jones of Wildlife*, Alan Rabinowitz has changed the world in ways that cannot be adequately measured or repaid despite our heartfelt gratitude. Dr. Rabinowitz is quick to shrug off this and other monikers like hero, and say simply: "It is they (the animals) who are the heroes." His modesty does not do justice to his legacy. In the more than twenty-five years of his fight to save the tiger and other big cats, he has encountered danger and hardship and had to negotiate with some unsavory individuals, groups, governments and military. He is often bone tired, injured or sick but nothing stops *The Boy Who Saved Tigers.*

The small, silent and private world of a misunderstood boy has grown into a roar heard 'round the world. Tabby or tiger, bunny or bison, butterfly or eagle, hamster or horse; they speak to all who have the ears to listen.

When I asked this extraordinary man, "What is your fondest wish?" He said, without hesitation, "I want to go to my grave knowing that tigers will not be extinct."

When our conversation came to a close, I thanked him for his dedication and passion, wished him safe journeys and safe returns to his wife and children. They, too, have sacrificed by selflessly loaning us a husband, a father and a friend of many people and to all tigers and big cats. Rabinowitz brings to mind the words of the poet Ella Wheeler Wilcox (1850–1919). They are adapted here, in part:

> *"I am the voice of the voiceless. Through me the speechless shall speak. 'Til the deaf world's ear be made to hear the cry of the wordless weak, I am my brother's keeper, and I will fight his fight and speak the words for beast and bird 'til the world shall set things right."*

How to Talk to Children about Animal Death

Death comes to all of us. We are all touched and often wounded by it throughout our lives and, ultimately, invited to it ourselves.

The pain of loss can come in many forms - From the death of parents, siblings and other family members, friends, teachers, religious and community leaders, colleagues, entertainers and others.

Among the better ways to refer to dying, death or assisted dying is, *help to die*, *help to leave his broken body and*, my personal favorite, *change worlds*. I do not, nor do I recommend that one avoid the use of "dying" and "death." Still, there are times when a softer, gentler expression is both desirable and also in keeping with my philosophy that is rooted in kindness. Woven deep within the tapestry of the layers of *worlds* in which we live, move about and die, there is also a final exit. Hence, when we move from one world to another, we *change worlds*.

Loss is most often associated with death but loss and death have many forms. We lose our ideals, dreams, honor and childhood. We lose our autonomy and body parts. We lose trust and hope, and belief in ourselves and each other. We live with the potential of recurring life-threatening illness in ourselves and those we love. We struggle in frozen anticipation of impending death, terminal illness and institutional care. We lose control, opportunities and even memory.

Children are at risk when coping with all of these losses and the consequences can be unmitigated and damaging if the risks are unrecognized or are poorly managed by those who can help.

The challenges of mourning are varied and often seem insurmountable. They require that we journey from an active relationship of the present to a comforting relationship of memory. This is not an easy journey for anyone to make. It is made more difficult if it has to be made alone and is especially complicated for a child.

It is believed that children begin to understand death at about age six. This will vary among children and some will do so earlier. Even if a child displays some understanding of death, the absolute finality of it can remain a mystery to them.

Although it is well known that adults cannot fool children for very long, many endeavor to do it despite the fact that generations of people have never found success with this strategy.

In feeble efforts to avoid addressing the subjects of catastrophic illness and death, some persist in giving children mixed and inappropriate signals that result in fear, rejection, confusion, and guilt. The wish to protect children from the harshness of serious injury, illness, dying or death is natural. But attempting to act on this impulse can be dangerous because it leads to isolating children from reality. Children are better served with a measured and well thought out exposure to facts. Such exposure is more likely to produce children who can surmount their personal history and learn to appreciate themselves and others, including the animals with whom we share the planet.

The unnecessary hasty removal of a sick or injured animal *can* and often *does* teach children that animals' lives are cheap and replaceable. From there, children may easily internalize that they, too, can be *dispensed with* if they are sick, misbehave or cause displeasure.

A responsible approach to bringing an animal companion into the home must begin by teaching children that we are *guardians*, not *owners* of our animal companions. Adults must also take into account an acknowledgement of the mortality of the animal friend-to-be. Many schools have class or school mascots or other animal residents and they must be cared *for*, cared *about* and treated in ways that are kind. That is the least they deserve. Similarly, at home, we can help children by actively displaying kindness and responsibility to our companion animals as well as all others.

"*Kindness in words creates confidence. Kindness in thinking creates profoundness. Kindness in giving creates love*"
... Loa-Tzu (570-490 BC).

When an animal companion or mascot is removed from the home or school and children are not involved, they can feel that they have been excluded because of something they may have done wrong and can bear the guilt of that perceived wrong-doing for years. Too many children experience the Sherlockian mystery of *The Case of the Disappearing Animal*. In the home setting, the child arrives home from school or other activity and the family companion animal is not there. They ask, "Where's Mandy?" It is then that the mystery turns into a horror story of deceit, lies and pain when they are told, "You know that Mandy was getting too old to walk up the stairs" or "You know that Mandy could never learn not to wet the floor, so while you were away, we gave her to a nice farmer where that won't be a problem." These scenarios are played out after a companion animal has been either helped to die due to illness or the decision has been made for her to be relinquished to a shelter or pound. In the latter, the cause is likely to have been a behavior problem that the family did not know how to remedy and were unwilling to address through the help of an experienced animal behaviorist.

When, after much questioning that includes, "When is Mandy coming back?" or "When can I go to see her?" the child learns that the situation is final and he has no control over it.

In addition to the shock and sadness the child endures, he will likely suffer from guilty thoughts including, "I should have taken her for more walks like I was supposed to," or "Maybe she would have been able to walk better if I didn't play so hard with her. Then they wouldn't have sent her away."

When the sadness and pain are no longer apparent, parents may think that they have convinced the child of the veracity of the farmer story. They may even feel reassured that all is well. But they have fooled only themselves. In most cases, the child never believed the story and never will. He instinctively understands that there is no saving farm or farmer and a bond of trust between parent and child is broken. In some cases, the child believes the story temporarily, only to recognize the lie later on.

The Case of the Disappearing Animal can take place in the school setting and is equally damaging. It is often needlessly born from events over a weekend or holiday break. Here, again, adults have the choice to either attempt to delude the children or provide them with an experience that guides them without deceit.

Parents and other adults must examine their motives for deceit. Perhaps their own insecurity in contemplating a talk with children about this difficult subject outweighs their protective instincts altogether. Often, they are trying to protect themselves from the uncomfortable task of talking with their child about death and dying. It remains, however, that a gentle and sincere discussion of loss, dying and death is probably all that most children require. By their own actions, children will limit and control the amount of information they receive. A child may respond to being informed by saying,"Okay," and then return to the activity they had been doing. In such instances, it is best not to insist on delivering the whole speech one might think they need to give. Children, not unlike their animal friends and siblings, will reply with non-verbal responses that speak as loudly as the audible voice. Adults must learn to be sensitive to these cues. There are many such forms of non-verbal communication and each parent, adult or educator must learn to recognize the important communications transmitted. These communications include but are not limited to:

- Appearing to be tired or sleepy.
- Rubbing the eyes or yawning.
- Loss of or refusal to continue eye contact.
- Sudden and seemingly inappropriate distractions such as returning to play as though nothing has happened and other things unique to each individual child.

When recognized, adults should go no further and say, "If you want to talk about this or ask any questions, we can do that later or whenever you feel like it." This leaves the door open for the child to return to the subject as much and as often as needed.

Do not expect or demand any particular kind of reaction. Allowing children free expression and even *no* expression is best.

The finality of death is hard to accept both for children and adults. Explanations in simple terms help but questions regarding the possibility of a companion animal's return may still come up. This is natural and normal.

The joy of bringing animals into the lives of children does not have to be overshadowed by death education 101.

Like people, animals can die suddenly, be accidentally killed or need assistance in dying because no hope of recovery for a meaningful life exists. In the case of sudden or accidental death, children are often witnesses. Adults should address these situations with care, honesty, and compassion. The words, death and sleep must *never* be interchanged. This is typified in the common phrases used to describe assisted dying for companion and other animals. The phrases are: *going to sleep*, *put to sleep*, and possibly worst of all, *put down*. There are better ways to articulate the loving choice of assisted dying even amongst adults. But, certainly, sleep terms should never be used with children. Children take words quite literally and may develop sleep phobias.

How to Explain Death in Simple Terms

The sleep metaphor often comes into play even when there is no reference to the phrase as regards assisted dying. People use it to explain the appearance of death. We should make clear to children why death is not really sleeping at all.

In a children's story I offer here, *Me 'n' Duke*, I crafted a parable for communicating this idea and others. It covers a particular set of circumstances but it holds important guidelines that can be adapted to suit many individual circumstances and families. I invite all readers to use it as best fits their particular situation. A cautionary note to educators: Do not read this story to children without the expressed and written permission of a parent or guardian.

Me 'n' Duke

It all started a long time ago... fifteen years. Before me and before Daddy. When Mommy was an art student away at school and a little lonely, she found a tiny, fluffy puppy under the stairs of the school library. She could tell that he was sick and took him to a veterinarian; that's a special doctor for animals. The doctor said that, although he was very sick, she thought that after a few days in the hospital, he could get better and be able to go home and be okay if Mom would take very special care of him.

Mom went to visit him in the hospital every day, and every day, just like Dr. Green said, he got better and better. On the fifth day, he was well enough to go home.

Mommy took him home, gave him medicine, special food and lots of love and attention. He was a very special, little dog. He was so special and so little she decided to give him a *big* name - Duke!

Duke got well. He grew and grew and grew. He became a great, big, one hundred thirty-five pound, beautiful German Shepherd. He and Mom were best friends. They went for long walks and played together in the park. Duke kept Mommy company while she painted her pictures and studied. On school breaks and summer vacation, Mommy and Duke would go home to Grandma and Grandpa's house so they were never apart from each other. Duke was not just Mom's friend. He was like a brother, too. He helped her by barking at strange sounds in the night and carrying her newspaper.

One day when Mom and Duke were in the park, they met a man who liked them both very much. They spent the whole day together and were together a lot after that, too. That man was Daddy. The next winter they got married.

They didn't want Duke to be left out of the wedding, so they got married at Grandma's house in the country and instead of Duke carrying a newspaper, he carried the flowers.

When I was born, Duke watched me all the time and even slept next to my crib in his own bed. Mom and Dad said that Duke and I were good pals right away.

When I was little (I'm seven now,) we had a party at Grandma's house. There were lots of people and everyone was very busy and didn't see me crawling across the front lawn. Everybody except Duke, that is. He saw me and picked me up by my jumper and carried me back to Mommy. Good thing, too, 'cause I was crawling right towards the road.

Duke was the hero of the day and when all the excitement was over, we all ate big bowls of pink, strawberry ice cream and Duke had some, too.

Duke would let me ride him like a pony and even when I would accidentally step on his paw or tug on him tightly, he was never mad. I know, now, that I must *never* pull any dog or cat's tail because it hurts them. Animals have feelings just like kids and can get scared or worried just like us.

Duke and Mommy were always waiting for me at the corner where the school bus stopped. One day, I came off the bus and Duke wasn't there, just Mommy. We walked home and she told me that Duke wasn't feeling well and couldn't walk that day. I knew that his back legs were very tired. Mom and Dad helped him get up and down the stairs, and Grandpa made a special staircase so he could get into the car. Duke even had special treatments called acupuncture to help keep his back legs as strong as they could.

Mommy said that as soon as Daddy came home, we would take him to see Dr. Green. Daddy left work early and got home a little while after we did.

Daddy carried Duke to the car in a blanket that used to be mine and I helped by tucking in all the edges. I sat in the back seat with him and Mom and talked to him all the way. I told him how much I loved him and sang a little song for him, too.

Dr. Green spent a long time carefully examining Duke. When she was finished, she asked Mom and Dad if they wanted me to wait outside. They said, “No” because we were a family. Duke was my friend, too, and we have no secrets from each other.

Dr. Green said that Duke was not going to get well. He would not be able to walk again or do any of the things he loved to do. He would not want to eat and be very, very unhappy.

I asked why she couldn’t fix him like when Mommy first brought him to her and when he cut his paw on a sharp stick. She explained why that was different. Duke was much older now and his body was very tired and worn out and could not be fixed any more.

Mommy was crying and I was getting scared but then she told me that the thing we could do for Duke was to ask Dr. Green to give him a special injection that would not hurt. It would take away all the pain and when the pain was gone, Duke would be too.

The injection was not like the others Duke had gotten before. It was not like any injection my Mom or I ever had, either. This one would make his heart stop and he would die.

We all hugged and kissed Duke and cried a lot because we understood that, even though it was the best thing to do, we would not be the way we always were and we would miss him very much.

Dr. Green gave him the injection and a kiss, too, and he looked like he was asleep. Mommy, Daddy and Dr. Green all explained again that Duke would not wake up and that he just *looked* like he was sleeping but he was dead.

Being asleep is very different from being dead. When you’re asleep, your body is working and moving and can feel things and wake up. When you die, your body is not working and you don’t move. You don’t feel things and you don’t wake up. You also don’t feel scared, or hurt or sad or anything at all.

We stayed with Duke for a while and touched his head and kissed him some more and then went into Dr. Green’s office. We all listened to Dr. Green tell us about the different ways to take care of Duke’s body now that he was dead. We could bury him in a cemetery for animals and be able to visit his grave almost any time we wanted to because it was close by. I thought it would be better to bury him in our garden under the willow tree where he liked to play and sleep in the place where the sun came through. That way, he'd be really close.

Dr. Green explained that even though that seemed like a good idea, it was not allowed by the rules of the town. She also explained that it is not allowed in other towns and cities, too. Then she told us about cremation. That's when you take your dog to a place called a crematory where they put him on a special metal tray that goes into a machine that is very hot and after a little while, what is left is called cremains. Most people call it ashes but it's not really ashes; it's cremains. It's okay to call them ashes if you want to. The cremains are put into a beautiful container so people can take them home to be close by from then on. The containers are called urns. We talked for a while and decided to cremate him so we could have his cremains.

Mommy cried the most and was extra sad. I thought maybe it was because she loved Duke more than me and Daddy did. But Daddy told me that it was because she and Duke had been such good friends for so long. They were together before she knew me and Daddy and they had a special love. Even though we all loved each other and we all loved Duke, Mommy's sadness was different. Everybody's sadness is different when somebody they love dies.

Even though we did all the good, special things for Duke, we still felt sad and cried a lot. That's okay because when someone you love dies, sadness is one of the things you feel. You can feel lots of other things, even being mad but it's all okay. Crying is also okay 'cause it can help make you feel better even if you don't feel like talking.

We did other things to help make us feel better. We made a special place for Duke's urn. We put in on the mantle over the fireplace in the den. We lit a tall candle and put it next to the urn and found all of Duke's pictures and put them in a pretty box to make them ready to put into an album.

We didn't really know what to do with his leash and we didn't want to throw it away or leave it hanging on the pegboard where it was. Then Mom came up with a good idea. We'd get a grapevine wreath from the craft store and braid the leash into it. We also decorated it with little dog biscuits, silk flowers that looked just like the ones he loved to sniff in the garden and other things to remind us of him and we hung it on the front door.

I missed Duke a lot and wanted to have another dog but I was afraid that Duke might feel I didn't love him anymore if we had another dog. Mommy said that she and Daddy were too sad to have another dog right away but that no matter what, Duke would not feel like we stopped loving him and we never would.

Always loving Duke did not mean that we couldn't love another dog. Daddy reminded us that Duke would want us to be happy again like when he was alive and that he was sure that Duke knew he would never be forgotten and he never will.

The next spring came and so did my birthday. We still missed Duke like always but we weren't sad in the same way anymore. It was time for another dog and what a great birthday present that would be.

We went to the shelter to see the dogs there. Dogs in shelters don't have a home. They are waiting for people like us to come and take them home with us. I saw a cute puppy at a shop in the mall that sells puppies and kittens but Mom and Dad explained that it was much better to adopt a dog from a shelter than to buy one from a store.

At the shelter, we saw lots of dogs and cats, too. Big ones and small ones, loud ones and sleeping ones. Then we saw one that was very small and very noisy. She was white with a wiggly tail and a black circle around her eye. We took her home and named her Jesse. Jessie 'n' me are gonna be special friends forever and I think Duke would like her, too!

Creating Rituals

Rituals can involve anything from a formal burial in an animal cemetery to a simple candle lighting at the home if the animal friend has been cremated. I suggest that you take freely from whatever personal or family rituals are already in place in the family system and build on them. These may include rituals and memorials from religious, cultural or family traditions or any new ones that seem appropriate.

Encourage Children to Participate in Ceremonies

Discuss the possible roles children can play in memorials and allow them to choose or create their own versions. The choice *not* to choose or participate is also a valid one and should be honored. In the case where a child does not want to participate, the ceremony or ritual should be carried out just the same, leaving the child free to change his mind at any time he may wish to do so. A child's desire often changes and they may involve themselves more deeply along the way.

Adults must avoid turning invitation, inclusion and encouragement into coercion as children mourn. Coercion can be as traumatic and damaging as exclusion and deceit.

Teach and Encourage Mourning

Children look to models for expressing their feelings. Adults' crying and open sadness can teach children that sad feelings are normal and that expressing them is natural and welcome. It is particularly true for boys, who still struggle against the stereotypes that *boys don't cry* and *big boys*, especially, *don't cry*. Often, their fathers and other male role models perpetuate the unhealthy myths. A stunning example is when they are told, "You're the man of the house now" following the death of their fathers. This is usually accompanied by an instruction to "Take care of your mother" or "Now you have to take care of your mother because you're the man of the house." Deep damage is done to boys and young men as these responsibilities are feats that no child or young man can manage. These are burdens from which they may never recover when taken literally and children do just that; take things literally.

Conversely, girls and young women must not be expected to fulfill their stereotypical role of being more emotional, crying freely and expressing great sensitivity. Not every girl, young woman or woman grieves this way and it should not be demanded or expected of them.

Teach your children well…"*For in the end, we will save only what we love, we will love only what we understand and we will understand only what we are taught.*" … Lao-Tsu (Circa 6th Century BC).

Chapter Five

The Brutal Truth

"We have not two hearts – one for the animals, and the other for man. In the cruelty toward the latter, there is no other difference than in the victim." ... Alphonse de Larmartine (1790 - 1869).

The magical link that binds us to animals and each other is like the web of a spider. It is beautiful, complex, exquisitely designed, and very powerful. It can warm the heart and delight all the senses. Like all powerful bonds, the links between and among us are not always pretty, friendly, benevolent or healthy. This chapter takes us on a journey through much of it.

"The truth is heavy; therefore few care to carry it."
... Hyman Polano, 19th Century Scholar.

It is not easy to learn the truth because, once known, there is usually an imperative to do or stop doing something. This is why ignorance and the pretense of not knowing are held on to so strongly. Under the veil of not knowing or not being aware, lurks a deeper knowing that denies awareness in order to avoid taking action and responsibility. There are also those who truly do not know. When they learn the truth, while shocked and disturbed by the ugly and painful reality, they will embrace and welcome it. For many others, there is a knowing deep inside that is cloaked in not wanting to know and being inconvenienced by the truth.

Through the magic of their oneness, animals can influence and teach us to become better than we are. Love, empathy, kindness, respect and compassion are like water; you cannot spill it on others without getting some on yourself.

Hope can be found in the ashes of cruelty, sadness and pain if we look for it. We can change if we choose to do so and everyone can do something!

Animals Used for Food, Clothing and Sport

With gratitude to People for the Ethical Treatment of Animals (www.peta.org) and their tireless mission to raise consciousness, educate, investigate and expose cruelty, legislative action, and *make a difference!*

Down on the Factory Farm

The idyllic image of farms with rolling, green pastures and happy animals engaging with each other in barnyard bliss is a notion of imagination and distant fantasy.

Before continuing, it is essential to know that the widely-held belief that the sole goal of animal advocacy organizations is to abolish or outlaw the consumption of meat, fish and all animal products and by-products. This is a false notion. For as long as it remains the practice of society to raise animals for food consumption, the primary goal of such groups, their members, supporters and other individuals is to advocate for a more humane and compassionate treatment of *food animals* and animals who are *used* for all other purposes, as well. Accompanying the primary goal is also to educate people about their choices and offer encouragement and alternatives for a more cruelty-free and healthy lifestyle.

Another erroneous belief is that some groups also have the goal to abolish sharing our lives with companion animals. While there *may* be a philosophical discussion to be held on this matter, it is only that – a philosophical discussion. This false belief may have come from out-of-context or misunderstood comments carelessly taken from interviews or magazine articles. The exact source or sources are unknown to me but the potentially damaging rumor is untrue. In the case of animals raised for food, sadly, it is well understood that the practice is highly unlikely to be discontinued. What *can* and *should* be discontinued is the cruel and unconscionable ways in which they are treated.

Today's mechanized, factory farms are combinations of filthy, windowless sheds, wire cages, gestation crates and other unspeakable confinement systems.

Animals who live on these farms will never raise their young, root in the soil, build nests or do anything that is natural to them. They are often given so little space, they cannot even turn around or lie down comfortably. Deprived of exercise so that all their energy goes toward producing flesh, eggs, or milk, they often cannot manage under their own weight and are severely crippled. Some die only inches from food and water. They are given drugs to fatten them up quickly and kept alive in conditions that would otherwise kill them. They are genetically altered to grow faster and produce more product than they ever could or would, naturally. The only time they see the light of day is when they are loaded onto trucks bound for slaughter.

> "*As long as there are slaughterhouses, there will be battlefields.*"... Leo Tolstoy (1847 – 1852).

Cattle are castrated and their horns ripped from their heads. Third degree burns are inflicted on their flesh in the form of branding. All of this is done without anesthesia or pain control.

Milk cows are drugged to produce unnatural amounts of milk. Their babies are stolen from them shortly after birth and sent to cruel veal farms for an abbreviated, miserable life. Cows suffer from chronic mastitis which is a painful bacterial inflammation of the udder in dairy cattle. They are given large amounts of antibiotics to treat it. This is not done for the benefit of the well being of the cows but to try to control or prevent the clotted and bloody milk that mastitis produces and is unsaleable. If gangrene sets in, cows can die and profit is further reduced. Antibiotic residue is often found in the final dairy products consumed by children and adults throughout the country.

More than nine billion chickens are raised on factory farms every year. Their cages are stacked one on top of the other and the excrement of the chickens in the higher cages falls on those below.

Chickens have part of their highly sensitive beaks cut off so that they cannot peck at each other as a result of the anxiety and frustration they experience from unnatural confinement.

Photo Provided by PETA

Because male chicks are unable to produce eggs, they are killed. Every year, more than one hundred million male chicks are ground up alive or tossed into bags to suffocate. At the slaughter house, chickens have their legs snapped into shackles. Their throats are cut and they are immersed in scalding, hot water to remove their feathers. Without federal, legal protections, most are still conscious during this process and many others are scalded to death in the feather-removal tanks after missing the throat cutter.

"*Nothing more strongly arouses our disgust than cannibalism, yet we feed on babies; though not our own.*"
... Robert Lewis Stevenson (1850 -1894).

Many people who really know pigs, have come to view them much in the same way most people see dogs: friendly, intelligent and loyal. Pigs are naturally clean animals and, when given the opportunity, pigs will spend many hours playing, exploring their surroundings with their powerful sense of smell and lying in the sun. The reason they are often seen covered in mud is that their skin is very sensitive to the sun and, to protect themselves, they bathe in the mud and also enjoy it.

Piglets on factory farms are taken from their mothers when they are less than one month old. Their tails are cut off and the males are castrated without anesthesia or pain control. They spend the rest of their wretched lives in overcrowded pens on a small slab of concrete.

Breeding sows live in tiny metal gestation crates where they cannot turn around. Shortly after giving birth, they are once again, forcibly impregnated. This cycle continues for years until their bodies give out and they are sent to be killed. Many die from heat exhaustion in the summer and freeze to death in the winter because they are transported in trucks that travel for extended drives through extreme weather. It is estimated that more than one million pigs die annually during transport and an additional 420,000 are injured or crippled. Cattle raised for beef are usually born in one state and fattened or *finished* in another and slaughtered in a third state. They, too, are transported hundreds of miles in extreme weather and many die along the way. Those who survive are shot in the head with a bolt gun and then hung up by their legs and taken onto the killing floor of a slaughter house. There, their throats are cut and they are skinned. Some remain fully conscious throughout the entire process.

Ducks, geese, turkeys and rabbits fare no better. Ducks and geese are some of America's best known and most beloved animals. They are as adept on land as they are in water. Ducks live in pairs or groups, while geese mate for life. They mourn for a significant amount of time when their mates die, and they are highly intelligent.

Duck and Ducklings

Grey Goose Family

Despite our society's seeming appreciation for them, they are the victims of extreme cruelty in the making of foie gras, an expensive delicacy eaten by many people. Translated from French, foie gras means fat liver. Foie gras comes from intentionally subjecting fowl to a highly pathological and painful state known as hyperlipidosis. Ducks and geese must endure the pain of having a tube forced down their throats several times a day so that three pounds of grain (the equivalent of force-feeding forty-five pounds of food to an adult human) can be forcefully pumped into their stomachs with each forced-feeding. The process begins several weeks before slaughter and, during that time, the ducks and geese are also deprived of swimming water. The result of this cruel and unhealthy procedure which forms the basis of foie gras, is a diseased fatty liver that grows to about ten times the normal size, causing extreme suffering. The making of foie gras is not only cruel, it can also present a health hazard in the final product. In 2007, a study revealed that protein fibers found in foie gras, speed the onset of secondary amyloidosis, a disease that can be fatal to humans. Accordingly, the Animal Legal Defense Fund (www.aldf.org) filed a legal petition with the United States Department of Agriculture, urging that foie gras products carry a label to warn consumers of the potential threat. Your author suffers no illusion that a warning alone can stop foie gras production or prevent people from eating it (or any other animal product), but consumers *do* have a right to know what they are *really* buying and be warned about the cruelty and risks involved. Moreover, to stand by and do nothing is unconscionable. Every step taken, no matter how seemingly small or inconsequential, is a step in the right direction.

In August 2004, California became the first U.S. state to pass a law (effective July 1, 2012) banning the production and sale of foie gras. Foie gras is also banned by more than a dozen countries including the United Kingdom, Germany, Italy, and Israel. Additionally, a growing number of retailers, such as Whole Foods Markets and Wolfgang Puck's restaurants refuse to sell it.

The Folly of Fashion

Wool

Wool comes from sheep, goats or Tibetan antelopes. The product may be called wool, mohair, pashmina or cashmere, but no matter what it is called, the result is very bad news for the animal from which it came.

Weeks after birth, lambs have their tails chopped off. The males are castrated without anesthesia. Flystrike, a maggot infestation propagated in wrinkly skin, is intentionally bred into sheep to produce more wool. Many ranchers use a barbarous mutilation called mulesing to rein in the flystrike that, if left uncontrolled, can damage the end product. In 1923, Mulesing was invented by a farmer named Mules. It involves the carving off of skin and flesh the size of a dinner plate from the back end (rump and areas surrounding the anus) and sometimes the shoulder and face of lambs. The folds of the skin that attract the blowfly to lay eggs are thus eliminated. This cruel and very painful technique is performed without anesthesia or pain control of any kind. It is still used in Australia, despite the fact that there are many other management methods to prevent and control flystrike. Undoubtedly, mulesing is preferred based on time and financial concerns. The mulesing method is without cost, except to the lambs who suffer greatly.

John Auty is a veterinarian with vast experience in sheep farming and management. He said of mulesing, "It is similar to flaying (peeling), and the pain will be experienced for weeks and months afterwards. Mulesing does not free the sheep from blowfly strike but proper husbandry practices including close inspection of sheep will reduce and virtually eliminate flystrike."

Leather

Leather is not a slaughterhouse by-product as many think. Instead, it is a vital and driving force for the cattle industry in its own right. Leather accounts for two thirds of the value of slaughtered cattle. Even the hides of baby cows (veal calves) are made into high-priced calfskin products. The economic success of factory farming and slaughterhouses is directly linked to leather.

Fur

> "*No one in the world needs a mink coat but a mink.*"
> ... Murray Banks.

Image Provided by Barbara Meyers

With thanks to The Humane Society of the United States (www.hsus.org) for decades of devotion to animals, animal welfare, animal rights, legislative action, and more.

Fur farms are much the same as any other farm whose purpose is to breed and slaughter animals for their body parts. Mink and other animal victims spend their lives in cages deprived of all natural activity, only to die by the cruelest of methods.

If they are not in captivity, they are trapped by the millions each year in steel-jaw leghold traps, body-crushing traps, and strangling snares. Terrified and injured animals caught in traps try to escape by lunging away and biting the traps and their own limbs. In some states, trappers are not required to return and kill the trapped animals (often by beating or shooting them in the head) for several days.

The steel-jaw leghold trap is the most commonly used trap in the United States. They are banned by at least ninety nations in the European Union, but, except for eight states they remain in unrestricted use in the United States. New Jersey is the only state that enacted a complete ban in effect since 1994. Seven other states have partial bans with exclusions for "human health and safety, animal damage, research and wildlife control." It is the opinion of many (including your author) that the exclusion is tantamount to no protection at all!

The fur industry claims that ranch-raised fur is humane. Yet, they continue to utilize killing methods that include gassing, anal and genital electrocution, neck breaking, and poisoning.

Many informed people have made the decision not to wear fur and, if they have fur in any form, they have given what remains of its former inhabitant, a proper burial in an appropriate forum or in their own back yards.

Selling or giving fur to charity clothing drives or thrift shops is not the act of charity it may seem to be. The practice merely recycles the victims and fails to rectify the cruelty and bloodshed. The Humane Society of the United States (HSUS) has instituted a program named Coats for Cubs. Coats for Cubs returns the fur back to the animals in a unique form. Coats are collected and sent to wildlife rehabilitators who cut them into appropriate sizes and use them to warm and comfort orphaned and injured wildlife. (Video: http://youtu.be/bQs--yKHrcY).

It is estimated that more than two hundred rehabilitators across the United States and Canada participate in this or similar programs. Locating a participating wildlife rehabilitator may not be easy to do. However, I encourage you to use the power of an internet search to find one. If you are not successful, please do not reconsider giving it to a thrift shop, consignment boutique or other sources where it will be sold and the cycle of cruelty will continue. Let your conscience be your guide.

Fish and Fishing

"If fish could scream, the sound would be deafening."
... Barbara Meyers.

Aquaculture, or fish factory farming, is the world's fastest growing agricultural industry. By weight, more than one-third of all aquatic animals eaten in the United States are raised in aquaculture facilities. According to the Los Angeles Times, these farms confine 50,000 to 90,000 fish in a single 100' x 100' pen. The exact number of aquatic animals killed for food goes largely unreported, but annual estimates record more than 10 billion.

There are no regulations regarding the treatment of fish. It is estimated that as many as 40% of aquaculture fish die before they are slaughtered. Those who survive are starved for as long as ten days before being killed in order to reduce waste contamination in the water during transport.

There is no effort to stun and render fish unconscious when they are killed. Thus, they are fully conscious when they start down the slaughter line.

Gills are severed and the fish are left to bleed to death, convulsing in pain. Large fish, such as salmon, are sometimes bashed on the head with a wooden bat called a *priest*. Many are seriously injured but still alive when finally cut open. Smaller fish, like trout, are often killed by simply draining the water from the tanks, leaving them to suffocate, or by packing them in ice while still alive.

Commercial fishing is no better. Commercial fishermen commonly use nets several miles long to trap tens of thousands of fish in a single pull. These nets are not discriminating, and about one in four fish caught in the gear dies as a *bycatch* (unwanted or unintentional catch). When the catch is brought to the surface, many fish experience decompression during which their organs can burst even before they suffocate on the deck of the boat.

Commercial fishing is an extremely hazardous endeavor for people, too. It is regarded among the most dangerous jobs in the world.

The Sport of Kings

Though horse racing has been called The Sport of Kings, the horses are not always treated as royalty. Visions of horses turned out to pasture to enjoy their lives in comfortable retirement when their careers are over are all too often, an illusion.

Ferdinand was the winner of the Kentucky Derby in 1986 and was Horse of the Year in 1987. Two years later, he was retired to stud where champion horses are expected to earn millions of dollars in stud fees and breeding shares through their offspring. Ferdinand did not prove a successful stud. In the high stakes often ruthless thoroughbred breeding business, an unsuccessful stud is considered worthless. They are treated as criminals and punished by deportation. Ferdinand was sold to Japanese interests and, ultimately, he was *disposed of*, jargon for killed in a slaughterhouse. Horse meat is considered a delicacy and is in high consumption in Japan, France and Belgium.

Ferdinand is not the only champion horse to die in an overseas slaughterhouse. Jockey Club Gold Cup winner Exceller was slaughtered in Sweden, and Kentucky Derby winners Alysheba (1987), Strike the Gold (1991), Sea Hero (1993), and War Emblem (2002) are now at stud in foreign countries where they may ultimately meet the same fate when they have outlived their usefulness.

Horse slaughter has been illegal in the United Sates since 2007. This legal reality only adds to the misery of horses as they are not slaughtered here but are shipped to many other countries where the practice is lawful. One need not, necessarily, ship overseas; our neighbors, Canada and Mexico have not outlawed horse slaughter. Consequently, making slaughter illegal in the United States has not changed the number of healthy, young horses sent to the kill-pens at auctions where they are bought by kill-buyers and sent to slaughter. The best hope for horses is federal legislation that would ban the export of horses for slaughter. As of this writing, there are no horse slaughter operations in the United States. But in the state of Montana, there is a bill pending to allow them. Unsatisfied, Governor Brian Schweitzer stated that the bill hides "unintended consequences" for the right to challenge companies' operating permits of slaughterhouses. He has also stated that, as a livestock and horse *owner*, he supports processing horses in a humane way to produce meat for human consumption. Schweitzer further stated that he would support a horse slaughterhouse in the state, but that the bill would do nothing to bring one there. In addition, "Not a single person has come forward from anywhere in the world to say they'd like to build a horse slaughter plant in Montana."

Horses suffer both while being transported and being slaughtered. They are hauled in trailers designed for cattle. They are overcrowded, often injured, and may go for days without food or water. Horses not destined for human consumption end up as dog food or other products.

Killing a horse is not an easy thing to accomplish. It is very difficult to render them unconscious even with a captive bolt gun. Many slaughterhouses dispense with the bolt gun procedure altogether. The horses are slaughtered while fully conscious by having their throats cut and being left to bleed to death. Other slaughterhouses use the practice of stabbing the spinal cord multiple times. The procedure is performed on horses in tight confinement; and the person doing the stabbing is in a safe position above the horse. Stabbing the spinal cord is used to paralyze horses so, though fully conscious, they cannot fight when their throats are cut.

Trainers who sell horses into this horrific death usually earn less than $350. Because legally, trainers and or owners *own* horses as property, they retain the right to sell them in any way and for any purpose they choose. A horse can be humanely euthanized by a trained equine veterinarian for as little as $60. This service, however, is usually available as a courtesy fee by equine veterinarians near to or associated with thoroughbred racing tracks. It is meant for horses who have suffered a serious injury or illness from which they cannot recover; not convenience killing for profit. Rendering companies will often accept dead horses for processing into dog food and other products such as soap for no fee at all. Geography permitting, some rendering companies offer staff that will come to a farm and shoot horses and then take them away for a small charge. Though hardly what any healthy horse deserves, the service at least allows a horse to avoid the torture of transportation followed by brutal slaughter. In today's *Sport of Kings*, race horses are truly running for their lives, but the same sad end awaits many other horses as well.

There are those who would have us believe that horses who find themselves in the killing pens at auctions are there because they are old, sick or at the end of their natural lives. This Is not so. Often horses one finds in the pens are young and healthy. Their only crime is that they are not earning big money and, therefore, viewed as disposable.

Thoroughbred horses capture the attention of the public when it is learned that they have been brutally slaughtered for a few dollars and their flesh. It remains, however, that more quarter horses are sent to slaughter by The American Quarter Horse Association and its members than thoroughbreds.

It should be noted that racing and track safety present a serious threat to race horses. Many believe that racing tracks could be made safer if dirt tracks were eliminated and replaced by all synthetic surfaces. Others advocate that horses should not be raced on any surface until they are at least three years of age, when they have they fully developed their skeletal growth and strength. Breeding practices that focus exclusively on speed rather than soundness and durability also contribute to tragedies such as those publicized by the breakdown and death of Eight Bells in the 2008 Preakness. Others like her remain anonymous but have suffered similarly.

Two champion thoroughbred horses captured the hearts of America as no others. They are Seabiscuit (1933-1947) and Barbaro (2003-2007). Neither succumbed to the fate of others before and after them.

Seabiscuit

In the late 1930's, after a decade of world chaos and in the midst of the *Great Depression,* Seabiscuit brought enthusiasm and hope to Americans. Seabiscuit had many physical defects and a heedless temperament, hardly the qualities of an ideal racehorse. But, beneath it lay the heart of a champion, and a champion he was!

High-strung and sensitive horses like Seabiscuit are often calmed and comforted by goats. Seabiscuit was given a goat named Whiskers but the great steed was not impressed. He did, however, have other companions – a little stray dog named Pocatell, a Native American Cayuse Pony (also known as a cow pony) named Pumpkin and JoJo, a spider monkey who had been left behind at a racetrack. They became so close that JoJo slept in the crook of Seabiscuit's neck while Pocatell lay curled into his tummy. Note: Horses are able to sleep both standing up and lying down. In fact, they are only capable of reaching REM (rapid eye movement or *dream sleep*) while lying down.

Seabiscuit had an illustrious career that ended with winning the Santa Anita Handicap in 1940–the one race that had eluded him in the past. Seabiscuit then retired and lived out his life as a beloved member of the Charles Howard family. His burial site was never disclosed except to Howard's sons.

Seabiscuit
By Fred Stone

You will read more about equine artist, Fred Stone in Chapter Eight.
www.fredstone.com

Barbaro

Barbaro won the Kentucky Derby in 2006, but shattered three bones in his right hind leg after breaking down on the track. Despite all efforts to save him and his gallant battle to regain his health, a series of complications made it impossible for Barbaro to go on. He was released from his broken body on January 29th 2007.

On the one year anniversary of Barbaro's death, his family, Roy and Gretchen Jackson, announced that a memorial would be built at Churchill Downs. A life-sized bronze statue of Barbaro was commissioned by the Jacksons and added to the memorial where his cremains are housed.

A beloved champion horse will often be buried whole or cremated, and the cremains will be returned to the horse's family. The practice of burying the head, heart and hooves of a horse is also considered a burial of honor. It is believed that the essence of the horse is found in these body parts. The remainder of the horse is usually cremated with this type of burial, and the cremains are returned to the horse's family.

A Legacy of Hope
Barbaro
By Fred Stone

"Until he extends the circle of his compassion to all living things, man himself will not find peace."
... Albert Schweitzer (1875–1965)

Making a Difference!

"We all owe a great debt of gratitude of those who keep the flames of hope burning."... Barbara Meyers.

Random acts of kindness can be found everywhere. Many seem small and are viewed by some as not making much difference: a drop in the bucket or a futile attempt that does not solve the problem completely.

The best argument countering this narrow view is represented in a well known, often told story about an old man seen throwing starfish from the beach into the sea.

A young man, walking along the seashore, saw, far ahead of him, the distant figure of someone who was walking, stooping down, and apparently throwing something into the sea.

His curiosity aroused, he hurried to get closer. As he drew nearer, he saw that the figure was an old man who was stopping every step or two to pick up a starfish and fling it into the ocean. The young man noticed that the beach was littered with thousands of starfish stranded there by the tide. He thought that what the old man was doing was pointless, and he walked over to explain as much.

"Why are you doing this?" the young man said. "You can't save them all. It's useless! What does it matter?"

The old man paused for just a moment, looked down at the dying starfish he had just picked up, tossed it into the sea and only then, answered. "It matters to this one!"

This philosophy is shared by many who have devoted their lives to the rescue of animals in peril. Two such people are Christy and Ricky Sheidy. Together, they founded Another Chance for Horses in Bernville, Pennsylvania (www.ac4h.com).

The pair have been rescuing horses and educating people on how to responsibly care for them for more than a decade. In 2004, they gained official 501 (C)(3) status as a non-profit organization and they also formed The Horse Rescue Coalition, a nation-wide network of approved horse rescue groups.

The Sheidys go to the killing pens at auctions and rescue as many horses as their limited finances will permit. They then rehabilitate the horses from the trauma they have endured, and find permanent homes for them with people who are committed to a life-long, responsible, loving relationship with horses.

The Sheidys and their like-minded and like-hearted coalition teams are making a difference one horse at a time. There is no question that to each horse saved "from stable to table in 7 days," the couple's work matters.

Christy Sheidy was featured in the HBO Real Sports expose on horse slaughter "*Hidden Horses*" with journalist, Bernard Goldberg. In my conversation with her, she said, "though finances remain our greatest challenge, we will continue to save as many horses as possible and work with legislators to achieve federal laws to protect horses from transportation to slaughterhouses." When asked about her wish list, she was quick to reply that she had no such list for herself but only for the horses.

In this chapter, I have touched only *some* of the exploitation and systematic abuse of animals. It reaches deep into the dark, hidden places of puppy mills, greyhound racing, dog and cock fighting pits, rodeos, fishing, laboratories where unspeakable animal experimentation is conducted in the name of medical research that is often both cruel and unnecessary, cosmetic and product testing centers, poaching of exotic and other wildlife, marketplaces for animal body parts and trophies, and *canned* hunting grounds.

A *canned* hunt is one in which hunters pay a fee in exchange for the opportunity to kill animals for pleasure and trophies. Their victims have no chance of escape because they are confined by fences, tethered, or launched into the air as hunters stand ready to kill. *Canned* hunts often target exotic animals such as bears, tigers, Siberian ibex, zebras, and many more.

Hunters are also frequently offered a money back guarantee if they do not make the promised *kill.* Further complicating the entire subject of animal abuse and killing is the matter of *human exceptionalism.*

Black Bear at Yellowstone National Park
Photo by Laura Cowen

Human Exceptionalism

Human Exceptionalism refers to a widely held belief that human beings have a unique, special, and *higher* status in nature. It serves as a dangerous justification for vastly diverging ethical and moral standards in the treatment of animals. It has permitted people to dominate the planet by, among other things, ruthlessly and destructively exploiting Mother Nature and *all* her children (both flora and fauna) without conscience. Exceptionalism, with its highly questionable *uniqueness* philosophy, is, in my opinion, a cornerstone on which speciesism has been built.

Speciesism is defined as discrimination against or exploitation of animals by human beings based on the assumption of humankind's superiority. Speciesism, like other *isms*, gives rise to and license for cruelty, abuse, neglect, hideous animal experimentation and mass extermination of sentient living beings. Historically, humankind has been victimized by other powerful *isms: racism*, *ageism*, *sexism* and, the newest, *lookism*. Indeed, *isms* account for historical moments of infamy: the Tuskegee syphilis experiment, the experiments conducted by Nazi doctors in concentration camps, and ethnic cleansing in various countries throughout the world. Sadly, the infamy continues in far too many places today.

A compelling argument against exceptionalism was made by Donald Griffin, Ph.D (1915-2003). Griffin was an American zoologist often called the "father of cognitive ethology" - the study of animal minds. He proposed, demonstrated, and defended the ability of animals to adapt to unpredictably changing conditions, showing they are conscious and able to assess what is needed to be done in a given situation. In an even less enlightened age, Griffin argued, perhaps at the expense of his own popularity, that the great complexity and adaptability of animal behavior indicates that animals are not mechanistic automatons. From the sophisticated food-gathering behavior of chimps, to the clever fishing techniques of herons (two of many examples), he maintained that animals are thinking, feeling beings, even if and when they are thinking about different things in entirely different ways from humans.

In closing this chapter, let us look to the words and wisdom of Albert Schweitzer: "*Anyone who has accustomed himself to regard the life of any living creature as worthless is in danger of arriving also at the idea of worthless human lives.*"

Chapter Six

Fables and Facts

"The land of fairy tales is charming to those who view it at a distance, but, like all other landscapes, the charm fades on close approach and the thorns and briars become visible."
... Adapted from Washington Irving (1753-8159).

Animals and Violence in Fairy Tales and Film

Fairy tales have the ability to enchant children and adults. They are, however, often brutally violent and filled with monsters, wicked step-mothers, fathers who abandon their children to evil forests, girl-eating wolves and other *bad* animals.

According to the fairy tale *Hansel and Gretel,* under the instruction of a domineering stepmother, Hansel and Gretel's spineless father takes his children into the forest and abandons them there to either die of starvation or fall prey to any number of other possibilities. The children find their way to a cottage inhabited by a cannibalistic, wicked witch who fattens them up so she can cook and eat them. Before her plans reach fruition, the children escape by pushing the witch into the flames of her oven. They take her gold coins and then return to their abusive father, only to learn that their stepmother has died. The children then turn over the coins to their father, and everyone "lives happily ever after." Looking critically at the fable, is this really a good example of forgiveness?

Similarly, popular film can also send the wrong messages. Often, dogs, rabbits and cats are murdered by deranged neighbors or obsessive stalkers.

Bambi's mother is murdered by a hunter leaving Bambi and the children who view it, terrified throughout most of the film. In *Old Yeller*, a boy whose dog contracts rabies while saving the family from disaster has to shoot his dog in order to prove he is finally a man. In *Finding Nemo*, Nemo's mother and 498 fish brothers and sisters are eaten in the first ten minutes. In *All Dogs Go to Heaven*, Charlie, the canine lead character is run over by a car.

In the television remake of *The Yearling*, a man kills a deer in an attempt to make antitoxin from her entrails. Her orphaned fawn becomes a friend of the man's 11-year-old boy. The fawn subsequently grows up as a beloved friend of the child, but makes the error of breaking into the family garden for a snack, after which the mother shoots and wounds him. The shot is not fatal, and the boy is required to kill his friend as another senseless act of becoming a man. Surely there is a better way to teach children how to learn to take responsibility and mature into strong, sensitive, empathic adults.

Eight Below is a tear-jerker about eight sled-pulling dogs left to fend for themselves in Antarctica. A completely avoidable accident puts both the involved men's and dogs' lives at risk. The men are rescued but the dogs are left behind without food or water. They manage to survive more than 170 days in the depths of Antarctic winter. Two dogs die, one of them while playing with the vision of the Aurora Borealis. This plot device is nonsense, and an example of a gratuitous, senseless cinematic death inaccurately portraying the danger of abandonment. The truth is that sled-pulling dogs in this region of the world are quite familiar with the sight of the Aurora Borealis and very much in touch with the particulars of their environment. It is unlikely at best that the event leading to the dog's death could ever take place. Nevertheless, viewing this scene, both children and adults are reduced to uncontrollable sobbing, and many leave the movie theatre deeply disturbed because of it. Others came away from

Eight Below convinced that Huskies and Malamutes would be great family dogs and wanted one for themselves. This erroneous conclusion constitutes a decision not to be taken lightly.

Damian, Siberian Husky
Photo by Barbara Meyers

Like so many other breed-specific dogs, Siberian Huskies and Alaskan Malamutes are wonderful and appealing. Those experienced with them will, however, tell you that there are significant challenges to tackle when providing for their care.

The Siberian Husky is predisposed to hip dysplasia and a number of inherited eye diseases. The most prevalent are progressive retinal atrophy (PRA), corneal dystrophy and inherited cataracts. Inherited cataracts (also known as juvenile cataracts) are manifested as early as three months of age. The Alaskan Malamute is prone to a number of serious health problems. The problems include but are not limited to varying seasonal exercise needs, hip and elbow dysplasia, several neurological conditions, and bloat or gastric dilatation and torsion (GVD), the latter often being fatal. They are also not recommended for apartment life. Many of the dogs purchased and taken home as family companions ended up paying for the fantasy created by film by later being surrendered to shelters. There, they are unadoptable, killed or passed along to breed specific rescue groups who must struggle to rehabilitate and find proper homes for them, often without success.

The Dalmatian has suffered the same misfortune as a result of animated films.

Bling, Rescued Dalmatian of Jessica and Justin Braun
Photo by Justin Braun

Though unlikely to be the intention of the filmmaker, the call for family Dalmatians following the release of *101 Dalmatians* increased exponentially. This demand led to breeding practices that produce genetically deaf or seizure-prone dogs. In addition, Dalmatians are also pre-disposed to cystic and urethral calculi (stones in the bladder and urethra) which can result in extreme pain, urinary obstruction, and death if not treated aggressively and immediately. All breed-specific dogs should *not* be bred to simply be good-looking. They must be sound in health, behavior and personality. Thus, many carelessly bred dogs have serious health and behavior problems built into them.

Even cinematic classics are not immune from sending mixed or wrong messages about companion animals. No one who has seen the *Wizard of Oz* can forget the wicked witch of the west threatening Dorothy and Toto with, "I'll get you, my pretty... and your little dog, too!"

Wolves are often depicted as evil, thieving, murderers, with *Little Red Riding Hood* being a classic example. Red Riding Hood is on the way to visit her sick grandmother when she encounters a wicked wolf. The wolf eats Red's grandmother and disguises himself in the grandmother's clothes, fooling Red Riding Hood with his impersonation. This accomplished, he eats Red Riding Hood, too.

As if that were not violent enough, a hunter arrives to save the devoured girl by cutting the sleeping, satisfied wolf open with a pair of scissors, and *magically* releases Red Riding Hood and her grandmother. Red Riding Hood then fills the wolf with stones to prevent him from running away. When he finally awakes, he collapses under the weight of the stones and falls dead. The humans are delighted, and the hunter cuts off the wolf's skin and goes home with it. Is this a charming little story? Not all fables, fairy tales and film are so repugnant in nature. Androcles and the Lion stands as a shining example.

Androcles and the Lion

Androcles and the Lion is a fable about a Roman slave, Androcles, who escapes and runs into the forest. There, he encounters a lion moaning and roaring pitifully. He sees that the lion is holding out his paw. The paw is covered with blood, very swollen and has a thorn pressed into it. Androcles swiftly removes the thorn. The lion licks Androcles' hand in friendship and thanks. They stay in hiding together, and the lion brings food for them to eat.

One day, soldiers come and take the pair away. Later, Androcles is thrown to the lions to meet certain death in the arena. The signal is given to release the very same hungry lion Androcles had befriended in the forest. The lion runs to his old friend, but only to lick his face and hands.

The Emperor is so taken with what he sees that he releases both of them to permanent freedom.

"*Gratitude is the sign of noble souls*."... Aesop (4th century Greek slave and author of Aesop's Fables)

Animal Abuse and its Association with Other Violent Crime

"The tendency to cruelty should be watched in children. The tormenting and killing of animals will harden their hearts toward man. Children should be brought up with an abhorrence of killing and tormenting animals or they will delight in doing so." Excerpted in part... John Locke (1632 - 1704).

Joshua K. Marquis (www.costada.com) has been District Attorney of Clatsop County Oregon since 1994. He is a former president of the Oregon District Attorney's Association, is currently a vice-president of the National District Attorneys Association in Alexandria, Virginia and serves on the Board of Directors of the Animal Legal Defense Fund.

It is to him that we owe a great debt of gratitude for his commitment, hard work and contributions to the following:

Prosecutors, law enforcement professionals and advocacy groups who work on behalf of victims of elder abuse, child abuse and domestic violence all recognize the undeniable association between crimes against animals and crimes against people.

Marquis quotes one of Mahatma Gandhi's most famed and profound statements; "*The greatness of a nation and its moral progress can be judged by the way it treats its animals*." He goes on to remind us that the truth in that statement should prompt police, investigators and prosecutors to vigorously investigate and prosecute, to the fullest extent possible, those who abuse animals. Cruelty to animals is a crime in all fifty states. Some associated crimes carry felony sentences in forty-three states and the District of Columbia. In the past, animal abuse crimes were rarely investigated or prosecuted. Fortunately, that practice is now changing.

The well-worn excuse that "it's *just* a dog," and we should focus on crimes against people betrays a frightening lack of understanding for the ramifications of animal cruelty and its insidious effects on targeted companion animals, their guardians and other law abiding citizens. Victims may also include wildlife in the vicinity of the home. Animal cruelty can be linked to the vast majority of serial killers, many habitual violent offenders, and most children and teens who kill.

If we pay attention to children, teenagers and young adults who perform acts of cruelty on animals and take immediate action to stop their behavior, future crimes can be prevented and lives may be saved. Here is a very short list, but a part of a much longer list, of serial killers and others who workshopped their future criminality by torturing and killing animals in their early years. Their early actions seem to have been ignored. Had someone paid adequate attention to them by taking their animal abuse seriously, seeking the help of law enforcement and others who appreciate the seriousness of the aberrant behavior, many lives could have been saved.

- The school shootings that took place between 1997 and 2001 (in Perl, Mississippi; West Paducah, Kentucky; Jonesboro, Arkansas; Springfield, Oregon; Littleton, Colorado; Conyers, Georgia; and San Diego, California) all contain a common element. Prior to killing their classmates and teachers, all the boys who perpetuated these school shootings had performed acts of animal cruelty.
- Albert DeSalvo, the Boston Strangler, killed thirteen women. When he was a boy, he put cats and dogs into orange crates and shot arrows thorough the slats to kill them.
- Ted Bundy was a serial rapist and killer of at least thirty women. As a youth, he tortured and killed animals.
- Jeffrey Dahmer killed and cannibalized at least seventeen people. As a boy, he killed and impaled the heads of cats and dogs on sticks.
- Dennis Rader, the BTK (Bind, Torture, and Kill) killer in Wichita, Kansas, killed at least ten people. He abused and killed animals for practice prior to killing people.

The lesson to take away is that many potential killers can be recognized in their youth. Boys who torture and kill animals are not just *boys being boys* or going through a phase. Animal abuse is a serious warning sign. Anthropologist Margaret Mead once noted that "*One of the most dangerous things that can happen to a child is to kill or torture an animal and get away with it.*" The results of doing little or nothing is chilling.

Animal Cruelty and its Link to Domestic Violence, Child Abuse and Elder Abuse

The strong link between people who abuse animals and also commit acts of domestic violence, child abuse, elder abuse and other familial or personal violence must be recognized.

There is an alarming association between people who torture, abuse and kill animals and also torture, abuse and kill their spouses and or partners, children and the elderly. In one national study more than 80% of women entering domestic violence shelters reported that their partners also abused or killed a family companion animal. Researchers found animal abuse in 88% of those families in which there was child abuse. Numerous other studies indicate that there is a high correlation between animal abuse and all forms of domestic violence. Some women will not leave their abusive spouse or partner because they fear for the life of their companion animal. Fortunately, there are an increasing number of organizations that work with victims of domestic violence to either shelter them and their companion animals, or in partnership with another group, provide care and protection for the companion animals who are also at risk. Thanks in part to this assistance, victims of domestic violence are more willing to leave their abusive environment, secure in the knowledge that their companion animal will be safe.

Often, those who abuse elders are their caretakers. They also abuse the elder's companion animals. Even when not outright abusing them, caretakers frequently threaten to injure an elder's animal family as a means of extorting something from her. The threat or act of animal abuse can also be used by the abuser to force their victims into silence regarding other abuse taking place in their homes. The threat of animal abuse is frequently enough to make a child, adult or elder victim keep quiet about any abuse that is taking place. When a police officer or animal control officer receives a report of animal abuse, it should raise a red flag of alert. When the officials respond, they should not only investigate the charge of animal abuse, but also check for signs that spousal, child or elder abuse may also be taking place. Regardless of the extent of the criminality, if animal abuse, family violence, or both are taking place, the abuser should be arrested and prosecuted.

Other Forms of and Facts about Animal Cruelty

Dog and cock-fighting is a felony crime but still exists across America and elsewhere. Dog-fighting is banned in all fifty states, the District of Columbia, Puerto Rico, Guam, and the U.S. Virgin Islands. The possession of dogs for fighting is also a felony crime in forty-seven states - New York, Texas and Washington are *not* included. It continues in abundance and is often well-organized. Fights are usually staged in facilities equipped with a *pit* and space for spectators. It is noteworthy that as a result of the *pits* in which the fighting is staged, the beautiful American Staffordshire Terrier has become known as the dreaded *pit-bull*.

Jake, American Staffordshire Terrier
Photo by Barbara Meyers

American Safffordshire Terriers are highly intelligent and loving dogs who have been victimized by the people who intentionally breed them with disregard for temperament and also teach them to be aggressive. When they have the benefit of guardians who educate, respect, love, rehabilitate and value them as friends, they are as desirable a breed as any other. Returning to the subject of dog fighting - The fights also take place at neighborhood schoolyards, dead-end streets or in rural barns and other secluded locations. These fights not only promote and foster animal abuse, they create a breeding ground for other crime, including drug and gun trafficking, money laundering, etc. Children are frequently present at these events. Prosecutors and police are increasingly committing themselves to end cruel and illegal animal *blood sports* and the criminal activities associated with them.

The thirst for this reprehensible cruelty is not confined to any economic, social or cultural class. It is indulged in by sports figures as well as other well-known public and private individuals. In my opinion, there is no acceptable excuse or apology for it. Those who have been caught and prosecuted for their crimes include people who have brutally murdered dogs because they are not *winners* or prove otherwise unacceptable to them. Undercover investigators and others who witness it, report that the perpetrators find a sinister *enjoyment* or *pleasure* in the carnage accomplished either by their own hands (strangling, neck twisting, throat cutting, and repeated bashing against a hard surface) or by gunfire from illegal weapons and other methods. As if the lives of these animals are not filled with enough suffering, they also die a horrific death. It is my opinion that attempts to rehabilitate damaged reputations stemming from actively engaging in and promoting this *sport* of unspeakable cruelty is nothing more than financial *damage control* on the part of the culpable and under-punished. This author acknowledges that the perpetrators *are* sorry; sorry they got caught!

Even non-criminal activities can constitute abuse. For example, puppy mills thrive because they are owned and operated by those who profit from animal abuse and torture. At the mills, female dogs are kept in cages all of their lives and used for breeding from the onset of their first *heat* until they die from over-breeding. They are rarely let out of their cages and are consistently kept in filthy conditions. They lack adequate food and water, and they receive no affection or veterinary care. Puppies born at mills are packed into unheated or non-air conditioned trucks to be carted away. Many die in transit to the destinations where they are sold. A large number arrive alive but sick, only to die where they are sold or soon after they are purchased. Without knowing the origin of *those cute puppies* and the lifelong health and behavior problems that will accompany them, people continue to patronize businesses that sell cruelty and heartache. Think before you act. Adopt or rescue an animal friend.

"When you buy, others die."

Chapter Seven

With a Little Help from My Friends

"Generosity gives assistance, rather than advice."
... Marquis De Vauvenarques (1715-1774).

To most people, the two best known assistance animals are guide dogs for the blind or visually impaired and hearing dogs for the deaf or hard of hearing. Over the last two decades, the number of dogs used to assist people with other challenges has risen exponentially, and there is now a remarkable diversity of canines that come under the heading of Assistance Dogs. They are categorized as Guide Dogs, Hearing dogs, and Service or Assistance Dogs.

Assistance Dogs International, Inc. is a coalition of not-for-profit organizations that educate and place Assistance Dogs. Their mission is to establish and promote standards of excellence in all areas of Assistance Dog acquisition, education and partnership. The coalition also strives to facilitate communication and learning among member organizations and educate the public on the benefits of Assistance Dogs and ADI membership.

Anyone seeking an Assistance Dog would do well to be certain that they obtain one from an accredited member of ADI (www.assistancedogsinternational.org).

Guide Dogs

Guide Dogs assist blind and visually impaired people in avoiding obstacles, stopping at curbs, navigating steps and negotiating through crowds. The typical U-shaped harness and handle fosters communication between the guide dog and his or her blind partner. Some guide dog programs may educate dogs from shelters or other rescue situations, but I know of none. Labrador and Golden Retrievers, as well as German Shepherds, seem to be the preferred breeds and are generally the products of their own breeding programs.

According to the International Guide Dog Federation, the earliest history of the special relationship between dogs and the blind is lost in the mists of time (www.igdf.uk)

Historians have some evidence of ancient connections as depicted on a mural in the buried remains of the Roman Heculaneum. A wooden plaque survives showing a dog leading a blind man.

The first recorded systematic attempts to teach dogs to assist the blind came about 1780 at the Les Quinze-Vingts Hospital for the Blind in Paris. Thereafter, in the modern era, guide dog relationships were refined during the First World War when thousands of soldiers were returning from battle blinded, often by toxic gas. A German doctor, Gerhard Stalling, had the idea of teaching dogs to help them. While walking with a patient through the hospital grounds, he was called away and left his dog with the patient as company. When he returned, he observed that his dog seemed to be looking after his blind patient.

Dr. Stalling started to explore ways of educating dogs to become reliable guides, and, in August 1916, he opened the world's first guide dog school in Oldenburg. Unfortunately, this pioneering venture closed in 1926. By then, however, another center had opened in Potsdam.

Around that time, an American woman, Dorothy Harrison Eustis, was already educating dogs for the army, police and customs service in Switzerland. Through her energy and expertise the guide dog movement was launched.

In her work, she visited the Potsdam Center for several months, coming away so impressed that she wrote an article about it for the Saturday Evening Post in America in 1927. A blind man named Morris Frank heard about the article and bought a copy of the magazine. He later said that the magazine cost of five cents "bought an article that was worth more than a million dollars to me. It changed my life." He wrote to Eustis telling her that he would like to help introduce guide dogs to the United States. Eustis took up the challenge by teaching a dog named Buddy and bringing Frank to Switzerland to learn how to work with him. Frank went back to America with what many believe to be the nation's first guide dog.

The success of this experience encouraged Eustis to set up guide dog schools at Vevey in Switzerland in 1928 and, shortly afterwards, in the United States. She called the schools L' Oeil qui Voit, or The Seeing Eye. They are widely recognized as the first modern guide dog schools.

In 1930, two British women, Muriel Crooke and Rosamund Bond, heard about the Seeing Eye and contacted Eustis, who sent over one of her Seeing Eye canine educators. In 1931, the first four British Guide Dogs completed their special education, and, three years later, The Guide Dogs for the Blind Association was founded. Since then, guide dog schools have opened all around the world, and more open their doors every decade.

Hearing Dogs

Hearing Dogs assist the deaf and hard-of-hearing by alerting them to a variety of household sounds including door-knocks or doorbells, alerts from alarm clocks, oven buzzers, telephones, baby cries, name calls and alerts from smoke alarms. Each dog is educated to make physical contact and lead their deaf partners to the source of the sound.

There are many organizations that provide Hearing Dogs, but Dogs for the Deaf (www.dogsforthedeaf.org) in Central Point, Oregon, is the oldest in the country. It was founded in 1977 by the late Roy G. Kabat. His daughter, Robin Dickson, is his successor and the current CEO and president. She has surrounded herself with the best and the brightest staff available, and is the driving force that maintains Dogs for the Deaf as the gold standard of excellence in the field.

Dogs for the Deaf Hearing Dogs are chosen *exclusively* from shelters where they would otherwise face execution for the crime of being unwanted. The organization's mission statement is: "Rescuing and professionally educating dogs to assist people and enhance their lives, maintaining a lifelong commitment to all dogs we rescue and all teams we serve." Notably, Dogs for the Deaf has remained faithful to its credo, saving dogs and changing people's lives without compromising its ethical standards. The group is fully accredited by Assistance Dogs International and it has been awarded the highest possible rating from Charity Navigator (www.charitynavigator.org). It is also rated the Best in America by Independent Charities of America (www.independentcharities.org).

Dogs for the Deaf provide Hearing Dogs, *Miracle Mutts*, *Harmony's Hounds*, *Career Change Dogs*, and *Autism Assistance Dogs*. Hearing Dogs are usually mixed-breed dogs up to thirty-six months of age. Dogs who are friendly, energetic, healthy and confident are candidates for this program. Many dogs relinquished to shelters fit that description quite well. Each dog is carefully and individually evaluated. Good candidates are brought back to Dogs for the Deaf for a thorough medical exam, and are given whatever they may need to bring them to optimum health. All dogs are microchipped, spayed or neutered and then begin the four-to-six months of the special education they will require to become skilled as Hearing Dogs.

When ready, the individual dogs and their educators travel to the homes of the recipients for one-on-one education. This usually takes about five days. Follow-up includes continued coaching with written advice, in-home visits, and other methods.

Each Dogs for the Deaf Hearing Dog is an every day hero because they bring sound awareness, independence, freedom and security. Some have even performed extraordinarily remarkable deeds including alerting a woman to a fire in her kitchen, pushing a man out of the way of an oncoming car, and leading a young mother to a child with a dangerously high fever during the night. Nacho, a little mixed-breed Chihuahua, was murdered by burglars after awakening her family. Posthumously, Nacho was awarded the coveted Stillman Award by the American Humane Society.

Candy and Clara were two Hearing Dogs who changed life for Elke Gonzalez of San Antonio, Texas. Though not recipients of the Stillman Award, they were *heroines* nonetheless.

Elke and Candy Gonzalez
Photo provided by Elke Gonzalez

Candy and Clara were succeeded by Minor who is Gonzalez's third Hearing Dog. Though now retired, Minor remains a precious companion to both Elke and her two rescued cats, Sofie and Kali. Candy and Clara *changed worlds* but not before changing Elke's world here on earth. Each of the pair brought freedom, love and a new life for Elke that she describes as, "beyond words." An extraordinary person herself, Elke is deserving of an award for her courage in the face of all adversity and the resilience never to give up or give in.

No Dogs for the Deaf canine is ever returned to a shelter, even if they ultimately do not qualify as a Hearing Dog. Dogs for the Deaf remains devoted to its lifelong commitment to dogs and people and many of the dogs go on to become *Miracle Mutts, Harmony's Hounds* or *Career Change Dogs.*

Miracle Mutts or *Special Dogs for Special People* are canine friends who provide companionship, motivation and emotional support to people who need a helping paw. *Miracle Mutts* help to minimize loneliness and depression by providing people with a reason to get up in the morning, the motivation to exercise and the inspiration to feel life more worth living. Special care is taken to insure that no dog is ever placed into a situation that is hazardous or inappropriate for either the dog or the recipient.

Harmony's Hounds Dogs or *Dogs with Special Needs* have special physical or emotional needs of their own. It is necessary for them to have someone to care for them in a stable, loving home where their needs are provided for in abundance. Some of their needs include those stemming from chronic medical conditions, advancing age, anxiety, allergies and seizures. In the right, loving environment, these dogs can and *do* thrive, and they provide the companionship and love of any other canine member of the family. They also bring with them the opportunity for people who are willing and able to nurture a very special someone with whom to share a lifetime bond.

Harmony was one such special dog. She was a spunky, little Boston Terrier who came back to Dogs for the Deaf when her Hearing Dog recipient could no longer provide an adequate home for her. A thorough veterinary exam revealed that Harmony had mast cell tumors. The tumors were surgically removed. Because of the possible consequences associated with her recovery and also for her own well-being, she would not be placed again as a Hearing Dog, and, thus, the search for someone willing to provide a home for a special dog with an uncertain future and special medical needs began.

A couple in California, Donna and Tony, read about Harmony and wanted to adopt her. When they met her, it was "love at first sight." They took Harmony into their home and into their hearts, and a happy ending was secured. Because Harmony's happy ending is the goal and wish for every dog with special needs, Dogs for the Deaf decided to call these special dogs, *Harmony's Hounds*.

Career Change Dogs are well educated and loving dogs who do not make ideal Hearing Dogs but are wonderful companions, partners, and friends for people who make significant career changes in their lives such as retiring. As a result, they may, for the first time, enjoy a lifestyle with stability and time to share their lives with a dog and rise to the level of a loving guardian.

Autism Assistance Dogs

In their efforts to rescue more dogs and help more people, in 2009, Dogs for the Deaf started an Autism Assistance Dog Program as part of its services. The program allows the organization to rescue a totally different type and size of dog from shelters to help children and families affected by Autism.

This program provides safety for a child when he or she is in public. The assistance dog wears a harness, and there is a strap that goes from the harness to the child and around the child's waist. If the child tries to suddenly run, the dog will sit and stay, serving as an anchor. The utility of this action is that it gives the parent or guardian time to control the situation and avert potential disaster.

Once a child and his dog are bonded, a powerful calm can emerge in the child's daily transitions from one activity or environment to another, preventing *meltdowns* or tantrums that typically happen during this time. Even when tantrums continue to occur, they are diminished in number and intensity due to the child's work with and connection to his or her dog.

Autism Assistance Dogs have also been shown to increase a child's ability and willingness to connect and communicate in new and previously unavailable ways. Children who are reluctant to make eye contact and bond with people (including a parent) will often learn to incorporate these attributes when relating to their dog. Some children also may become more verbal just by trying to give their dog a direction or praise. Out of a desire to enrich their relationship with their canine friend, an autistic child may also discover an increased tolerance for physical contact with humans.

For more than two decades, it has been my distinct pleasure and privilege to serve on the advisory board of Dogs for the Deaf as their grief therapist. Dogs for the Deaf was the first and remains the only assistance dog organization to recognize the importance of and preparation for loss and grief when Hearing or other Assistance Dogs or their partners come to the close of life or retirement. They are unique in establishing a system *not* exclusively limited to internal staff.

Some people regard their Assistance Dogs as mere mobility tools and they are replaced as needed. Many more embrace them as beloved, valued members of their family. Dogs often seem happy in their various roles as Assistance Dogs. In my experience, however, no Assistance Dog is happier or more well adjusted than Hearing Dogs.

At Dogs for the Deaf, dogs learn their helping roles by being rewarded with love, praise, affection, toys and games. They are having fun doing their work, the enjoyment undoubtedly contributing towards creating the joyful lives they live and provide for others.

All Dogs for the Deaf dogs are placed free of charge to the recipients but, on average, the financial investment for each dog amounts to at least $25,000. The funding to cover the cost of this special work comes from donations from individuals, service clubs, bequests and businesses.

"The one true deafness is the incurable deafness of the Mind."
... Victor Hugo (1802 – 1885).

Service Dogs

Service Dogs assist people with disabilities other than those of vision or hearing. They have been educated to work with people who use power or manual wheelchairs, have difficulty with balance, or various types of autism. They also alert or respond to seizures or medical conditions such as hypoglycemia (low blood sugar) and some psychiatric events.

Service dogs retrieve objects that are out of their partners' reach, pull wheelchairs, open and close doors, turn light switches on and off, bark to indicate that help is needed, find help when their partners are in need, assist people to walk by providing balance and counterbalance, and complete other individualized tasks as needed.

Dogs who act as protection, personal defense or comfort do *not* qualify as Assistance Dogs. They may play an important role in the lives of their partners, but they do not enjoy the public access and privileges of an Assistance Dog. It is the right of a person with a disability to be accompanied by his or her Assistance Dog in all public accommodations. Public access is granted to the person, not to the dog. Therefore, Assistance Dogs have public access only when accompanied by their disabled partner.

Facility Dogs

A Facility Dog is a specially-educated dog who works with volunteers or professionals specially trained to work as a team with the dogs. The work of a facility dog can include visitations or professional therapy in one or more locations. Facility Dogs (and other animals performing this service) are more often recognized as being in the category of Animal Assisted Therapy or Visitation. Public access is permitted only when the dog and handler (the trained volunteer or professional), is directly working with a disabled client.

It is important to understand the distinctions among the many kinds of Assistance Dogs as the groups, coalitions and organizations are varied and great in number. They can be found throughout the entire United States and in nearly every other country. Those who have earned accreditation can be found through Assistance Dogs International, Inc.

More than one group offers Assistance Dogs to veterans who have been injured and disabled as a result of their service in Iraq and Afghanistan. These dogs can do everything other Assistance Dogs are capable of, but they are specifically offered to veterans.

Not Just Dogs

Dogs make up the majority of assistance animals but cats, birds, rabbits and tropical fish are also residents of or regular visitors to numerous, nursing homes, adult day-care centers, rehabilitation and assisted living facilities, dispensing therapeutic interaction to resident adults or children with special needs.

A Horse of a Different Color

Therapeutic Riding, also known as Equine Assisted Activity, is an emerging field in which specially selected horses can provide people with opportunities for physical therapy, emotional growth and learning. Many people experience a unique connection when riding a horse that cannot be duplicated by other sporting activities. For riders who cannot walk, a horse provides more than just transportation. Horses offer the sensation of free movement, improve balance and creates a bond of friendship and trust between rider and horse that is equal to none other.

Horseback riding gently and rhythmically moves the rider's body in a manner similar to human gait. For people with physical disabilities, therapeutic riding often results in improvement in flexibility, balance and muscle strength. Individuals of all ages with a wide range of physical, cognitive and or emotional disabilities can benefit. Therapeutic Riding Programs can be found throughout the country and the world, and are easily located through an internet search.

Guide Horses

The Guide Horse Foundation (www.guidehorse.com) founded in 1999, provides miniature horses as assistance animals. These horses make excellent alternatives to dogs, especially for blind people who have grown up with horses and understand equine behavior. People develop a strong bond with their guide animals and experience overwhelming grief when their assistance partner dies or must retire. Horses tend to live far longer than traditional canine guides. A miniature horse can live to be more than fifty years-old, with the average lifespan being 30-40 years.

Miniature horses have an exceptionally docile nature and physically disabled people may find them easier to handle. These little giants are also strong enough to provide physical support in helping people to stand or sit. Educated horses have a calm and focused demeanor and remain even-keeled in chaotic situations.

Historically, cavalry horses remained calm even in the heat of battle, and in today's stressful situations, Police Horses are similarly unfazed by most events.

Horses have excellent vision because their eyes are on the sides of their heads. They are the only assistance animals capable of independent eye movement and they can track potential danger with each eye. They are naturally safety-conscious and are always on the lookout for danger. Horses also have a great natural propensity to find the safest, most efficient route and use excellent judgment in obstacle avoidance.

Miniature guide horses are not for everyone and not every miniature horse is a good candidate for becoming a guide horse. There are stringent requirements for each species (equine and human) before a partnership can be formed. The Guide Horse Foundation properly sets the standard for determining these qualifications. An example of one requirement is that while horses can live without other equine companionship, they do better and are happier with another equine friend to come home to after work. The Guide Horse Foundation considers the well being of the horse and always places a companion horse with each Guide Horse.

Helping Hands of Monkeys

Capuchin Monkeys may be the best known monkeys in the world. They are often fondly remembered as *Organ Grinder Monkeys*, the highly intelligent and mischievous partners of street entertainers who were a common sight for decades.

There are two possibilities regarding the linguistic origin of the name given to the Capuchin Monkey; the French word for a skullcap, capuce, or from the Italian word cappuccino. Cappuccino, recognized as a type of coffee drink, also means "hooded one". Supporting the argument for the French origin, the heads of Capuchin Monkeys bear markings resembling the small hats (capuche) worn by an order of Franciscan Monks.

There is no argument, however, that monkeys look very much like we do. They have large, intelligent eyes and amazing hands and feet featuring thumbs and big toes that are opposable. They are swift, nimble and capable of performing remarkable tasks.

Monkeys are natural tool-users and, in the wild, have been observed creatively using rocks to crack nuts. They also use other objects (twigs, branches, etc.) as tools to perform a variety of tasks. They have remarkable problem-solving abilities, and learn quickly both by instinct and through guided education by humans.

How It Began

Dr. Mary Joan Willard was a behavioral psychologist and Professor of Rehabilitation Medicine at the Boston University School of Medicine when she met and befriended a quadriplegic named Joe. She visited Joe daily, brushed his hair, brought him drinks, put cassettes in his tape player, and completed other simple tasks. This sparked within her the belief that an intelligent animal with "hands" could learn to perform these simple but important tasks. Thus, the idea of educating Capuchin Monkeys was born. Helping Hands Monkey Helpers for the Disabled (www.monkeyhelpers.org) has grown from an innovative idea into a thriving national, non-profit group offering independence and hope to those with severe spinal cord injuries or mobility impairments.

Photo provided by Helping Hands Monkey Helpers

The group does this by providing such people with highly educated Capuchin Monkey Helpers. The first Monkey Helper was placed in 1979. In 1982, Helping Hands became a 501(C)(3) corporation.

To ensure that no monkeys are taken from the wild, Helping Hands Monkeys come from a closed breeding colony now housed at Southwick's Zoo located in Mendon (near Boston, Massachusetts) which is owned and operated by the Brewer family. When the hand-raised monkeys are ready to begin their education, they live at the *Monkey College* in Boston and learn a wide variety of tasks and activities to assist their human partners.

They are educated with positive reinforcement that consists of verbal praise, affection, and food. If they have difficulty learning, or make little mistakes, they are never punished in any way. Rather, they are simply given more time to practice. Most earn their *Monkey Helper Ph.D* within twenty-four to forty-eight months.

Each graduate is carefully matched and placed with a human partner. To be a candidate partner, it is required there be a willing and able family member or other aid in the household who will learn what it takes to lovingly and properly care for a Monkey Helper.

Monkey Helpers do not work twenty-four hours a day. At day's end, they sleep in indoor enclosures in the home they share with their partners. The enclosures are properly sized and well appointed to insure that needs and comforts of the monkeys are accommodated. They include polar fleece blankets and favorite toys.

Capuchin Monkey Helpers have a lifespan of thirty to forty years. Helping Hands makes a lifelong commitment to its monkeys. This commitment includes insuring that the monkeys live in appropriate, loving and stimulating homes, and that they get the highest quality of medical care for their entire lives. How many of us can be assured of that?

Loss and Grief Surrounding the Death or Retirement of an Assistance Animal

People and animals share a wide variety of relationships. Many stand out because of the circumstances that underlie their deeply entwined bonds.

Assistance Animals, because of the special education they receive, provide freedom and independence to their guardians, and, not surprisingly, uniquely strong bonds are formed. When such a bond is interrupted by illness, retirement, or death, the impact on the surviving guardian is as unique as the relationship itself.

Some people view their animal assistants as mere tools of mobility and do not necessarily share a partnership that includes deep love and companionship. But, for those who do not hold this less common utilitarian view, the loss is substantial and multifaceted. When an assistance animal dies, her guardian loses both friend and freedom in the same blow. Many individuals report an overwhelming experience of becoming blind, deaf, or immobile again, confirming that their assistance friend had released them from the prison of their disability.

How does a person cope with such grief? What and who should be grieved, and in what order - the death of a beloved friend and companion or the sudden loss of freedom and independence?

The tasks of this distinctive type of mourning can be arduous, and time is required to get in touch with the shock and pain, to pass through a sea of emotions, and to regain the strength and desire to invest in another relationship. Many service animal recipients do not have the gift of time. Sometimes, their circumstances and practical needs demand that they quickly obtain another service animal. This crisis often does not allow adequate time to grieve or prepare for reinvestment.

The new assistant, rushed into service may be overly burdened as well. She must perform and bond to a naturally reluctant person and, for a time, work in the shadow of a ghost.

There are those who resist reinvestment, and these individuals may require a high level of support for their decision. Although this resistance is not inappropriate, it *does* require the relinquishment of some degree of independence. Others may take a "never again" attitude and choose to return to a more limited lifestyle without an animal assistant.

An otherwise healthy, blind person may develop another physical condition such as destructive arthritis in the shoulder or a permanently unstable knee that limits ability to walk with a dog. The limitation may be so great that their assistance friend may even become a safety risk to the person. This scenario is another circumstance in which a relationship can be interrupted, causing great emotional pain from the loss of a friend and personal freedom, as well as from the demands of learning a new mode of mobility.

In the absence of preparation and a support system, the death of a service animal can so greatly affect a person that it may produce a stress-induced exacerbation of any underlying illness or condition he or she has. Preparation for loss must be carefully woven into the human-service animal relationship from an early stage. It is most effectively addressed in the earliest phases of consideration as a candidate for an animal assistant.

This can be difficult to achieve given that the desire for an assistant can overrule some of the practical thinking about a relationship that is still in its embryonic stages. Nonetheless, preparation for loss should be as much a part of the planning as it is for the overall health care of a new partner.

This is not to say that grief therapy is not an indispensable intervention following a loss. But a broad-based and comprehensive inclusion of death education during orientation better prepares everyone involved for the impact of loss. This includes organization leadership, staff and assistance animal recipients.

We have a natural resistance to the discussion of dying and death. This resistance is not difficult to understand, but it remains a major obstacle to the acquisition of a full and authentic picture of ourselves and the world we share. In my opinion, it is the responsibility of every ethical assistance animal organization to take a hard look at loss and begin to reevaluate themselves with a view towards including appropriate death education. Optimally, both staff and assistance animal recipients should receive ongoing education in the form of workshops and seminars conducted by experienced specialists in the field of grief therapy and the human-animal bond.

The older a program is the more cumulative the grief and mourning will be among staff members. Cumulative grief is often unrecognized due to a self-imposed demand to diminish or underestimate it. For this reason, even when there is no outward sign of trouble, inner turmoil persists. Failure to address grief only complicates and postpones the inevitable. Assistance Animals, like their guardian partners, will get sick, grow old, and develop physical disabilities that interfere with their roles as assistants. There is no greater sadness or irony than the Hearing Dog who becomes deaf, the Guide Dog or Horse who becomes blind or the Service dog or monkey who becomes disabled.

In our rapidly moving world, animals may become involved in vehicular accidents, retire, or even be murdered! Though difficult to imagine that anyone would intentionally take the life of an assistance animal, such travesties occur and I have experienced several such occurrences.

Organizations that provide assistance animals usually have a *replacement* policy and protocol. A *replacement* is not enough after a loss. The policy must be paired with support and time for healing. It is a long and often rocky road from the death of a friend to a second animal. No dog, horse or monkey can be *replaced* like rusted rakes or shovels. For this reason, I strongly suggest that the word *replaced* be entirely eliminated from use in this context.

Every human-animal relationship has a quality of its own, and the loss of this unique treasure must be recognized and honored. When properly understood, it becomes clear that the bond between physically-challenged people and their assistance animals is a special and cherished friendship that is tightly linked to personal freedom.

To appreciate this freedom, one need only to reflect what life would be like if we were not free to reach for a light switch or pick up a dropped item. Suppose the dropped item was a mouth stick, the only mobility tool for a quadriplegic? Suppose you were deaf and could not hear the doorbell or a child calling your name? How small and unsafe the world would become.

Some people will temporarily resist reinvesting in another service animal. These people require the highest level of support for their decision as they temporarily also relinquish some independence. Others may say, "never again" and return to a limited life-style without an animal assistant. Proper death education at the earliest possible time can bring palliation for the grief and shock. It may even eliminate the "never again" attitude entirely. This reversal has a higher chance of success if the person has had the benefit of death education during the initial pairing with their assistance animal.

Most assistance animal organizations have an *in-house*, staff-based grief support system for both recipients and staff. It is built on their experience and they report being confident it is adequate. I am aware of only one assistance animal organization that has, on its Advisory Board, a Certified Grief Therapist (your author) who specializes in animal related-grief; Dogs for the Deaf.

While death can be a truly shocking experience, the retirement of an assistance animal may also be difficult though usually less traumatic. After retirement, there may be the option to retain the assistance animal as a companion while still having the benefit of a new working friend. Where that is not possible, recipients are reassured that their retired friend will be placed as a companion or take on another less demanding role with someone who needs and wants them just as they are.

Ethical Concerns Regarding Assistance Dogs

It is of fundamental importance to recognize that there is legitimate disagreement, if not outright controversy, about guide and assistance dog organizations' policies to breed dogs for their programs while millions of healthy dogs are being executed in pounds and shelters. Many shelter dogs could be well suited for guide or assistance dog education if there was the will to evaluate them.

There is little, if any, evidence that Retrievers or Shepherds are the only dogs with the ability to learn the requisite skills. Moreover, Golden Retrievers are among the most popular assistant and companion dogs and are known to have exceptionally high incidences of cancer, heart and eye disease. Because more than half of Golden Retrievers die from cancer, The Morris Animal Foundation has launched the *Golden Retriever Lifetime Study* (www.morrisanimalfoundaton.org).

The study and its results are expected to provide valuable information on prevention strategies, early diagnosis and new treatments. Though the long-term study is focused on Golden Retrievers, it is anticipated that it will benefit the health of all dogs.

The precise number of dogs who do not, ultimately, succeed at the task for which they are bred is not known. These dogs are made available for adoption to the general public. Because of the appearance of their altruistic origin, they are more likely to be adopted as companion animals, thus leaving thousands of perfectly healthy, young dogs with good temperaments to continue to languish in misery or die in shelters and pounds.

There is an example of a better, more thoughtful and kind approach that is superior and successful in every way. Dogs for the Deaf exclusively rescues dogs from pounds and shelters for assistance futures. They do not have or participate in breeding programs of any kind and never have. Their mission to serve people and dogs is in perfect balance and leaves no losers.

Controversy Surrounding Assistance Animals

A sizable number of people regard the entire matter of assistance animals (dogs, horses, monkeys and others) as imposed bondage or slavery, and they are deeply troubled by it. These are not people who regard animal life as more important than human life. They hold that all life is valuable and worthy of recognition, rights, freedoms and protection. Though they may be regarded as radical by the under-informed, they are not. They seek inclusion and embrace a philosophy that is, in fact, centrist and neither left, right or radical. Valid arguments can be made that those who *use* animals as assistants and in other ways are the more radical.

To that point, Gary L. Francione, Distinguished Professor of Law and Nicholas deBellville Katzenback Scholar of Law and Philosophy at Rutgers University School of Law-Newark, New Jersey has made the case. Francione is the author of five books including *Animals, Property and the Law* (Temple University Press, 1995 and *Rain Without Thunder* (Temple University Press, 1996). Francione makes a stunning and compelling argument employing an abolitionist approach to the use of animals in our society (www.abolishionistapproach.com).

On his website, Francione's mission statement states, in part, "The mission of this website is to provide a clear statement of non-violent approach to animal rights that,

1. Requires the abolition of animal exploitation and rejects the regulation of animal exploitation.
2. Is based only on animal sentience and no other cognitive characteristic."

We have a moral imperative not to carelessly subject animals to harm, abuse and exploitation. Those, like Francione, who have the courage to champion this philosophy should not be dismissed or labeled "radical *humaniacs*" or painted with another denigrating label. Historically, the early abolitionists, including John Brown, Harriet Beecher Stowe, Booker T. Washington, Levi Coffin, and Frederick Douglass, recognized the need to abolish human slavery in our country and devoted their lives to the cause. They, too, were considered radical troublemakers and risked their lives or had them taken for their beliefs and activism. John Brown was an example, executed by hanging in 1859. Though he, ultimately, perished for his ideas, he left behind a more just society.

Returning to the subject of justice for animals, though many service animals enjoy the love and companionship of their human partners and share in a mutually beneficial relationship, what of the others? Many are essentially treated like a carpenter's tool belt. At the end of the work day they are simply put away until needed for the next job. They are given what is necessary to keep them in working condition, but nothing more.

In any serious discussion of this importance, the tendency to focus on ideal partnerships must be balanced with a recognition of the less romantic possibilities.

In a society that is only just beginning to appreciate the damage done to animals by using them for all manner of things that includes selfish, thoughtless, and misguided purposes or financial gains, we must steadfastly scrutinize the roles and lives assigned to all service animals. This examination extends to the deplorable treatment involved in the use of circus animals, horse and dog racing, the capture of dolphins from their natural habitat for demeaning, clownish amusement and "Swim with the Dolphins" features at resorts, dog and cock fighting, rodeos, and more. There was also a time when we thought nothing of treating other humans in exactly the same way. Sadly, and too often, some still do. Nonetheless, we must fight for progress for people and animals alike until justice and peace prevails.

"Never give in - Never, never, never, never in nothing great or small, large or petty, never give in except to conviction of honour and good sense. Never Yield to force; never yield to the apparently overwhelming might of the enemy."... Sir Winston Churchill, 1941 Speech, at Harrow School. (1874-1965).

Chapter Eight

Animals in Law Enforcement

"When we are in partnership and have stopped enslaving each other, we will stand together and be friends, comrades and brothers and we will begin the march to the grandest civilization ever known."

Excerpted in part... Eugene Debs (1855–1926).

Equine Partners in Law Enforcement

It is no exaggeration to say that the history of the United States and the world rides on the back of horses. From Brown Beauty, (the horse that Paul Revere rode in 1775 to warn that "The British are coming"), The Pony Express, and the U.S. Cavalry, to the Royal Canadian Mounted Police and other mounted divisions of law enforcement throughout the world, horses and their riders have brought courage and heroism, as their riders sought to bring news and order to a tumultuous world.

The military funeral tradition of the riderless horse is one of the most poignant and solemn sights. It consists of a single, riderless horse following the caisson with boots reversed in the stirrups. This ceremonial horse is called the Caparisoned Horse, a reference to the ornamental coverings with a detailed protocol all to themselves. The *Cap Horse* follows the casket of an Army or Marine Corps officer who holds the rank of Colonel or above.

The *Cap Horse* also follows the casket of a President, by virtue of having been the nation's military Commander in Chief. The specially-assigned officer walking beside the *Cap Horse* is known as the *Cap Walker*.

Abraham Lincoln was the first President honored with this ceremony. Images of the *Cap Horse* remain emblazoned in the memories of millions of people who watched President John F. Kennedy's funeral procession in 1963. Moving from the military to other governmental agencies, one finds the familiar everyday, but majestic, Mounted Police Officer with her or his equine partner. Fewer know, however, that there are mounted divisions of the United States Park Police.

The United States Park Police Horse Mounted Unit is one of the oldest police equestrian units in the country. It was established in 1934 with only one horse and one stable. The value of the mounted unit was quickly proven and the program was expanded to give protection to the Washington D.C. metropolitan area, San Francisco and New York.

Training for horses and officers takes place at the agency's headquarters in Washington, D.C. Established Park Police Officers request duty to the units. The course lasts for ten grueling weeks. Despite popular assumption, there is no requirement that applicants be experienced riders. In fact, it is strongly preferred that applicants be rank novices or have minimal abilities. This permits an education free of the need to unlearn or relearn riding habits that are not suitable for the work they are to begin. Simply put, it is easier and more efficient for both horse and rider to get it *right* from the start.

All the horses are donated to the Park Police by private individuals, thoroughbred-racing operations and horse coalitions. If they are good candidates, they spend anywhere from six to ten months being evaluated and educated for their future as Law Enforcement Partners at Edgewater Stables, the training facility in Washington DC. Horses who do not fully qualify at the end of the orientation and preliminary education are returned to the donors. This procedure is an essential part of the agreement, ensuring the well-being of all horses considered for this highly specialized work.

The United States Park Police Mounted program is one of the most well known and respected throughout the world. As a result, the program receives numerous requests from outside agencies to provide training for their own programs. The Park Police have assisted the Army and Secret Service as well as police departments in Maryland, New York, West Virginia, and many others.

The English saddle is standard issue for the Park Police. As part of preparation, officers learn to ride bareback and sometimes without stirrups or girths. This practice teaches them to ride as one with their equine partners and not the saddle.

The recruits ride through smoke, in mud, at night and in the rain. They must also complete obstacle courses over timber jumps and creeks. As part of their tutelage, officers learn to groom their horses and clean and polish every bit of silver and brass. They soap every piece of equipment in their tack and become proficient in equine first aid. When they *earn their spurs*, they have truly earned them!

Regarding the spurs used, they are not the *rasp* variety found in rodeos and western film; they have no sharp edges. They are blunt and used only as an additional contact guide when necessary for the protection of the horse, the rider and others around them.

Park Police Mounted Police Officers also carry side arms and, while they rarely use them, they are well trained and polish their skills on a regular basis with range practice.

Mounted patrols ensured public safety during parades and festivals, which they still do, and they helped keep peace during demonstrations in the politically explosive 1960's.

Today's mounted police are known not only for crime-fighting and crowd control, but for equestrian showmanship. Both horse and rider perform feats unimaginable to most riders. The horses are routinely exposed to sirens, gunfire, horns, drums, fireworks, throngs of people, busloads of children and sign-waving demonstrators. They must also deal with a perhaps surprising terror: balloons! Experts believe that the horse's natural instinct to detect and avoid unnatural objects in their environment is the cause of their fear of balloons. Releasing balloons into the air for celebration or remembrance may stir emotions, but the practice can be terrifying to horses and also amounts to an environmental hazard of a serious nature.

What goes up must come down, and when the balloons come down, they fall over protected woodland or into the sea. Marine life, fresh water fish and both land and seabirds and other animals can die an elongated and painful death as a result of ingesting the deflated balloons or being caught up in their string and ribbon. In my opinion, the practice of releasing balloons should be banned.

Turning back to equine subjects, in Staten Island, New York, "the borough of parks," at the Gateway National Park site in Fort Wadsworth, I had the privilege to spend time with Park Police Mounted Officer Dan Firce and his horse, Sinkme. Sinkme is a 19-year-old Bay Thoroughbred. At 1,200 pounds and standing 16.1 *hands high*, he is a majestic sight.

Photo by Sgt Wm. Wilkens, USPP

According to popular legend, ancient horse traders needed a method of measuring horses. Stacking one man's fist upon anther was the simplest system. Thus, horses came to be measured by the hand unit. Each *hand* is about four inches. Thus, if a horse is sixteen hands high (hh), then he is sixty-four inches or 5'4" tall. One must remember that horses are measured at the withers. The withers is the prominent ridge where the neck and the back join. A horse's height is measured vertically from the withers to the ground because the withers is the horse's highest constant point. His neck and head, of course, extend far above that point. Because of the height and sight range provided by Sinkme, Officer Firce is able to detect activities at a distance unmatched by a Motor Officer.

A single look into Sinkme's eyes reveals a proud, confident horse with a gentle spirit and a generous heart. Sinkme was donated to the U.S. Park Police in 1999. He had been assigned to the National Mall in Washington, D.C. where he worked several high profile demonstrations. He has also participated in many parades in and around New York City and still does.

Together, Firce and Sinkme are a formidable pair. Their effectiveness at crowd control is due in part to the uncertain reactions they engender. Most people know little or nothing about horses, or the scale of their physical presence. To experience a horse and rider in person as they advance toward you can be deeply intimidating. And yet, horses, in other situations may bring out great affection from the public. The equine nature is a tapestry of gracious, compassionate tolerance combined with a benevolent power. It is this balance that draws the immediate attention of adults and children alike. They want to know the horse's name, if they can touch him, and are fascinated by everything about the horse. They barely notice that they have failed to ask the officer *his* name or anything about him unless it relates to the horse. It has been observed that if a regularly patrolled area has a change of horse, it is immediately noticed. If the officer astride that horse changes, it might not be.

Whether on beach or park patrol or at a parade, festival or honor ceremony, Park Police horses and their riders remain alert to unsafe activities or conditions. This can range from the use of glass or broken glass, unauthorized fire, dogs off leashes or unruly or criminal human behavior. Dan Firce shares his life with Sinkme, his wife, Vilma and their canine companion; an engaging and spunky, short-haired Daschund named Pablo.

The mutual respect, love and partnership shared by Firce and Sinkme is primary, but Sinkme also enjoys the company of his stable-mate, Brigadier General. "*The General*," as he is affectionately known, is the Partner of Officer Robert O'Brien. He is a Chestnut American Saddlebred, standing 17.2 hh, making O'Brien a stunning example of rider who is truly tall in the saddle atop this magnificent steed.

The American Saddlebred with its conformation, personality and stamina is suited to accomplish any task requested and is known as the peacock of the horse show world. Saddlebreds are high-stepping, very sensitive and alert. Their wide-set, expressive eyes and gracefully shaped ears are positioned on a well-shaped head set on a long, powerful neck. The average height of the American Saddlebred is fifteen to sixteen hh, and *The General* exceeds his exceptional qualities even in his height. I was very fortunate, indeed, to visit the mounted division when *The General* was twenty-five years old and approaching retirement.

Brigadier General and Sinkme
Photo by Officer Dan Firce, USPP

When a horse is ready for retirement, he is released to his partner, assuming that person has the means to care for him or her. Those who can, do so. Those who cannot are comforted by the knowledge that their partner will be adopted into a leisurely and happy retirement with someone who is well matched and well suited to the job. Some partners retire at the same time, and it is not unusual for them to literally *ride off into the sunset* as the team they always were and remain together permanently. O'Brien was far from retirement and unable to remain together with *The General*. Nonetheless, *The General* had a bright future. Normally, retired horses return to Headquarters in Washington D.C. The *horse country* in nearby Virginia and Maryland provide most of the retirement homes for Park Police horses.

The General's retirement was to be as unusual as the way O'Brien and *The General* met and became partners. Like all USPP horses, *The General* was donated to the Park Police in the early to mid 1990's and worked with his former partner (who transferred to other activities within the department) until 2001. In February of 2001, O'Brien went to headquarters to begin his instruction as a mounted officer. There, he met *The General* for the first time. He was one among twenty horses in the stable. With touching and articulate words and animated facial expressions, O'Brien described to me how he was immediately drawn to *The General* and, silently, said to himself, "you're the guy I want to take home with me." As though pre-destined, that is exactly what happened.

As per the requirements, O'Brien could have expected to ride each of the horses (usually about 20) for no more than five or six days. This would have allowed him to become proficient with each horse and sharpen his skill to do so in the field, A mounted officer must ride any available horse at a moment's notice without the benefit of growing accustomed to the style, needs and unique qualities of any partner.

Due to complex and unusual circumstances, O'Brien and *The General* spent three full weeks together. O'Brien worked with other horses over the ten weeks he was there, and, like all U.S.P.P. Mounted Officers he is at home and confident with any horse. But the rare opportunity to be with *his* horse so frequently set the stage for a partnership of nearly a decade of wonderful years. When the famed Sigmund Freud said, “There are no accidents,” he must have had O’Brien and *The General* in mind! Over the years, the pair worked many high profile, potentially dangerous, special events including a KKK rally, The International Monetary Fund Conference, The Million Man March and others. Their relationship is one based on mutual, love, respect, admiration and trust. Eventually, the perfect retirement home was found for *The General*, and in another unusual turn of events, he would not return to headquarters in Washington, D.C.

Through a network of special organizations and individuals, O’Brien was able to find a retirement home for *The General* in nearby New Jersey. O’Brien and *The General* spent nearly a decade together in unbroken friendship. O’Brien’s love and regard for his horse will allow him to see *The General* off to a well-deserved retirement. Being so close by, O’Brien would be able to visit *The General* and maintain their unbroken bond. What they will share in the future will, undoubtedly, be different but equally precious.

Brigadier General in Retirement
Photo by Officer Dan Firce, USPP

O'Brien's new partner joined him when *The General* had a thorough veterinary exam and was issued a health certificate. The certificate affirmed that he was free of contagious illness, current on his vaccines, and in good oral and dental health. *The General* was also examined by his farrier (a specialist in equine hoof care), who certified that he was ready for travel to the Garden State. O'Brien's new partner, George (affectionately known as, *Gorgeous George*), is a sixteen-year-old Bay Thoroughbred standing 16.2 hh. Not surprisingly, George came to the service of the Park Police through an unusual and circuitous route, fitting the pattern established by his predecessor.

There is no concern over whether George can fill *The General's* shoes. *The General* will continue to fill his *own* shoes wherever he is. George and O'Brien will make and leave their own special tracks along the new trails they will ride together. The hoof-prints etched into O'Brien's heart by *The General* are permanent and untouchable.

The heart touched by the love of an animal can be broken, but the *magic* that animals bring with them also opens the heart to make room for another.

O'Brien shares his life with his wife, their two children and their canine companion, a Boxer named Nala.

Canine Partners in Law Enforcement

"He is your friend, your partner, your defender, your dog. You are his life, his love, his leader. He will be yours, faithful and true, to the last beat of his heart. You owe it to him to be worthy of such devotion."... Anonymous.

K-9 units in law enforcement are not uncommon. Many state and city police departments have their own K-9 education centers. Many more do not, though they still require education for their units even if their police force consists of as few as two or three officers and their K-9 partners. These departments look to private professionals to fill their need.

FRED STONE

"Partners"

A GRATEFUL AMERICA

HONORS ITS FALLEN FIREFIGHTERS

Fred Stone

Fred Stone is recognized as the world's most famous and gifted equine artist. Partners portrays exhausted fire-fighter Anthony *Skip* Fernandez III with his protective arms around his search-and-rescue dog, Aspen, at the scene of the bombing of the Alfred. P. Murrah Federal Building in Okalahoma City on April 19th 1995. Though equally exhausted and in need of rest, Aspen remained upright and at her partner's side, where she continued to hold watch over him as he briefly succumbed to his desperate need for rest after their twelve-hour shift.

From his magnificent work in oil, Stone then created the poster to honor Fernandez and Aspen and all fire-fighters and search-and-rescue teams. The poster depicts Aspen's authentic paw print and, thanks to the generosity of Fred Stone, has raised more than a half-million dollars for charities and the families of New York City firefighters who died on September 11th 2001.

In November of 2008, after a gallant battle with cancer, Aspen changed worlds at home, in the arms of her partner. As in the anonymous quote that opens this section, Aspen was faithful and true to the last beat of her heart and Fernandez is, indeed, worthy of such devotion.

A signed lithograph of "*Partners*" hangs on the wall of my consulting room. There, Aspen and Skip and the love that binds them together are forever captured in Stone's unforgettable image.

The K-9 Global Training Academy (www.k9gta.com) fulfills that need. It is located near San Antonio, Texas, on over 140 acres. Law enforcement officers of K-9 units are referred to as handlers and these grounds provide an ideal place for both K-9 and handler education.

On October 1st, 1984, GTA was founded by Jim Parks, Dan Hayter, and Ken Nelson. The trio came from careers in the United States Air Force where they met, became friends and went on to form GTA upon retirement from the military. They were well prepared for their chosen careers as private citizens, bringing their experience from the Air Force. To date, GTA has educated over 3,500 dogs. Over the years, their program has garnered a solid reputation of success. For example, two of their Drug Dogs are listed in the Guinness Book of Records.

GTA's expertise is especially recognized in the highly specialized field of De-Mining Dogs. De-Mining Dogs can detect land mines that, sadly, still exist in very large numbers throughout the world maiming and killing people every day.

GTA has twenty-six K-9 educators and at least seven full-time staff members whose job it is to look after the needs of the dogs and their living quarters.

GTA has worked with various breeds over the years but has chosen three as preferred breeds. They are the German and Dutch Shepherd and the Belgian Malinois. Most people are quite familiar with German and Dutch Shepherd, but less well acquainted with the Belgian Malinois. They each have similar appearances but an experienced eye recognizes the differences among them. The Malinois is a medium-sized, very hard-working, square-proportioned dog in the sheepdog family. They are distinguished by their short, brownish-yellow coat and black cheeks, muzzles and ears that stand at full attention. The Malinois is highly favored in Belgium, Germany, the Netherlands and other European Countries. They are primarily bred for protection, detection, all police work, search and rescue and the sports of Schutzhund, French Ring and Mondio Ring. The United States Secret Service uses the Malinois exclusively. The Israel

Defense Forces strongly favor the slighter build of the Malinois to that of the formerly-used German Shepherd and Rottweiler.

All the dogs at GTA are educated with precision guidelines that put their health and well-being first. Food rewards are not used and they learn their work from patient, loving leaders and educators who reward them with praise and affection.

Key verbal signals are taught in Dutch: Sit is "*Zit*;" stay is "*Blijf*," and article search is "*Zoek*." This is because the greater majority of GTA dogs come from Holland and, thus, handlers need to learn to give directions in the native language of the original caregivers of the dogs. This adaptation is easier and proves less confusing than trying to teach a new *work* language to a dog, especially one that is trying to adapt to a new home, a new handler and a new job. Moreover, at GTA, dogs learn to respond only to their handlers. The use of Dutch provides an extra layer of on-the-job security; it is unlikely that criminals will know the foreign words or that other officers will give accidental directions.

During education, dogs do not wear the bullet-proof vests they may wear once deployed. Later, they will adapt to their protective gear if it is provided by the agency to which they are assigned.

For dogs who detect people, drugs or chemicals, the greatest reward is that of the *find*, itself. This is always enhanced with praise, but the dogs love success and there is no greater reward for them than accomplishing their goal.

For this reason, following the events of September 11, 2001, many volunteer Cadaver Dogs (dogs who find deceased or dismembered human remains), who came to assist at Ground Zero, had to be taken away from the search of debris. Remains, small and scattered, were throughout the area and, though the remains could be detected by the dogs, a solid *find* eluded the fatigued dogs and their partners. Though frustrated and weary, the dogs would not stop working. Left on their own, they quite literally could have worked themselves to death under the circumstances. To say that those dogs and their equally dedicated guardian partners are heroes and love their work is an understatement. GTA with nearly a century of combined experience, is licensed by the Texas Commission on Private Security and registered with the Drug Enforcement Administration, the Texas Department of Public Safety, and the Bureau of Alcohol, Tobacco and Firearms. The group provides many government and law enforcement agencies with specially-educated dogs and also provides handler courses for all members of future K-9 assisted teams. These courses include training for the following applications:

Bomb Dogs

When GTA was founded there was no standard for Bomb or Drug Dogs in the civilian community. GTA established the standard for Bomb Dog Certification in 1984. This standard was developed from that used by the founders during their careers in the United States Military. It has stood the test of time, and GTA remains recognized as a leader in educating Bomb Dogs and their handlers. GTA Bomb Dogs can detect just about any explosive.

Narcotic Detection Dogs

GTA also educates Narcotic Detection Dogs for partnering with law enforcement. These dogs find illegal drugs like marijuana and controlled substances such as cocaine, heroin, methamphetamine and others.

Patrol (attack) Dogs

Patrol dogs are proficient in handler protection, attacking with or without command if their handler is assaulted. They guard criminal suspects while the suspects are searched by their handler and scout for criminals in open areas, buildings and other locations. Multi-discipline education to include patrol duty may appear to be a simple dual or cross education. It is, however, a highly complex combination of skills. Not every dog, in fact very few, are suited for attack roles. As Parks said, “they just don’t have the heart for it.” Only dogs who are really good candidates for patrol are chosen for the dual roles. Every specialty can be combined with patrol skills and GTA is experienced in matching only the *right* dog for the dual roles that may be needed by any specific law enforcement department or agency.

Handlers are carefully trained on how to responsibly and safely handle a dog with patrol capacities. Dog and handler become a team driven by mutual love, respect and skill enhanced by the special bond they share.

Arson Dogs

An Accelerant Detection Dog (Arson Dog) is one who learns to detect minute traces of accelerants that may have been used to start a fire. Every year, billions of dollars worth of property damage and hundreds of lives are lost to arson, a crime that has an impact on all communities. An Arson Dog is a highly valued asset in fighting this crime.

Drug and Bomb Search Dogs

Many schools, prisons and civilian companies have the need for drug and bomb searches but do not have an internal ability to perform it. GTA has teams who provide that service and it was from such a team that a very special dog, a Malinois named Rex had his roots.

Unlike most dogs who come to GTA for a career in law enforcement at eighteens months of age, Rex was three years old on arrival. This was due to his being a KNVP (Koninklijke Nederlandse Politiehond Vereniging, Royal Dutch Police Dog Association) educated and titled dog. A KNVP titled dog is one who has successfully completed a rigorous, multi-tier study program rarely achieved before age three.

Rex had been diagnosed with hip dysplasia and the prognosis (based on x-ray findings) was poor. He was, however, symptom and pain-free and had excellent mobility. X-rays revealed that his hips were certainly less than perfect, but *he* was perfect in every other way. Rex was intelligent, quick and eager to learn, and a *natural* at everything he did or was asked to do. In addition, Parks said, "everyone at GTA just fell in love with him immediately."

Rex

Photo by Jim Parks

All GTA dogs come with their health certificates and radiographs (x-rays) of their hips taken while they are still with their breeders. GTA does not rely on those initial reports exclusively. They immediately have each dog examined by their own veterinarian, and digital radiographs are taken again. This avoids discrepancies from less-than-current radiographic images. Physical as well as psychological changes can and *do* take place as dogs grow. The original radiographs may not be of the highest digital quality, and GTA spares nothing to ensure the health and happiness of their dogs.

Canine Hip Dysplasia (CHD) is a developmental disease in which an abnormal formation of the hip leads to *looseness* in the hip joints. This causes cartilage damage and leaves dogs lame, in pain and also subject to complicating, painful arthritis. There are good surgical procedures available to help these dogs if the disease is diagnosed early, monitored carefully, and surgery is recommended. Some dogs have CHD but it does not progress to the point of debilitation. Only careful ongoing monitoring by a Board Certified Veterinary Orthopedic Surgeon will reveal the progression of the disease even if a dog remains asymptomatic.

Every dog at GTA goes through the process of radiographs and reevaluation. The new radiographs are sent to The Orthopedic Foundation for Animals (www.offa.org) to be certified as free from CHD. Dogs who are found not to be appropriate candidates for their work can be returned to their breeders. It is, however, well known that if a dog is returned, they face a grim future. Once it has been established that they have a defect like CHD, breeders usually consider them *worthless* as they cannot be sold. They are often destroyed rather than fed another bowl of kibble. This fate was *not* awaiting Rex!

Parks and his partners decided to make Rex a member of their own team or keep him as a companion despite expert opinions that CHD would inevitably develop in Rex. According to Parks, "we also decided not to tell Rex about it." By all accounts, Parks and his partners were true to their decision and Rex remained happy and pain-free. He had an illustrious thirteen-year career as the partner and companion of Parks' daughter, Cindy Taylor, and lived at home with her after working hours.

Rex came to be known as "*The Million Dollar Dog*." This was because his skills at detecting narcotics was so keen that while on loan to a Sheriff's Department in Oregon, Rex made a *bust* worth well over a million dollars. Rex was also fully proficient as a Patrol Dog, but worked exclusively as a Narcotics Detection Dog.

He retired from active duty and lived happily and quite well as Cindy's non-working companion until he was fifteen. This outcome is not ordinary but Rex was an extraordinary dog!

Parks emphasizes that while CHD is commonly found in large dogs like Shepherds, Rottweilers, Labrador and Golden Retrievers, Mastiffs and St. Bernards, it and can also be found in smaller breeds and should not be a death sentence. The disease, because of its genetic basis, must be eliminated by more responsible breeding practices.

Until that has been accomplished, the demand for *perfect* hips will continue to send dogs like Rex into the "junk pile", breeder jargon for dogs who can not be sold. This practice is both cruel and unnecessary since, with proper care, they can have happy and productive lives. Some, like Rex, can even have productive working lives if given the opportunity and work that suits them. Sadly, single-minded profit and greed stands as a roadblock. The public is also victimized when breeders sell non-professional, unsuspecting people similarly affected dogs. By the time they discover their predicament, their canine companions have become obviously lame and the disease is well in progress.

Parks' greatest wish is that the entire matter of CHD be more responsibly addressed by a three-tier program. First, the condition must be eliminated by better breeding practices. Second, a more compassionate management of the condition must be provided for working dogs who are more likely to have their lives ended prematurely and unnecessarily. Third, and possibly the most urgent part of the program, stronger efforts need to be made to re-home retired working dogs who cannot be adopted as companions by their partners. This re-homing will insure the dogs can live out their lives in an environment of leisure and love.

Jim Parks, the family of GTA, and his own immediate and extended family have proven that the *business* of dogs does not have to be fueled only by profit motive. They truly love dogs, love their work and have woven that love and compassion into the fabric of their lives.

Parks and his wife, Darlene, live in Texas with their Samoyed, Yukon. Several in their extended family of children and one grandchild are among those involved in the operations of GTA. Others serve in the military or law enforcement.

Chapter Nine

Understanding Animal Behavior

"Those who cannot be wise and kind,
cannot and must not lead."...Yiddish Proverb

The leading cause of death for dogs and cats is not cancer, kidney disease, illness or accident of any kind. It is unwanted and misunderstood behavior.

Every year millions of healthy cats and dogs are relinquished to pounds and shelters where they are executed for the *crime* of being unwanted, unadoptable, or *inaccurately* labeled as unadoptable, vicious, dangerous or sick. In many situations, *sick* can refer to a condition as minor as ringworm in an otherwise young and healthy cat! *Ringworm* (dermatophytosis) has no association with *worms.* It is a fungal infection in the superficial layers of the skin, hair or nails that is both treatable and curable.

Before we continue, it is important to establish a working definition of the terms used when describing shelters, pounds, sanctuaries, euthanasia vs. killing policies, etc. For the purposes of some foundational clarity, your author offers you the following:

- An animal shelter is a place, center or establishment, generally supported by charitable contributions, that provides temporary homes for cats and dogs (and sometimes, other animals) that are voluntarily relinquished to them.

- An animal sanctuary is a facility where animals are rescued and taken in, to be given protection for the rest of their natural lives. The mission of sanctuaries is to provide a safe-haven where animals are not bought, sold, or traded, nor are they used for animal testing. The residents of a sanctuary are given every opportunity to live and behave as naturally as possible in a completely protected, caring and compassionate environment. Some sanctuaries will also offer animals for adoption.
- An animal pound is generally understood as a city, state or local municipality enclosure for stray or unwanted animals. Pounds are also usually understood as *kill-centers* where attempts to encourage adoption *may* be made but the adoption rate is far too low and the killing far too high.
- Euthanasia means painlessly, and with loving compassion, ending the life of the mortally wounded or dying and those with a hopelessly terminal illness causing unrelenting suffering no longer manageable with hospice care. By definition, euthanasia does *not* mean premeditated murder because of behavior, difficult or challenging medical conditions that are not life-threatening if well managed, illness, medical costs associated with the illness, or an inability to be adopted due to advanced age, unpopular breed, disability or disfigurement that does not compromise or interfere with quality of life. While there are those who will argue against it, your author identifies these killings as premeditated murder.
- Unadoptable is a term with a plethora of meanings that vary from one facility to another. Labeling an animal unadoptable can produce results that are both capricious and cruel. For example, a dog can be defined as *unadoptable* simply because he was growling when a *dog-catcher* put the snare of a *catchpole* around his neck, dragged him across the street and threw him into a dark box inside a truck dispatched to collect stray dogs.

- A *catchpole* is a long stick with a snare at the end. It is used to reign in an animal. In practice, the user of a catchpole will put the snare of the pole around a dog's neck, tighten it and pull or drag the dog, now suspended by the neck, into a cage or transport vehicle. A catchpole can also serve as a benevolent tool to facilitate the rescue of an animal trapped in an otherwise inaccessible place. However, those content to use catchpoles for non-benevolent purposes, literally throw frightened, starving, confused, and abused animals into a hostile environment such as a municipal pound. At the risk of restatement, many subsequently-labeled *vicious* or *unadoptable* animals were merely reacting, as anyone would, to the horrific and terrifying circumstances of their entrapment and confinement.
- A *vicious* classification can mean many things. Some shelters and pounds, in assigning the fatal signet, rely on a *temperament test*, which, in my opinion, is flawed, unreliable and unconscionable. The test involves observing a dog's disposition after he has been subjected to a series of frightening and, sometimes, painful provocations that include being slapped with a rubber hand at the end of a stick, prodded with a stick, and teased with a treat that is then snatched away. Some *testers* even hang a dog upside down to gauge the reaction elicited. In addition to the harshness of the tests, there is a level of absurdity; a reaction of a curl of the lip or a brief snarl equates to failure, and the dog, having behaved as one expects, is, nonetheless, killed for being *vicious*. Cats are also misjudged by different but similarly ridiculous methods. As I see it, these *tests* are, in and of themselves, cruel, do nothing more than simulate the abuse many of these animals have already suffered, and create a fear-provoked natural defense response. They have no value in determining the personality, characteristics, or potential of any living being. Moreover, they are not an acceptable determinate of who will live

and who will be killed. The use of the words, euthanize or euthanasia, have no place in the ethical or moral reality of these murders.

Having defined the terms of the analysis, the parameters of the problems involved with animal care and rescue, and the policies in place at responsible, no-kill shelters are perhaps more easily understood. Responsible, no-kill shelters do not accept companion animals with known behavior problems because they are considered to be *unadoptable*. Adoption and long-term solutions remain the goal of these shelters and, therefore, this makes some sense.

Behavior problems are rarely, if ever, disclosed by people relinquishing their unwanted cat or dog to a shelter or private adoption. Many minimize known problems and fabricate reasons why the problems do not comport with their lifestyle. More often, problems are not revealed at all. This is because people are aware that their attempt to relinquish their *problems* to a shelter or private individual will be unsuccessful if they tell the truth. Among the many false *excuses* are: "I can't keep him any longer because I have to move and the new place doesn't allow *pets*. Sometimes he's a little grouchy while he's eating, but he's a great dog, smart as a whip..." Translation: "I'm not really moving anywhere. I just can't deal with him any more. He's ungrateful and tries to bite me if I go near his food bowl." Another example: "She's the most beautiful cat in the world, but my son is allergic to cats and we can't just keep her any more." Translation: "She pees any place she feels like and she's ruining my house. I don't want this cat."

People who use deceitful, irresponsible and unkind methods to *get rid of* and pass their problems on to others usually behave this way in order to rationalize their unscrupulous behavior. They tell themselves that they gave their *unfriended* animal to a "good place" where they will find another home, thereby freeing themselves from the legitimate guilt that should be associated with their behavior. They are also reinforcing the self-serving view of themselves that they are even thoughtful and kind. Many also convince themselves that they have "done everything possible" to correct the behavior problem. Nothing could be further from the truth. The truth is they have, in all likelihood, *not* consulted an expert animal behaviorist, relying exclusively on myth, nonsense, punishment, and archaic methods to treat problems. These methods are not effective and are guaranteed to make matters worse.

Shelters that do *not* use the ghastly *temperament testing* previously described often err on the side of good intention and rely on the information given by the person seeking to relinquish their companion animal. They take into account that behavior can change during and after travel and a *snippy* or unfriendly dog or cat is often believed only to be stressed by the car ride or a little *nervous* or shy in a new environment. In many cases, this assessment is entirely accurate.

But if there is a serious and intentionally undisclosed behavior problem, the reasonable conclusion that the relinquished companion is only expressing temporary strain, is both inaccurate and misleading. If a shelter animal is young and good-looking he has a good chance of being accepted for adoption. Because behavior can and will change in new environments, shelter staff may not see problems and they may be adopted. After the adoption is complete and the problems begin to reveal themselves to the unsuspecting adoptive family, as a general matter, the family will return the cat or dog to the shelter of origin, mishandle them through punishment, or simply abandon them in the street to fend for themselves or worse.

Beyond the tragic and disturbing situations already described, there is another, often hidden tragedy inherent at shelters. Some shelters that claim to have a no-kill policy do not reveal that they *do* have an "exchange program" with one or more shelters or pounds that *do* kill. This program entails exchanging those who are labeled unadoptable (for *any* reason) for others from a kill-shelter or pound who seem to be adoptable. The shelter that *claims* to be no-kill does not do the killing themselves, but those who have been deemed unadoptable have their fate decided nonetheless and are moved to a kill-shelter or pound where they will be executed.

If shelters are not the best answer for resolving the companion animal problems we face at home, where can we look? To begin, be wary of much of the well-meaning, but misguided, advice coming from a variety of sources including some *so-called,* professionals. It rarely works, postpones effective treatment and can complicate and escalate a problem. A particularly destructive example of this kind of advice is when you are advised to get a second companion animal to solve a behavior problem in first. On rare occasions, this very bad advice will actually be effective, but, when it is, it is purely by accident or *luck*. The more common result is *two* distressed, anxious and confused animals with behavior problems. Early intervention in unwanted or problematic behavior is best, but it is never too late to seek professional help. You cannot *give away* or *get rid* of a problem. If you do, the outcome is considerably less than desirable and especially destructive if there are children in the family. *Getting rid* of animals through modeling of parental behavior, teaches children that they, too, are disposable and may be given away if they behave badly. Children, not unlike like animals, bite themselves and others, engage in household destruction, have elimination accidents, and fail to get along with each other. While most people would never *get rid* of their children, the children do not know this and, instead, look to our treatment of animals as a template for how they will be dealt with. Children who learn by example to love and respect animals are learning kindness, compassion and empathy. These are valuable lessons they will take with them into the rest of their lives.

Every Problem Has A Solution!

A firm commitment, investment of time, love, energy, patience, money, and adherence to a care plan that has been designed especially for *you*, your lifestyle and *your* cat or dog, is the platform on which solutions are built. A care plan is not a one-size-fits-all *cookie-cutter recipe* for any and all animals. While basic principles and a deep, experiential understanding of animal behavior are always involved, a care plan should be personally crafted for each individual animal, his family and the lifestyle of all members of the household, both guardians as well as other companion animals. The plan must begin with a willingness to be open to and accept the truth that some of the myths and strongly held beliefs about why animals behave as they do are simply not so!

Examples of common myths are encapsulated by typical false conclusions such as: "He *knows* he's doing something wrong, acts guilty and this proves he knows it"; "She's doing it for spite"; "He's stubborn, spoiled, not too smart"; and on and on.

Everything animals *say* and do communicates important, but not always obvious, messages, and the way we react or do not react is equally important as a response. It is widely believed that behavior problems are the result of mistreatment or abuse. While this conclusion is certainly true for some animals, it is an assumption that should not be made without definitive knowledge that abuse has taken place.

The more likely cause of many behavior problems is the *hard-wiring* of a biological or physiological nature that takes place in the brain because of poor breeding practices and other behaviors of people not acting in the best interest of animals. You are probably *not* the cause of the unwanted behavior, but must understand that you may be reinforcing or even encouraging such behavior whether or not you are conscious of your actions and their results.

As a starting point, know that scolding or punishing animals in any way whatsoever will not help and will actually make things worse. While understandable that these responses to frustrating situations are *only human*, your efforts to permanently curb them with more effective and less cruel methods will prove worthwhile and rewarding in the long run.

To do so, first, we must all *get on the same page.* There is often disagreement among household members as to how to solve animal behavior problems. Opposing philosophies, diverging levels of tolerance, different understanding and problem-solving skills, and alternating styles and attitudes must all be respected and can be successfully managed without causing further difficulty or disagreement among family members. These differences must be resolved *before* a care plan that will succeed can be crafted.

Crafting such a plan is best accomplished in a consultation with an adept animal behaviorist. No behaviorist or any other animal care professional can help animals without first addressing the needs of their guardians. With diplomacy and skill, a really good behaviorist will uncover differences among family members in a balanced way that leaves no right or wrong sides. The ultimate collaborative care plan will blend solutions and harmonize the needs of the entire household, producing the achievable goal of a win-win outcome.

After everyone is on the same page, it is critical to learn exactly *what* we are trying to solve. For example, did you know that many behavior problems are not behavior problems at all? Instead, they are indications of physical illness. For this reason, it is essential that all animals who *seem* to have a behavior problem enjoy the benefit of a thorough veterinary evaluation to rule out any underlying physical ailment. This is especially so for those with sudden behavior changes involving frequency or volume of urination, house-soiling with urine and or feces, or, for cats, failure to use their litter box in the ways they previously did. Sudden behavior changes also include diminished or increased appetite or thirst and change in mood or level of activity.

The veterinary evaluation should consist of a careful physical exam, a complete blood chemistry that includes thyroid evaluation, a urinalysis with microalbumin, and a urine culture and sensitivity test from urine that has been taken directly from the bladder through sterile means. The latter is a common, non-painful procedure known as cystocentesis, which is accomplished for most animals without the need for sedation or anesthesia.

The reason to include the culture and sensitivity test through cystocentesis and *not* from a *free-catch* (urine you have collected in a container and brought to your veterinarian) is because *free-catch* urine produces test results that are not fully reliable. The diagnostic test results needed must absolutely confirm or rule out underlying infection, identify the exact bacteria causing the infection, and guide the veterinarian to the precise antibiotic needed to treat the infection. A full bladder is the ideal source from which to easily obtain urine by cystocentesis. If your animal friend is being cared for by a board certified veterinary internist who is experienced with the use of ultrasound, she will employ ultra-sound guided cystocentesis to withdraw an adequate amount of urine from a bladder that is minimally filled with urine. *Without* the benefit of ultrasound-guided cystocentesis, if your cat or dog does not have a full or adequately full bladder, he may have to remain in the hospital for several hours in order to allow the bladder time to refill. Additionally, if not in the care of a specialist, a primary care veterinarian may help speed the process along by administering subcutaneous (under the skin) fluids. It will, however, still require time spent in the hospital to administer the fluids and for the bladder to refill. While extra time spent in the hospital is not an attractive prospect, it is still far better than resorting to a *free-catch* sample that will not produce reliable results. Many animals (especially cats) who display any symptom involving inappropriate urination are, without the benefit of urine culture and sensitivity testing, treated with antibiotics as though they have a proven urinary tract infection. In fact, less than two percent of dogs and cats actually have infection. The true cause of the symptoms and behavior then remains undiagnosed. Moreover, being given unnecessary antibiotics is cause for concern on many levels. In particular, the indiscriminate overuse of antibiotics leads to antibiotic-resistant strains of bacteria known as *super bugs*.

The veterinary exam should also include a fecal analysis to help rule out internal parasites and any other procedure (such as x-rays or ultrasound) your veterinarian recommends in order to rule out underlying pathology that may be responsible for the behavior. On the chance your veterinarian does not recommend these additional tests, you must advocate for your animal friend and open the subject for discussion. Do not be deterred by imagining that you will insult your veterinarian by asking questions and seeking discussion. Your advocacy will very likely be a surprising and most welcome component in caring for your animal family and your veterinarian will appreciate the input. You may be asking yourself, "Why will my vet be surprised?" The surprise stems from the disturbing truth that a significant number of people who bring their animal friends to a veterinarian, do so far too infrequently or too late and with completely unreasonable expectations as to the cost of good veterinary medicine. Veterinarians are under great pressure to deliver high-quality care at very low costs and under extreme conditions. They are also expected to do this without the benefit of the diagnostic testing and procedures that permit them to properly do so. I know of no veterinarian who entered into the profession with goals other than to heal and help animals. After years of training and hard work, they are often faced with having to practice their skills with the equivalent of *one hand tied behind their backs.* On a daily basis, their advice is dismissed, they are accused of recommending "unnecessary" tests or referrals to specialists for financial gain and also asked to kill animals who, with proper care, could recover from illness, injury or have a behavior problem rehabilitated. While there are some veterinarians who *will* inflate their bills with unnecessary testing or procedures, it is less common than supposed.

Returning to the subject of behavior; sometimes, behavior that has its roots in physical illness, trauma or stress of any kind will continue even when the original cause has been resolved. These behaviors must also be compassionately and appropriately addressed. When animals continue to behave in unacceptable ways after the source of the problem is resolved, it is because they have been so deeply traumatized by an event that they remain in a state where their behavior is fixed in a pattern that they have no control over.

A common example of this is seen with cats who may stop using their litter box and urinate in various places to indicate that they have a painful, condition without infection such as interstitial cystitis, bladder stones, diabetes, or kidney disease. The condition may be treated, stabilized or resolved, yet they continue to avoid the litter box and urinate in places other than their litter boxes. It is not because they are stupid or getting even for something. Instead, they repeat their behavior because they still associate the pain they first felt at the onset of the illness with the litter box. With professional intervention from a practiced behaviorist, one who has a full understanding of the medical and emotional lives of animals, the behavior can be managed and, ultimately, even cured.

Animals (especially cats) are very stoic and hide their pain, illness, distress and anxiety quite well and for long periods of time. Often, by the time they reveal changes that have become blatant, they are well into their illness, whether physical or emotional. As a consequence, careful observance and sensitivity to change is needed to detect problems before they become full blown.

All unwanted behaviors, while complex in nature, are highly manageable and many are completely curable. A complete and in-depth description of all the elements of rehabilitation cannot be distilled into a single chapter or portion of a chapter, and every behavior problem is worthy of a book of its own.

It is this author's wish to provide you with the tools you need to better understand behavior and behavior problems. With these tools, you will become better informed about the challenges you and your cat or dog are facing, able to preserve your relationship with your animal companion, and be better able to appreciate the importance of proper diagnostics to rule out physical illness.

In this chapter, you will read examples of some of the most common feline and canine behavior problems and be given some basic tips on how to begin management. These examples are intended to help set a foundation of understanding, but they are by no means complete. Every cat and dog, their guardians and extended family members must have a care plan that is tailored, polished and perfected to meet their unique needs.

Canine Behavior

Pinky
Photo by Barbara Meyers

There are no bad dogs! A dog's deepest and fullest measure is to be social and cooperative. They behave cooperatively with each other, and we need to extend similar behavior to them. The idea that dogs have an innate desire to please people is at best misguided and, at worst arrogant. Rather than merely *designed to please others*, a dog's drive is to be in shared harmony with both their animal and guardian peers. This harmony can, however, be easily corrupted and misguided, leading to confused, fearful and anxious dogs.

The conventional notion is that dogs have a *job* or function to perform. These *jobs* are assigned to them by, perhaps, well-meaning, but poorly informed, people who fail to recognize and honor the true nature of dogs. Yes, some dogs are *working dogs* but most are not. Dogs do *not* need jobs. They need to feel and live their exquisite canine natures and, initially, need to be with their mothers and litter-mates until they are twelve weeks old. Some large-breed dogs *may* successfully leave their mothers and litter-mates at eight weeks of age but I am not at all comfortable in recommending it.

Categories of behavior such as dominant, possessive, territorial, etc. are surface readings that can be a useful guide but do not fully embrace or give meaningful definition to the whole dog. Dominance as a trait may *seem* undesirable, but is not, in and of itself, undesirable. To gain better understanding, it is necessary to delve deeper into the details.

You may be familiar with the term *dominance aggression.* It, along with *the pack theory* of canine and wolf behavior, has been bandied about for decades to describe a wide variety of behaviors that include aggression directed at other dogs or animals of another species, as well as aggression directed at their guardians and other people. Dogs, though similar in some ways, are not wolves!

Black Wolf at Yellowstone National Park
Photo by Laura Cowen

Dominance aggression is no longer considered an acceptable accurate term or description of motivating factors, and accordingly, it has been appropriately replaced with the term *conflict aggression.* This change is derived from an evolved understanding that the relationship between dogs and people is *not* driven by any over-simplified *pack mentality*. In fact, wild dogs and wolves do *not* organize their relationships with each other in this way, either. The notion of *the pack* and its ongoing demand and struggle for an *alpha* dog is a bit absurd. Instead, in canine social groups, each member of the group generally knows their social order or *arrangements* and they suffer no innate desire to overthrow or displace their elders or those who *seem* to be in a role of leadership. *If* and *when* disagreements occur, they are settled in the most peaceful way possible. This is usually accomplished by a respectful show of deference and holds no loss of perceived status or *place* in their group. Unlike humans, who often seek to *even the score*, dogs are wiser and avoid physical retribution while not suffering any shame or need for revenge. On the occasions where there is a stronger disagreement or conflict of interests, *conflict aggression* can take place.

It is not necessary to break a dog's spirit to redirect *dominance, conflict aggression* or any other unbalanced, unwanted or undesirable behavior. Ordinary and normal traits of dominance that are out of harmony, creates confusion leading to behavior problems. The relationship between dogs and people is as old as recorded time, and to imagine a world without dogs is unthinkable. Sadly, however, most people remain poorly informed about the true nature of dogs. Dogs are often described as jealous, vindictive, slow, stupid, stubborn, and more, but these are generalized qualities of humans, *not* dogs. Dogs are more likely to feel distressed, anxious, displaced or threatened by someone or something. Or, it may be that some canine behaviors are reactions to a lifestyle change such as a new home, new people, recently introduced other companion animals, etc.

Consistency from everyone in the household is a vital part of interacting with your dog. When change is unavoidable, as much consistency as possible is required. If *your* messages are unclear, your canine friend will become confused and distressed. Mixed signals and confusing messages are easily created. By example, it is not uncommon to hear someone say to their dog, "Come on, sit down." It easily escapes notice, that these four words contain three separate verbal directions: "Come," "Sit," and "Down." It is entirely unreasonable to expect any dog to properly understand and contextualize these words as delivered.

In response to these confusing directions, I have actually seen more than just one dog attempt to comply with the request by *sitting*, then going into a *down* position, and finally crawling in the down position in an attempt to *come*!

Along the same lines, a puppy who comes bounding into your lap will soon lose her charm when she is an eighty pound adult dog. She has no way of knowing that what she did for months and was encouraged and welcomed, is no longer acceptable. She cannot understand why people would react in such a strange way to what used to bring smiles of approval and affection.

Your dog is not going to *grow out of it*; whatever *it* may be. In addition, you cannot teach your dog anything but to be afraid of you if you try to punish her out of it or teach your dog *who is boss*. Punishment also seems to be used by many who *claim* to be knowledgeable and experienced trainers or behaviorists. I am adamantly opposed to it.

This raises an important point; not everyone who calls himself a trainer or behaviorist is either qualified or experienced. Even those who have managed to acquire some credentials may not be fully equipped to diagnose or solve problems with the more sophisticated methods now available. If you decide you need or want professional intervention, interview and select your professional very carefully. Begin with a phone call. Everyone you call should be willing and happy to spend some complimentary time with you to answer all basic questions including fee structure, provide you with meaningful credentials (not just testimonials) and, if they are conducting group classes, invite you to come to a class to observe. If the potential K-9 educator or behaviorist is not available when you call, they should return your call within no more than twelve hours.

If you decide to visit a group class, do not bring your dog with you. You could be putting him in a compromising situation and disturbing the group class as well. If the professional you speak with invites or encourages you to bring your dog or your children, this is not a good sign. The true professional should be protecting their existing group, as well as your dog and children, by asking you *not* to bring your dog or children. The presence of children can prove distracting during classes, and, while children should be a part of the learning experience, this kind of canine and family education is better served in a private, home environment and not a class or group setting.

Group classes are usually called "obedience classes." Obedience is not a term I care to use. The term implies a method of strict obedience rather than a more comprehensive shared education that will involve both you and your dog. A good education is one that enhances the bonds between you and your dog as you learn to be a kind, loving guardian worthy of your dog's respect. Your dog, in turn, learns to be a good canine citizen who is well- socialized and welcome everywhere.

Most obedience classes rely on *corrections*, *commands,* and the use of a restrictive collar or, worse yet, a *choke* or pronged collar. Some instructors may even recommend or insist on the use of a *shock* or spray collar for dogs who bark excessively and do not respond to a standard collar with what *they* think is adequate speed. The *shock* collar emits a shock upon barking or can be controlled from a remote, battery-operated device. The spray collar sends a spray of a citrus-scented liquid into the dog's face when he barks. Both devices will certainly get a dog's attention and may even *seem* to work to control the behavior in question. Of the two, the spray collar is less cruel, but neither, in my opinion, is necessary, kind, or as effective as building a relationship between dogs and their guardians. In building this relationship, there is no place for harsh methods of any kind.

The Clicker Method

The Clicker Method does not rely on punishment, nor is it harsh in any way. In combination with support from a savvy and experienced behaviorist, it is the most effective method to help resolve unwanted behavior challenges. It can be fun to use for both dogs and people, and has also been highly effective in species other than dogs. Clicker educators can be found in many cities and states, though they are not, necessarily, easily found in all areas.

For those who live on Long Island, New York, Helen Del Bove of SmartyPaws (www.smartypawsny.com) is a well-qualified clicker educator who is devoted to dogs and their guardians. Located in New Hyde Park, she conducts group classes for dogs *without* complicated behavior problems such as aggression. A class or group environment is *never* recommended for aggressive dogs. She will also travel throughout many parts of Long Island to make home visits when necessary. On the occasions when we work together to solve canine behavior problems, solutions are easily found and implemented despite our being located on two different islands of New York.

Helen Del Bove

Photo provided by SmartyPaws

Also in New York is Robert Haussmann, AKA *Dogboy* (www.dogboynyc.com). *Dogboy* is a certified, professional canine educator. He uses a multidimensional approach that *may* include the clicker method and designs a curriculum of education for you, your lifestyle, and your dog's special needs and situation. As a team, Haussmann and I (each of us doing what we do best), and in concert with the guardian families and veterinarians of the dogs involved, have worked together to rehabilitate some of the most complicated and dangerous canine behavior problems. Our team effort has produced consistent, happy results and re-cemented bonds that were in peril because of canine behavior problems.

Robert Haussmann
Photo provided by Dogboy

A clicker method canine educator in your area can be found at www.clickertraining.com. A few words of caution: Be wary of anyone who claims to be a clicker method educator and continuously relies on food reward. Food reward is only a very brief introduction to the clicker method and is to be discontinued as quickly as possible. The same principle applies across the board for *all* canine education. For effective and lasting results, you must not rely on food reward except for a very short time in the early stage of education. Note: On the subject of education-based food rewards and treats for *all* other uses, my exclusive recommendation is Whole Life freeze-dried treats.

Chicken seems to be the favorite of both cats and dogs. However, if your friend is allergic to or intolerant of chicken or any other Whole Life ingredient, it is not to be used. In general, this poses no problem as the treats are available in a wide variety of choices at www.wholelifepet.com.

Whole Life Freeze-Dried Chicken
Photo provided by Whole Life

Returning to clicker education: In rare cases, it is possible for some people to employ clicker education on their own without professional assistance. On the whole, however, a clicker method canine educator, in conjunction with a care plan designed by a behaviorist, produces a swifter, more successful result. This is especially so in cases of complicated behavior challenges. These challenges include lunging, excessive barking, fear and panic, thunderstorm and other noise phobias, household destruction, separation anxiety, lead pulling, excessive guarding of food or objects, biting and aggression towards other animals or people, snatching or *stealing* food or other prized objects, pica (an irresistible and uncontrollable desire to ingest foreign objects), etc. Dogs *without* these behavior issues are considered to have uncomplicated behavior challenges.

The determination of whether behaviors are complicated or uncomplicated should be made and confirmed by a behaviorist before you proceed with any educational curriculum. Because many complicated behavior problems are veiled and not easily recognized by all K-9 educators, it is best to consult a behaviorist. When it is determined by an expert behaviorist that your dog has an uncomplicated behavior challenge and requires only basic good canine citizen education, a behaviorist is still the best person to make the diagnosis. She will help you to resolve it on your own or recommend a first-rate canine educator who will be the *right* one with the *right* method for you and *your* dog.

Fear and Panic

This condition usually presents as fear of thunder, firecrackers, and other sounds, or specific situations or people, and it must be treated with great care. It requires the involvement of a behaviorist to make the correct diagnosis and a protocol of behavior modifications for you and your dog. There must also be a collaborating team veterinarian to prescribe the right drug or drugs agreed upon and monitor the general health of the dog. There is a progression to sound sensitivity (thunder storm phobia) disorders. It begins at the time of the first clap of thunder but, after a time and repeated events, dogs will panic at the onset of rain without thunder and then to any barometric change that even hints at the possibility of rain or thunder that may or may not follow. It is *not* possible to train, comfort or punish your dog to be free of the fear. In fact, such treatment only serves to exacerbate the existing problem.

Most of the garden variety approaches to solving fear and panic include intentional exposure to the source the fear that is known as *flooding*. Flooding is unkind, does not work and will exacerbate the condition and also create additional problems. An example of *flooding* is the all-too-frequently-made suggestion to play recordings of thunder storms to accustom a dog to the disturbing sound. In addition to *flooding,* another hopelessly useless method involves playing loud music or turning on a television or radio at an exceptionally high level of volume in hopes of masking the offending sound. Dogs' hearing is so sensitive that no attempt at masking can possibly negate their ability to hear thunder or other offending sounds. We know this for certain because fear of thunder storms and other acoustic trauma is experienced by hearing impaired and deaf dogs as well as dogs with normal hearing. Dogs respond to more than just the sound itself. They are able to detect changes in barometric pressure that signal rain or a thunder storm, and they will begin to panic long before the sound strikes.

There are also a variety of tight-fitting jackets and coats intended to alleviate this condition. I am skeptical of their claimed benefits, not comfortable recommending it as a solution and, therefore, do not.

Comforting dogs and telling them "It's okay" most certainly does not work. By doing so, you are, inadvertently, telling your dog that "It's okay" to be fearful and mortified.

Dogs will seek refuge from the sound by crawling into a corner or some other safe space and it is unwise and unkind to attempt to prevent them from seeking a safe-haven or try to remove them from it. Some dogs are in such an advanced state of panic that they will jump through a glass door or window, or attempt to get through another stationary object like a wall. This is known as *escape behavior* and is exactly what it appears to be; a futile and dangerous attempt to *escape* the offending sound. Dogs who do this are frequently seriously or mortally injured, or they become permanently lost, and remain confused and entrapped in an extended state of panic. If they manage to escape the home, they likely meet their fate by being hit and killed by a car or other vehicle.

Fear and panic is always an emergency and should be treated that way. When you first become aware of your dog's sensitivity to sound, run-don't-walk to a practiced behaviorist who will work closely with you and your veterinarian. Board Certified Veterinary Behaviorists are few in number, but some are available and they make up a rapidly growing, specialized field of veterinary medicine. If you do not have a behaviorist and collaborating primary care veterinarian available to you, a veterinary behaviorist can found through the American College of Veterinary Behaviorists (www.acvb.org).

The appropriate medication(s) combined with a comprehensive care plan that has been designed by a behaviorist is essential. Xanax is usually the medication of choice for thunder storm phobia but it must *never* be used without the guidance and oversight of a veterinarian. Xanax and other anti-anxiety (anxiolytic) medications are frequently found in the medicine cabinets of many people who benefit from them. Caution: It is a life-threatening danger to use them for dogs or anyone for whom it has not been specifically prescribed.

There are no harmless drugs! Every medication has the ability to do as much harm as it does good. One cannot exercise too much caution in using and handling them. Professionals as well as others would do well to keep the following paraphrased quote in mind, and not only as regards drug treatment: "*There are some we cannot help, but there are none we cannot hurt.*"... Carl Osborn, DVM, Ph.D, ACVIM.

Separation Anxiety

Separation anxiety is another condition that effects many dogs but *can* be successfully treated with multiple environmental changes, changes in the behavior of all the people who are part of the dog's life, and medication prescribed by a veterinarian who will work in concert with your behaviorist. Separation anxiety is characterized by an exaggerated attachment a dog has to his guardian that renders him incapable of being alone even for very short periods of time. When left alone, some dogs enter into a state of extreme anxiety causing them to engage in a variety of behaviors that include intractable barking, urinating, defecating, digging, destruction of furniture, carpets, and anything else they can get their jaws on and paws around. Household destruction presents a serious medical as well as psychological threat as dogs will ingest foreign matter such as plaster from wall board and sheetrock, paper towels, stuffing from furniture including anything from feathers and foam rubber, to electrical wires, cordless phones, and more. The ingestion of foreign matter can cause gastric obstruction, which will then require emergency hospitalization and even surgery. If not addressed quickly enough, death can result.

Dogs struggling with separation anxiety also scratch violently against doors, window frames, and any other object or surface in the home. They are capable of completely destroying a wooden door and its frame, or eating through baseboards and metal objects like crates. This, too, presents a serious medical threat as they can easily injure their paws and mouth from the splintering of wood and puncturing from bent or fractured metal objects.

Most of the symptoms of separation anxiety occur within the first twenty minutes following the departure of their guardian. In some cases, the anxiety will return after a number of hours and the cycle of symptoms will begin to manifest again. By the time the exhausted dog's guardian returns, he may appear calm and relaxed; he may even be found sleeping surrounded by destruction resembling the aftermath of a hurricane that had swept through the home.

Like with all behavior problems, a solution is *not* to be found with scolding or punishment. Neither will help at all, but both easily make dogs feel more anxious and confused, while leaving people feeling frustrated, guilty, angry and just as distressed as their dogs. Rather than relying on these fool-hearty methods, instead, properly identifying the problem as separation anxiety is the first step to changing it. It is *not* strong play, *spite*, or exuberance at work. To identify the problem accurately, you will need to answer a few simple questions that will quickly reveal if your dog is struggling with separation anxiety. Caution: *do not* make the diagnosis yourself, and do *not* rely *only* on the general diagnostic questions I have provided in the forthcoming passages. Though helpful, these questions are only to be used as a starting point. The desensitization technique that follows is entirely accurate in its basic concept but must be tailored for each dog and his family. Here, again, the proper diagnosis should be made by a seasoned behaviorist, and a care plan designed for you and your dog.

The Questions

- When separated from you, does your dog exhibit destructive behavior?
- Urinate or defecate in an inappropriate place?
- Display excessive vocalization: barking, howling or whining?
- Salivate excessively?
- Without being called, does he follow you around the house and try to maintain physical or visual contact at all times?
- Become distressed when you prepare to leave?
- Greet you with excessive energy when you return home?
- Become distressed with increasing physical distance from you and begin to pant, salivate, whine, or appear *shaky or nervous*?

If your answers are "yes" to some or most of these questions, your dog is likely to be struggling with some measure of separation anxiety.

The approach to managing separation anxiety is multi-faceted and must be designed for each individual dog. There are, however, some basics that will apply to all situations. They consist of multiple behavior modifications for both dogs and their guardians, the likely use of prescription medication, and the guidance of a skillful behaviorist to partner with you and your veterinarian.

As a threshold matter, one of several basic and imperative behavior modification techniques is to discontinue the cues that tell your dog to get ready to be alone and distressed. Without professional guidance, implementing this behavior modification is not likely to be adequate in solving the problem completely. However, it is still essential that you understand the modification and begin to see how it will enable you and your dog to better function.

Everyone has a pattern or routine they engage in when preparing to leave home. Most of us do not give it much thought, but we repeat our departure and arrival behaviors with reliable consistency. Departure routines generally include reaching for keys, putting on shoes, picking up a hand-bag or brief case, going to the closet where coats are kept, etc. They signal an unmistakable intent to leave. Your dog needs only observe *one* of these signals to alert him of your departure, thereby sounding the alarm for the separation-anxious dog. To prevent the cycle of panic, you should engage in the departure behaviors but *not* actually leave. This should be done several times a day for as long as it takes to disassociate the cues that represent departure. If there is *truly* not enough time to perform the routines in the morning without leaving, do so throughout the evening. However, I encourage you to *make* the time both morning and evening and certainly during all free time. It is a rewarding investment of time, not really as difficult or time-consuming as one might think, and is vital in eliminating a far more serious problem. In fact, without this desensitization process, success cannot be achieved. Once the initial cue is removed, perform the routine and actually leave, but only for few minutes while remaining outside your door. Then, repeat this step over and over again, observing the effects and increasing the time you play at leaving.

When you return, do *not* create a big fuss. In fact, ignore your dog and just go about the business of putting your things away and doing whatever you normally do. This protocol holds true for your departures, as well. Coming and going should be a *non-event*. Unless and until your dog is completely calm and relaxed, continue to ignore her upon departure and arrival.

If, during the process of rehabilitation, you come home to a destructive event, do *not* react. Do what you must to clean up. Under no circumstances should your scold or punish your dog. Even if punishment could have helped (and it would not), it is too late for your dog to associate *your* out-of-control behavior with her acts that took place hours before. Most people do not understand or refuse to believe that dogs do not associate punishment with an act of inappropriate behavior unless it takes place within no more than ten seconds after the behavior. Even within the ten second window, punishment is *never* an effective solution. In addition to being cruel, it will, without exception, *always* make problems worse.

Why? Your dog is responding to severe internal anxiety. Establishing a pattern of punishment, your dog anticipates it. Thus, *your* behavior is guaranteed to intensify the anxiety and escalate the underlying issues.

Biting and Aggression

There is little that is more frightening, disturbing or frustrating than having a dog who bites others, except, perhaps, when he bites you, too.

Dogs bite for a variety of reasons. Their targets range from strangers and other animals to people they know well and have interacted with successfully with in the past.

Biting and other aggressive behaviors do not necessarily indicate an abusive history or anything you may have done wrong in the past. While it is true that people often encourage unacceptable behavior or habits in their canine companions without knowing it, with biting, there are larger factors at play that are beyond your control but *not* beyond your understanding or repair with professional help. These larger factors are best seen through the prism of a dog's maturation as he develops his personality, natural tendencies, and general behavior over time.

Dogs, not unlike people, grow and develop socially, environmentally, intellectually, physically and sexually. Changes take place in stages at different times. A sexually mature dog who is able to produce puppies, is most often not a socially mature dog.

Though it may appear that a dog has bitten for no reason, it is *never* true. There is *always* a reason, and, most often, a number of reasons that have been building over time. With this in mind, and because biting and aggression are the most dangerous canine behaviors that threaten both people and other animals, aggressive canine behavior must be addressed as early as possible. At the very first sign such as a puppy who growls or snaps, you must seek professional help and, by that I do *not* mean a traditional *trainer*. You need a behaviorist! Remember, however, that puppies chew on all manner of things (including you) during the teething process. Do not confuse the normal chewing behavior associated with teething with biting, snapping, and growling. This can sometimes be a bit difficult to determine. Once again, a consultation with a behaviorist is recommended.

Feline Behavior

Jason

Photo by Barbara Meyers

Felis sylvestris catus is descended from *felis sylvestris lybica*. This marvelous creature is better known to us as our beloved friend, the cat! No other animal can mystify, engage, confound, love, touch and break our hearts like they can. Cats are the ultimate exquisite and magical beings. But they, like us, sometimes engage in behaviors that may be confusing, unwanted, unacceptable or even dangerous to themselves and others. Though there are other unwanted behaviors, the following are among the most frequently reported.

- Inappropriate use of the litter box.
- Household destruction.
- Biting, scratching, stalking, and aggressive behavior, including aggressive play behavior.
- Fear and shyness.
- Nocturnal activity accompanied by excessive vocalization that interferes with their guardians' ability to sleep.
- Awakenings with the infamous *five a.m. paw in the eye*.
- Inter-cat aggression seen in multi-cat households.
- Difficulties in blended (cats, dogs, birds, etc.) animal families.
- Behaviors associated with changes in the household: new spouse, partner or room-mate, long term visitors, new baby or children, home renovation, new dog or other companion animal.
- Behavior changes after hospitalization, illness, injury or trauma of any kind.
- Grief and mourning after the death of a guardian or house-mate.

Because inappropriate use of the litter box is the most frequently occurring and common feline behavior problem, the focus will be on that subject.

Cats are the most fastidious and clean animals on earth. They spend hours grooming themselves and each other. When they stop using their litter boxes or do not use them appropriately, it is not because they are stupid, lazy, or mean-spirited. It is *always* for a reason. They may be ill, distressed or in pain, or the litter box itself may be problematic - not clean or clean enough, located in a place that is not private or easily accessed, too small, shared by too many, have an unacceptable kind of litter in it, etc.

Most litter boxes and litters are produced with people, not cats, in mind. The boxes boast anonymity through design, and the litters advertised as providing a reduced need to clean, given added odor control and all sorts of extra ingredients. A litter box that has been properly maintained and cleaned will not accumulate odor. No amount of odor control additive or product will be sufficient for a litter box that needs, simply, to be maintained clean or changed. By *changed* I do not mean adding more litter to the mix. Rather, *changed* means completely empty all contents of the box and, if liners are used, disposing of these as well. If you use a hooded litter box, when changing the litter, also wash the box and the hood thoroughly with warm water and dishwashing liquid and rinse. Then, spray all surfaces with a ten percent solution of laundry bleach and water, let the box and all surfaces sit for five minutes, and rinse again thoroughly. From there, dry and fill the box with a liner (if you use liners) and the litter your cat(s) prefer. In general, this complete change should be done once a week.

Litter box Liners

Litter box liners should be expressly designed for a particular litter box, its size and shape. Ordinary plastic trash bags are not acceptable substitutes and never fit a litter box properly. Even when using a proper litter box liner, to achieve acceptable fit, they should be carefully placed in the box so that the liner is flush with the bottom and sides, creating a flat surface on which to put the litter. Cats do not like surfaces that create resistance when stepped on. Ill-fitting litter box liners will do just that.

Solid waste should be removed as soon as it is seen and careful observance of the condition of the litter box for liquid waste will determine if the box needs to be changed more often than once weekly. If you have only one cat, once weekly is likely to be more than adequate.

Number and Location of Litter Boxes

There should be at least one litter box for every two cats in the household. Litter boxes should be placed in easy-to-access, quiet, private places. Do not place them in any of the following locations: closets or crammed spaces that require a road map to avoid detours, near a noisy washing machine or dryer, hidden spaces obscured from your view such as in a basement or attic where you are more likely to begin to neglect litter box care.

If you are beginning to think this is all too complicated and too much trouble, it is possible you should re-think sharing your life with cats. On the other hand, this care is really far easier and takes less time to accomplish than it does to describe!

Most people are careful about what goes into their cats (food, water and treats) but are not aware of the importance of knowing what comes out of her. Vigilant observation of change in urine or fecal matter amount, frequency or infrequency of waste production; consistency, form and color, etc. are early indicators of illness brewing.

This attention to detail may seem like a lot to digest, but cats are worth it. As a grief therapist and animal behaviorist with a *super specialty* in feline behavior for more than three decades, I still and will always remain in wonder of these extraordinary beings. Their needs, normal but misunderstood, or unwanted behavior and preferences often clash with those of their guardians who struggle to find solutions. The single most frequently occurring group of challenges surround the litter box, cats' behaviors associated with it, its care and choice of litter.

Litter Box Design

You will find an endless choice of designs for litter boxes, including those with and without hoods, framed or unadorned, ball-shaped, contained in specially designed cabinets or planters, self-cleaning models, and even one that is flushable and installed into your plumbing system. There is also a simple device that will easily teach a cat to use an ordinary toilet! You have to flush the waste inside the toilet yourself, but the device works and cats will use it. It comes with alarming built-in problems, however. What will your cat do when suddenly faced with illness or injury and she has to be hospitalized without access to *her* toilet? What will your cat do if *you* are ill, injured, or hospitalized and she has to be boarded or cared for in someone else's home? How will he jump up to the toilet when he becomes advanced in years? These questions describe highly stressful situations that demand she learn a new skill to accomplish one of nature's most basic tasks. For this reason, none of these kinds of devices have my favor or recommendation.

Litter boxes that are too deep and require cats to climb rather than step into them are also not a good choice, especially for kittens, seniors, and those with temporary or permanent mobility challenges. A litter box that is angled with a very low front entry and gradually increases in depth as cats enter the box is ideal. Hooded litter boxes are a perfectly good choice provided that your cat displays no aversion to them.

Some models of litter boxes have plastic swinging-door entrances that require cats to push through them. These entrances are supposed to eliminate or reduce the litter that cats kick out of the box during normal use. Cats will kick and dig their litter to varying degrees depending on the individual cat. Also, the amount of kicking, digging and burying of solid waste has many variations. A cat who does not cover solid or liquid waste is not *sloppy* nor does he have poor hygiene. His actions are entirely within the range of normal behavior. The swinging door on the litter box may be easily accepted by some cats, but it also creates an environment equivalent an airplane rest room at the end of a long flight. Charming, isn't it? Similarly, filter-equipped litter boxes create the illusion of odor control. If they do anything at all, they simply prevent the normal odors of solid and liquid waste from wafting out of the box, thus trapping cats in another airplane-like bathroom. In the end, only one solution is really best for you and your cats - keep the boxes as pristinely clean as possible. That's all there is to it! You cannot have a litter box that is too clean. Truth be told again, most litters and other litter box products are designed for people, not cats. Cats are burdened with what appeals to well-intended people who use devises and products that are either useless, offensive and unnatural to them or are stress-inducing, counterproductive and counterintuitive to their needs and well being.

Healthy, happy cats are fastidious about cleanliness and grooming, and they are generally sensitive about their paws, claws and the surfaces they choose to touch or avoid. Some surfaces are so unacceptable to them they become anxious if they are forced to be in contact with them. These surfaces can even cause or exacerbate feline elimination disorder (FED). FED is a condition in which cats stop using their litter boxes and eliminate on surfaces of all kinds including carpet, bathroom or kitchen sinks, furniture, and other inappropriate places that can even include your bed! Once this syndrome is in place, and if what you are doing about it is not helping, you need the guidance of a feline behaviorist. It will *not* go away, it *will* escalate and it has the ability to fracture your relationship with your cat. Your cat is not *having fun* doing it. She is highly stressed and struggling with a legitimate problem that can be solved. The good news is that it is treatable and even curable. Run-don't-walk to a feline behaviorist with a proven track record of success!

Choice of Litter

The choices of litter are staggering. They range from clay, newspaper, wood, corn, and wheat-based litters to *pearls* and *crystals*, and more. Within those categories lies yet another layer of choices – scented or unscented, multi-cat or single-cat, clumping or non-clumping, flushable or non-flushable, and there are even recipes for home-made litter using sand, soil, ashes and all manner of substances. *Oh, my whiskers!* What to do?

First, remember that *if it ain't broke-don't fix it!* If what you are using is entirely satisfactory to both you and your cats, there is probably no reason to make a change. Keep it simple, keep it exquisitely clean, and maintain the correct amount of litter recommended by the manufacturer of the product you choose.

In general, I am not fond of clay and prefer wood or corn-based litters that are virtually dust-free. They also tend to track less and are *friendlier* to the respiratory system of cats, their guardians, and Mother Earth.

In the category of wood-based litters, my choice is Luv My Kitty by Luv Litters (www.luvlitters.com/kitty.htm). It is *not* found everywhere, but they will ship directly to you upon request.

It is made from 100% recycled wood products, is biodegradable, and feline, guardian, and earth friendly.

Photo provided by Luv Litters

On my list of non-favored litter features are additives or scents of any kind. However, there always being an exception, if you choose a corn-based litter, there is an easily found corn-based, lavender-scented litter that holds my favor.

Perhaps surprisingly, many cats like corn and will even taste or eat small amounts of corn-based litter. Provided that they do not ingest any more than *a taste* or tiny bit, it should pose no threat. Many especially enjoy eating corn directly from the cob. Please make sure to hold it for them so the cob itself is not eaten.

Raymond Eating Corn

Photo by Barbara Meyers

The corn was not held *only* while photo was taken

The cob is exceptionally difficult to digest and can cause serious gastrointestinal blockage. Even for dogs, this truth holds. More than one dog has snatched a whole corn from a table or picnic blanket and paid for it with his life. Cats are less likely to commandeer and ingest an entire cob on their own, but it is best to safeguard them from danger just the same. Additionally, corn should be viewed as an occasional treat and not part of a regular diet. Cats are *obgliate carnivores* and, therefore, *must* eat meat. Unless there is a specific medical reason for them to eat grain, their diets should consist of a high-quality, grain-free food such as Wellness Core. In addition to Core, Wellness makes other varieties of grain-free foods for both cats and dogs (www.wellnespetfood.com).

Wellness Core Canned and Dry

Photo provided by Wellpet

Returning to the subject of litter, more than one litter is advertised as *flushable* and they are. I very strongly prefer *not* to flush and I do not recommend it.

Why I do not flush litter

Flushing litter can be deadly to marine life! It is not common, but some cats host the deadly pathogen, *Toxoplasmosis gondii*. *Toxoplasmosis gondii* is very strongly implicated in approximately 40% of the deaths of California sea otters. The problem is so great that it is now illegal to flush litter in the state of California. Do not imagine that because flushed toilet water and its contents goes through a waste treatment plant it is safe to flush litter. It is not! When you flush a flushable litter, it gets taken to your local sewage treatment plant. Current water treatment facilities are *not* designed to eliminate this parasite and it moves into greater bodies of water alive, unharmed and is capable of killing sea otters. Other marine life is also at risk and studies are being conducted to document it. For the same reasons, people with dogs should not toss their used solid waste collection bags (or anything else) into a sewer or storm drain. Sewers and storm drains are designed only to collect excess rain water, help with flash flooding and are *not* for solid waste. As an alternative to flushing, you can scoop into paper bags or plastic bags that have been repurposed after primary use. You must, however, decide for yourself about flushing flushable litter. If, with the information provided, you remain comfortable with flushing flushable litter, be mindful of the amount you flush each time. Do not flush the entire box at once. If you have a multi-cat family, do not flush many clumps at the same time.

There will always be a cat who will reject any brand of litter, food, or toy for their own reasons. Their needs and preferences should be honored when, after proper introduction and a trial of use, they reject it.

Litter Catchers

If you live with cats, you live with at least some litter being tracked about. There are a wide variety of litter mats and other *gizmos* that attempt to catch and contain the excess litter that is tracked after litter box use. Some help a bit, some just make more work, and some make no difference at all.

...And then came Stikitty (www.cleanicity.com).

As emphasized earlier, cats are very sensitive to the touch of various surfaces and they generally dislike surfaces that are sticky. Stikitty is based on the *sticky factor* and, while it was interesting, I had strong reservations. I did, however, feel it was worthwhile to see for myself.

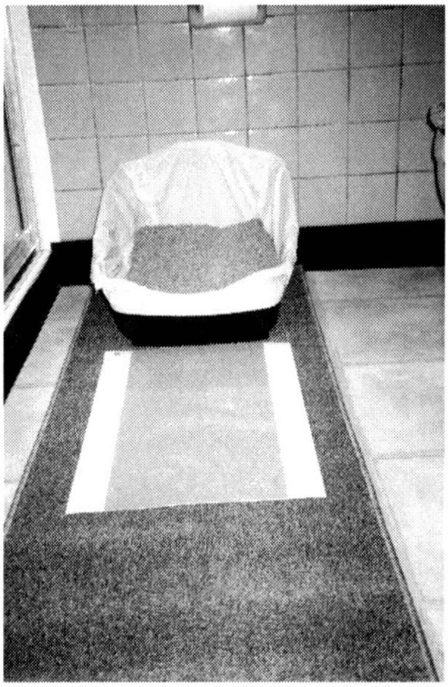

Stikitty Mat in Front of Litter Box
With Liner and Corn-Based Litter
All photos by Barbara Meyers

In the interest of creating a comprehensive study of the product rather than reliance a single, anecdotal experience, Stikitty was presented to nine known (my own feline family) cats. All were non-genetic members of the same feline family, of both genders and included both short and long-haired cats. Some had chronic illnesses that were well managed and stable. There was no inter-cat aggression or other social problems. There was no feline elimination disorder, and there was one litter box (there should never be less and, in some cases, more are necessary) for every two cats. All the litter boxes had low front entries and half were hooded. The boxes were in different locations with easy access unencumbered by a noisy washing machine or other intrusive objects. None was in remote location such as a basement or attic - How would *you* like to run an obstacle course to a distant bathroom when you need one?

The study took place over a forty-five day period and was used on tile, oak hardwood flooring, carpet, and linoleum with four different brands and types of litter.

Note: There will always be exceptions to any rule or finding. Not every experience can be expected to mimic my findings though I stand by my experience and I remain comfortable recommending Stikitty.

Study Results

- Swift acceptance with minimal initial hesitation by all cats.
- The *sticky factor* is adequate to fully perform its intended purpose, but not sticky enough to insult the paws. What a pleasant surprise!
- Tracking of litter is cut down by at least 80% or more.
- The overall performance of Stikitty is excellent.
- The more dusty the litter (like common clay litters) and the general environment, the more frequently you will need to change the Stikitty sheets.
- Multi-cat households with high traffic at any particular litter box location will require more frequent change of Stikitty sheets.
- Stikitty performs well with all litter, but the best results are achieved when using a high-quality, nearly dust-free litter. No litter is totally free from dust, though *virtually* dust-free litter does exist.

Like all solutions feline, the one that is right for *your* cat must be found and honored, and some creativity in use is always advisable. By example, it was my finding that there was no need to use the self-stick strips provided with Stikitty to hold it to the surfaces it was used on. Not using them during the study allowed for specialized placement of more than one Stikitty mat to accommodate a non-traditional or unusual space. In some cases, two smaller-sized Stikittys can be lined up to create length without width or width without length, and even a "T" formation.

Once the best placement for more than one Stikitty mat is determined, the self-stick feature can be used if necessary. Be creative! Stikitty lends itself to that with ease.

Raymond Evaluating Stikitty

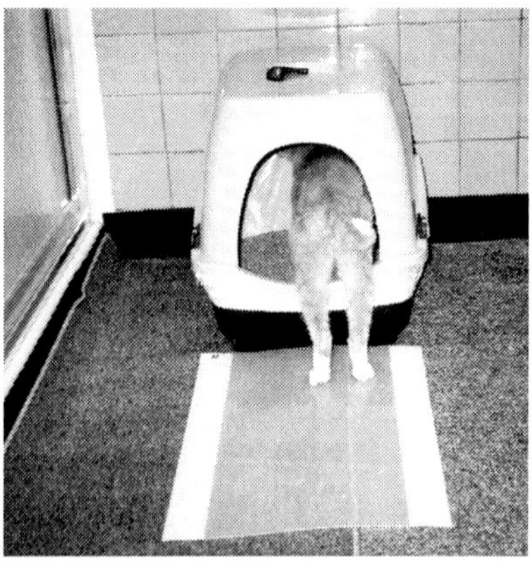

Raymond Entering Litter Box with No Avoidance of Stikitty

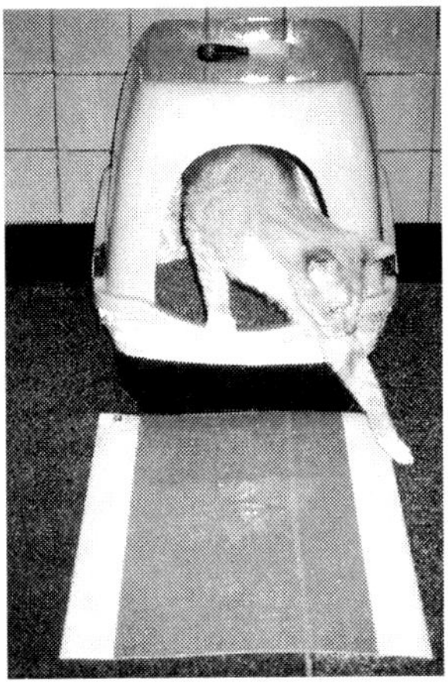

Raymond Engaged in Normal Pawing on Exit - Note litter collected by Stikitty

A note of caution on creativity; *never* subject your cat(s) to anything that is clearly causing them distress or anxiety. Some hesitation with new things is perfectly natural, but if it goes beyond that, it is stressful. Continued exposure to stress even with ideal and favored products, leads to serious distress.

With Special Thanks to Raymond, Beloved Friend and Stikitty Poster Boy

April 22nd 1996 – February 11th 2011

His heart failed but *he* never failed to be a daily source of delight, laughter, and fun. His antics, intelligence, the games he invented, and his endless affection for everyone he knew will be among the many things that will be missed. Clown, Ambassador, Chief Mischief-Maker, and Beloved Friend, it is impossible to remember Raymond and not find a smile to help soften the pain of his *changing worlds.*

"Everybody Loves Raymond."

Care of Scoopers

Be aware that scoopers must also be carefully maintained. Do not leave scoopers on the top of the litter box, prop them up against the side of the box, or in some corner out of sight. They, too, must be kept clean, and while you may not need clean with every scoop, scoopers should be placed back into a caddy that you have created for them or you can buy one that comes with its own caddy. To create a clean caddy for your scooper, find a plastic storage container or pitcher of the right size and shape. Note: Your author acknowledges that plastic is not an earth-friendly material. It is, however, a safety trade-off to avoid the dangers of broken glass. Continuing on with scooper care, remove and discard the top of the container you choose. Line the inside with a repurposed plastic bag and change the bag every few days. When finished scooping, place the scooper in its container, and remember to keep the scooper clean in the same ways recommended for the litter box. This simple method of using a disposable caddy liner allows you to have a clean scooper and caddy. Caution: Many cats are attracted to plastic bags and they will chew and swallow significant amounts of it. Cats who are attracted to plastic are not usually attracted to molded hard plastic objects such as litter boxes and containers. If your cat is an aficionado of plastic bags, do *not* use them as a caddy liner but, instead, keep the caddy clean with frequent washings.

Scoopers

Litter scoopers of all sizes and shapes can be found everywhere. They range in price from as little as two dollars to much more. An outstanding scooper, and my personal favorite, is the DuraScoop (www.durascoop.com).

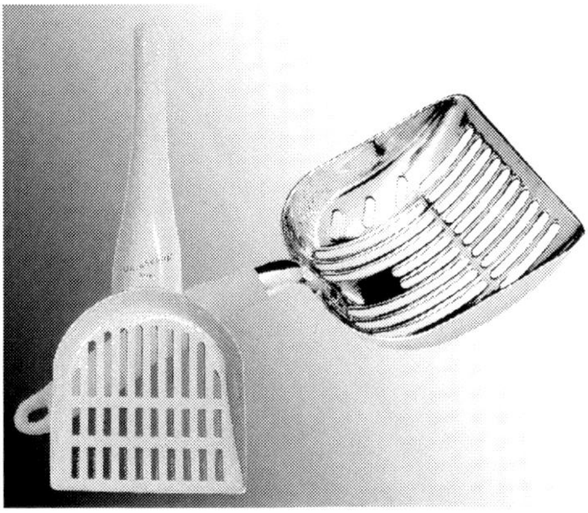

Durascoop
Photo provided by DuraScoop

There is a DuraScoop model for every preference and need, including one with an ergonomically designed handle (not shown) for those who must or prefer to sit while scooping. All Durascoop models perform at levels far and above the usual, and, depending on which one you choose, they are constructed from cast aluminum, powder-coated steel, or glass-filled nylon. They are widely available from a variety of retailers. I recommend that you visit the DuraScoop website to familiarize yourself with both the entire line and, specifically, the Ergo Kit extension handle so that you can make the best selection at the retailer of your choice. If you encounter difficulty in finding the Durascoop product you want, call Durascoop for their advice and direction.

Personal Styles of Litter Box Behaviors

We all have a personal style of elimination and bathroom habits. They are rarely, if ever, discussed, but if they were, we would learn the many differences among us. The same is true for cats.

Most cats will enter the litter box, dig about a bit, turn to face forward, and take a position to urinate. Others will prop their front paws on the forward edge of the box and urinate from that position. Some will not turn to face outward, instead urinating or defecating facing the back of the box. For male cats, because of their anatomy, these preferences can result in urine spilling over the front edge of the box and onto the floor, or if a hooded box is used, urine streaming onto the back of the hood, dripping outside the box and thoroughly soiling the inner side of the hood. If the litter box is not hooded, the unwanted but natural upward stream of urine will be, unintentionally, directed onto the surrounding wall and floor directly behind the box. This can create the illusion that your little boy has failed to use the box; yet he has not! It is simply a reflection of a normal variation due to anatomy.

As the above example demonstrates, it is, yet again, why it is so important to know the normal habits, behaviors and personal style of your cat and note any changes in the usual pattern. There is nothing to be done about this unwanted stream of urine except to provide an absorbent, disposable surface to collect the overflow and see to it that the edge of the box is kept clean. Absorbent under-pads that are found in surgical supply stores, work nicely when placed in front of the litter box. Similarly, the pads that are used to help puppies learn good house manners also work well. If your cat strongly prefers a non-hooded box and will not use a hooded box, protect the target areas by taping the absorbent pads in the appropriate places. It is somewhat easier to protect a hooded box from spill-over that is caused by anatomy but is a worthwhile endeavor for both you and your cat(s) and should be done in both situations.

You can create a backsplash for a hooded box by draping and shaping an absorbent, disposable material around the back of the box before placing the hood over it. The hood serves to hold the backsplash in place without tape or adhesives. The backsplash should reach at least to the level of the litter inside the box and extend over the back of the box by an inch or two. Two or three unseparated sheets of high-quality, paper towels work best. The sheets should be changed with every soiling.

Absent of any medical condition that would alter their routine, cats will (especially upon awakening) urinate first and then defecate. There are some cats who are so fastidious about their litter box habits, they may consider a box that has been urinated or defecated in as already too soiled to use again, and they will urinate or defecate outside the box. This behavior is not common, but it is also not outside the realm of normal. If there is no medical reason (constipation, obstipation, inflammatory bowel disease, colitis, etc.) for this, the addition of another litter box usually solves the problem.

Water

Water is essential to all life. The renowned veterinary endocrinologist Mark E. Peterson points out that though most people do not think of water as a nutrient, it remains the "king of all nutrients" (www.animalendocrine.com). Water serves a variety of functions, including transporting nutrients and oxygen throughout the bloodstream and into cells, moisturizes air in the lungs, regulates body temperature, and helps to eliminate waste products of metabolism through the kidneys and gastrointestinal tract. Water accounts for about two-thirds of a cat's body weight and is the hub of all chemical processes in the body.

Healthy cats normally do not have a strong thirst drive and do not drink very much water. Those who eat a high-quality moist or canned diet get most of their daily water needs from the food, and additional water consumption may be very low.

The exact amount of water any cat drinks will be dependent on various factors such as body size, activity, season, and state of health. Cats who prefer and exclusively eat a dry diet will need water supplementation, and illnesses such as hyperthyroidism, diabetes, and kidney disease will change water requirements significantly.

We are all familiar with the expression, "You can lead horse to water but you can't make him drink." With the basic belief that every problem has a solution, your author holds another perspective. Though it is true that "you can't *make* him drink," you *can* make him thirsty or give him another good reason to drink!

For cats, one of the *good reasons to drink* can come from the Drinkwell fountain. The Drinkwell fountain was invented in 1994 and, in my opinion, is the best one.

Drinkwell Platinum

All Photos provided by Drinkwell®

Many cats are enticed by and love to drink from running faucets. Inspired by her cat Buckwheat, veterinarian Dr. Mary Burns invented the Drinkwell fountain.
(http://www.petsafe.net/products/feeders-and-waterers).

In 1996, Dr. Burns made Buckwheat's fountain available to other cats and dogs. I was among the first to learn about the Drinkwell, still use it for my own feline family and continue to recommend it. Over time, the fountain evolved with many improvements. There are multiple models, sizes, shapes, and flow designs from which to choose.

You can even find Drinkwell systems equipped with a 360-degree or multi-tier design, high-capacity reservoirs, and a molded tray that goes under the fountain for those cats who are amused by playing with water and dogs who may be a bit *drippy* when drinking.

Drinkwell 360 – *molded tray not shown*

Many cats and dogs have benefited from the bond between Burns and Buckwheat and the creativity it inspired. The Drinkwell fountain is yet another example of *the magical link* that bonds us to our animal friends and family - a bond that changes us, them, and so much more.

Carriers

As in all things feline and canine, every cat and dog must have equipment and products chosen for them that are precisely tailored to their specific needs, preferences, sensitivities, life-styles and living situations. Carriers are available in every style, shape, material, size, and configuration imaginable. This includes stroller-type carriers and hard sided carriers with wheels that can be used similarly to luggage carriers.

When choosing a carrier, remember that cats are *not* luggage. Unless they express the highly unlikely preference for being transported as though they *are* luggage, do not treat them as such! While it may seem efficient and attractive to you, it is a bumpy and disturbing ride for your cat. Strollers offer a more comfortable ride, but even they may not be right for you or your cat's needs, purposes, and safety.

The best overall choice (my favorite and the one I use for my own feline family) is the hard sided, Petmate double door.

Petmate Double Door Cat Carrier
19.4" long x 12.8" wide x 10" high
Photos Provided by Petmate

The double door eliminates the need to *push* cats into the carrier through a single front door, later *dragging* them out through the same door to remove them. The top loading feature permits ease-of-entry and exit for the many who will not enter or exit voluntarily without great reluctance or distress. The carrier comes in two sizes: 19.4" long x 12.8" wide x 10" high or 24.1" long x 16.8" wide x 14.5" high. Kittens and most cats do very well with the smaller size. The larger size is a bit too high for cats as they prefer a *cozier* or tighter space, but it is ideal for small dogs and exceptionally large cats such as a long-legged, more than twenty-pound Maine Coon or a non-breed-specific cat who is of similar height and weight. You must decide for yourself which size will work best for you and your cat. When selecting a carrier, pay close attention to the space it will occupy in your home and car.

Be sure to put a comfortable liner in the carrier, and not newspaper, paper towels, or an ordinary towel. These materials do not stay in place, and your cat will find herself on the floor of the carrier with no *comfy* support. A washable, skid-resistant rubber backed mat (like the kind designed for bathrooms) is a good choice. These mats come in various sizes and colors. Purchase the one closest to the size you need and drape or fold as necessary to fit the carrier's interior for maximum comfort. Do not cut the mat as cuts will leave a rough edge that can fray. The *fray* is likely to consist of string-like material. Ingestion of string or string-like objects can, and often is, deadly. An even better option than generic mats are the Petmate bolster or kennel mats. They come in sizes that correspond to the size of the Petmate carrier you choose (www.petmate.com).

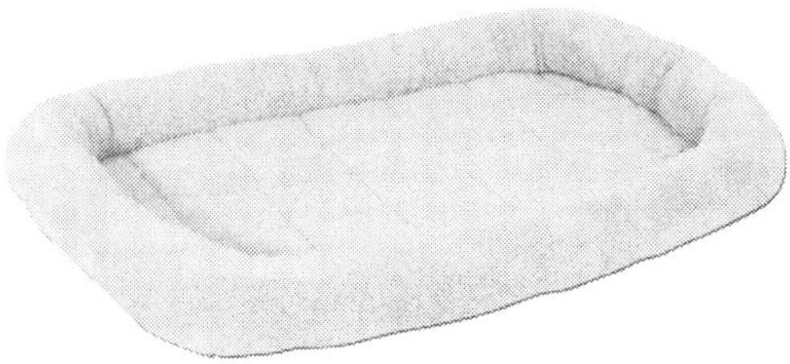

Petmate Bolster Mat

Feline Elimination Disorders

True elimination disorders are common, though completely unlike any of the normal variations described. If underlying physical illness has been ruled out, and you are diligently maintaining what you believe to be pristine litter box environment, and your cat is nonetheless, urinating or defecating outside the box, you very likely have a cat with feline elimination disorder.

The condition is frustrating, confounding, and, if left unaddressed, dangerous as it will create permanent damage both to your home and your relationship with your cat. It is, however, highly treatable and manageable. It requires precise diagnosis and a thorough care plan including most if not all of the following:

- Consultation with an experienced feline behaviorist who has the requisite academic knowledge, experience and a deep understanding and respect for cats and their guardians.

- Use of feline facial pheromones to help create a calming atmosphere. The best pheromone is Feliway, and is also sold as Comfort Zone. It is supplied as a spray as well as room diffusers. I recommend both the spray as well as the diffusers but you must learn how to use them for your exact situation. I am *not* comfortable recommending the use of the pheromone collar and, therefore, do not. Collars can generate health and safety issues. Your feline behaviorist will guide you through the selection, placement, and various uses of the other pheromone products. I do *not* recommend herbal alternatives in place of Feliway or Comfort Zone.
- Creation of multiple environmental enrichments.
- Use of prescription medications - there are several choices, and the right choice must be carefully selected on a case-by-case basis. Do not attempt to medicate your cat without the guidance of both a behaviorist and a veterinarian working in tandem. Even with professionals involved, from time to time, the first choice of medication may be rejected for different reasons - taste, form, or difficulty in administration. When these factors are not in play, the first medication chosen simply may not work, or work well enough. In these situations, a second or even third attempt to find just the right medication and dosage is necessary for a rewarding outcome.
- Disposal of thoroughly soiled furniture, carpeting, and other soft targets that must *not* replaced until the problem is completely solved. When organic material (urine) has completely saturated fabric and other surfaces like sheetrock, baseboards, etc., there is no treatment or remedy adequate to repair them. They are not only offensive and invite cats back to them for more soiling, they are also a breeding ground for bacteria, mold, fungus, and other toxins.

In applying the care plan, there are sound principles to keep in mind. If yours is a multi-cat household, the cat who has been identified as the culprit is often *not* the responsible offender. Whoever has the primary problem may be quietly in the background while others are drawn to the soiled spot. They will, naturally, re-mark it with their own urine lending to being misidentified. Though it takes a bit of detective work, there are methods available to identify the primary individual.

After stabilization is established, relapse or *break-through* events may occur. They are easily controlled with medication adjustment, and it is highly unlikely that a major problem will surface again. With the investment of time, love, patience, money, compassion, a team of experts to help you, persistence, and a shift in your own attitude, change *can* and *will* come. Cats with elimination disorders are *not* having fun. They are also not angry, spiteful or getting even with you. They are anxious, distressed, and in need of your help. Feline Elimination Disorder is *not* going away on its own. If you do not step up to help your cat, it is unreasonable to expect that anyone else will be willing to take on the challenge. So, know that your cat can be helped, and you can do it!

Claws for Concern

The subject of declawing cats for behavior problems or for any other reasons is highly controversial and emotionally charged. There are those are so strongly opposed to declawing, they have made it their personal goal to have it banished and outlawed. Efforts to accomplish it have proven successful in West Hollywood, California.

I am *not* in favor of the arbitrary removal (amputation) of cats' claws for prevention of their natural tendency to use them in ways that might be destructive. There are, however, situations where the removal of claws will spare a cat's home, future, and life. Declawing deserves as much consideration as any other elective procedure that will, when performed *properly* and for the *right* reasons, prove life-altering or life-saving. The two major reasons to consider declawing for cats are aggression accompanied by injury to people or other animals and cases where all other methods to redirect behavior that produces serious household destruction have been given adequate time to succeed but have failed. Declawing, on its own, is not the answer to the problems unless it is part of a comprehensive care plan that includes the behavior modification of people as well as cats, the possible inclusion of prescription medication, and a variety of environmental changes. At the very least, declawing can offer a window of safety during the time when all the other aspects of resolving the problem are in progress.

Cats who fall into these categories are at great risk of being banished to a single room or basement where what they destroy is of minimal value to their family, an unsafe outdoor life, surrendered to a shelter where they will be unadoptable or killed, or have their lives ended in convenience killing. *None* of these are good choices nor do they result in rewarding outcomes. They are isolating, cruel, ineffective and have damaging psychological effects on cats as well as people. If there are children in the family, these choices teach them that animal life is cheap and misbehaving may be risky for them, too. Not just a few children have concluded that they, too, will be sent away, banished to the basement, or left outdoors to fend for themselves if they misbehave.

Before delcawing, known as onchectomy, can occur, a more difficult and complicated surgery must take place - Radical mythectomy! A radical mythectomy is the removal of myth and nonsense that surrounds declawing.

Myth 1. Declawing will cause cats to bite instead of scratch. This is *not* true.

Myth 2. Declawed cats are less able to respond to danger and defend themselves when outside. Cats who are allowed outside are at great risk. The notion that a cat's claws will protect him from outdoor danger is utter nonsense. Cats with intact claws are very often severely injured or killed by other free-roaming animals and malicious people. With regard to cases of cats being killed by malicious people, the sad truth is that there are those who *truly* hate cats or have legitimate problems caused by *your* (or any other) cat using their gardens as litter boxes. It is very convenient for them to deter their unwelcome visitors with the use of poison-bated food. Unfortunately, this is a common practice! Claws are little defense when being assaulted by other aggressive animals and *no* defense against poisoning or an on-coming car.

Myth 3. Declawed cats develop litter box aversion and will urinate and mark the home. While true that litter box aversion may follow declaw, it is *not* due to declawing itself. It is more likely the post operative pain cats associate with the use of their paws to dig in the litter box. A properly performed surgery that is accompanied by adequate pain control prevents this. The *best* choice for removal of the claws lies not with traditional surgery but with laser surgery. It is a far less invasive procedure that produces significantly less trauma, bleeding and pain. The post operative recovery period is often as little as a few days. If, after careful research, you find that laser declaw is not available in your area and you are unable or unwilling to travel for it, a competent surgeon who uses the traditional method and combines it with safe, generous, modern and effective pain control drugs may have to suffice. The latter is *not* the preferred choice and I urge you to seek laser declaw even if you have to inconvenience yourself to secure it.

Cats who have undergone onchectomy with traditional surgery should not be given access to standard litters during recovery. In fact, I know of no veterinarian who will not caution against the use of standard litters. Instead, they advise the use of Yesterday's News, a very soft litter made from recycled newspaper that is appropriate for post operative use. Cats who have laser declaw do not require any special litter after the procedure.

Myth 4. Declawed cats have negative personality changes after the procedure and are never the same. If and when it may *seem* so it is not because of a well-done surgery or the loss of their claws; it is more likely the result of inadequate pain control. A technically well-done surgery is not *really* well-done if it is unaccompanied by the most sophisticated and generous pain control.

Cats who have not had the benefit of traditional surgery with generous pain control or the dramatically less painful and preferred laser declaw, may suffer complications such as aversion to their litter box as well as other behavior changes that stem from pain-induced stress and trauma. The behavior and trauma can be successfully treated even many months later. It should be done by a qualified and sensitive feline behaviorist in concert with a cooperating, empathetic veterinarian. Declawing is not the only surgery, illness, or injury that is subject to inadequate pain control and trauma. These maladies can produce post traumatic stress disorders but can be avoided with high-quality veterinary care.

Moving past the myths, when the life of your cat and the well being of your family are all at risk, think! Do not be misled by staunch proponents or opponents of declawing. Seek sound information, consult with unbiased professionals, and make informed decisions. Ultimately, the choices are yours and you are responsible for them.

Biting

Cats who cause injury to people and each other can do so with their teeth as well as with their claws. This is similar to the way people hurt each other. They may not confine their behavior to a slap or punch but may also kick and bite, too. Does this mean cats' teeth should be extracted? Sometimes, yes. If it is determined that there is a true need to disarm a cat by removing or limiting the damage they can do with their teeth, it should be understood that extraction is *not* the whole or only solution. It must be viewed as an important but still only a single component of a broad-based care plan for rehabilitation.

There is an excellent alternative to extraction of teeth for cats and, when necessary, is the *only* one I recommend. The procedure blunts the teeth without extraction or pain. It is known as crown amputation and pulp-capping. It can be expensive but well worth it. A consultation with a board certified veterinary dentist will determine if your cat is a good candidate for crown amputation and pulp-capping. The American Veterinary Dental College (www.avdc.org) can help you locate a board certified veterinary dentist in your area.

If you are on or within driving distance of Long Island, New York, *the* veterinary dentist to consult is Daniel E. Carmichael, DVM, Diplomate, AVDC. Dr. Carmichael can be seen at Veterinary Medical Center of Long Island in West Islip http://www.vmcli.com/veterinarians-dr-carmichael.

Daniel T. Carmichael, DVM
Photo provided by Daniel T. Carmichael, DVM

Dr. Carmichael is a nationally known leader and expert in the field of veterinary dentistry. The author of numerous scholarly papers and articles in veterinary journals, he is also compassionate, supportive and everything you could possibly wish for in a veterinarian and human being. Unfortunately, crown amputation and pulp-capping is ineffective for dogs. Some dogs may require and benefit from full-mouth extractions while their aggression is being treated. Indeed, it can save their lives.

General Dental Care

It is impossible to have good health without good dental and oral health. Do not be misled by findings that reveal your cat or dog *only* has some tartar on their teeth. Tartar (or more properly, dental calculus) is mineralized plaque.

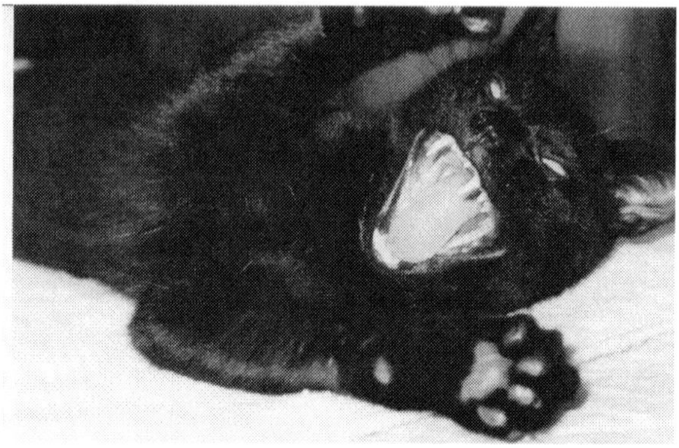

Jonah: "Look, Dr. Dan. No plaque"
Photo by Barbara Meyers

Plaque is composed of 70% bacteria. If dental calculus is apparent on oral exam, the very least that is needed is a thorough dental cleaning under general anesthesia. The photo is for your amusement. Do not expect your cat to willingly do what Jonah did. Even if he might, it is still not adequate to determine dental and oral health. Digital radiographs and a complete oral examination to screen for oral cancer are needed and must be performed with the benefit of general anesthesia.

Feline Tooth Resorption is the most common dental problem in cats. Studies worldwide have shown incidence rates of up to 75%. It is a painful condition. Signs associated with it include hesitation or unwillingness to eat or eat dry food, drooling, overall lethargy or other change in mood or personality. The most common sign of pain in cats is *no sign at all!* Cats are supremely deft at masking their pain until it is extreme or dangerously advanced. All teeth affected with this condition must be extracted. Some cats require full mouth extractions and do remarkably well afterwards. Most are immediately happier because they are free of chronic pain and infection. Soft foods like smooth baby food are recommended after the procedure but that changes fairly quickly. After full healing, they resume normal eating and those who eat a dry diet continue to do very well with it. A dental exam should be done at least once a year, and twice is best.

Scratching Posts

Most scratching and climbing posts are made with people in mind and are covered with non-removable and non-washable carpeting designed to match or coordinate with home décor. Be aware that giving your cats these posts may be creating unintended consequences because it is unreasonable to expect cats to distinguish between the carpet on the posts and your prized home furnishings.

Choose sturdy, well-balanced sisal scratching posts without fabric of any kind and climbing posts that have both sisal posts (for scratching) and comfy resting shelves or tunnels covered with fabric that is both removable and washable. Climbing posts should be *at least* five-to-six feet high and multi-leveled, with easy access from one level the other.

Cats have different preferences for scratching. Some like to stand on their hind legs and scratch vertically. Others prefer to stand on all fours and scratch horizontally. Some will enjoy both and cats without claws will continue engage in natural *scratching* behavior. It is best to provide your cats with the kinds of posts that will accommodate both preferences. Be sure to observe your cat's behavior and choices. You can then orient the posts accordingly.

Do not be tempted to *teach* your cat to use a scratching post by placing her paws on the post and mimicking scratching movements through your manipulation of her paws. Cats do not like this kind of handling and are perfectly capable of making their own decisions. If you pursue this learning myth, you will risk a negative association with both the post and you. Noteworthy is that contrary to popular belief, cats are not sharpening their claws through scratching behavior. They are removing the sheath surrounding the claw. This is necessary and normal. In effect, they are giving themselves a pedicure.

Cool Cats Really Like It Warm

Fahrenheit is the temperature scale proposed in 1724 by, and named after, the physicist Daniel Gabriel *Fahrenheit* (1686–1736). Normal body temperature for adult cats ranges between 100.4-102.5 degrees Fahrenheit. Newborn kittens have a body temperature of about 97 degrees Fahrenheit. Maintenance of body temperature is essential for good health, and body temperature is carefully monitored by veterinarians when animals are hospitalized for any reason and especially before, during, and after anesthesia.

Under conditions that are very hot, most cats will seek out cool surfaces such as those of tile floors, bathtubs, shower stalls, kitchen and bathroom sinks, and uncarpeted areas. In general, however, cats prefer warmth. For this reason, they are often seen wherever there is a sun spot or other source of warmth in the home.

Amanda in Sun Spot
Photo by Barbara Meyers

Warming Devices

We have all heard the horror stories of animals who were seriously burned or actually *cooked to death* by inferior or improper heating devices that were not especially designed for animals, their species-specific needs and safety.

Because of the ingenious warming devices made by K & H Manufacturing (www.khmfg.com), cats can bask in the warmth they love and be safe doing so. Lectro-Kennel and Lectro-Soft warming devices bring sunny warmth into your home even on rainy days.

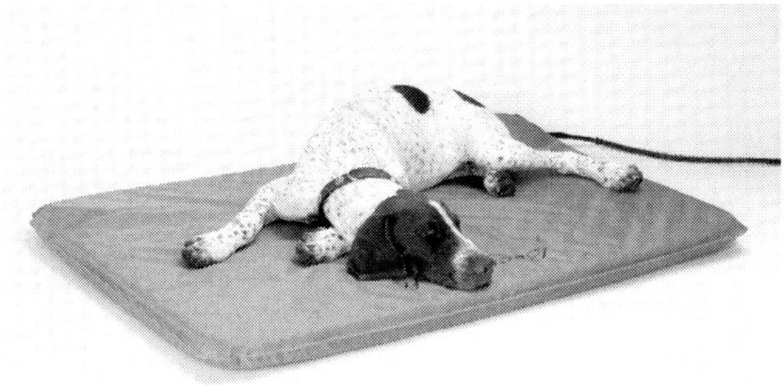

Lectro-Soft

K & H also makes an extensive line of warmers for dogs, heated bowls, a microwavable warmer and many other clever and easy to use warmers, including Thermo–Perch. As a consequence of cold, drafts, and air conditioning, birds are subject to serious illness. Because birds easily loose body temperature through their feet, Thermo-Perch helps to maintain consistent body temperature of companion birds.

Thermo-Perch

Caution: Lectro-Kennel and Lectro-Soft come with a specially designed washable cover that is constructed from a unique, open-weave fabric. *Never* cover your Lectro-Kennel or Lectro-Soft with anything but the Lectro-Cover. There is no substitute for it! These devices are safe to use *without* a cover but I recommend that covers *always* be used for additional comfort and cleanliness. Extra covers should also be obtained for the times when one is being laundered.

Thermo Kitty Sill
Photos provided by K & H Manufacturing

Many models of warmers are designed to bring warmth and comfort to outdoor environments, such as the interior of outdoor shelters in feral cat colonies. They work equally well indoors and your cat will love them. There is even a model called the Kitty Sill that allows cats to enjoy bird-watching and snoozing from a window sill. From the sill, a highly favored place for cats, they are kept warm even though the window area is cold because of the glass and its close proximity to the outdoors.

Chapter Ten

The Times They Are a Changin'

"My basic principle is that you don't make decisions because they're easy; you don't make them because they're convenient; you don't make them because they're cheap; you make them because they're right!"... Theodore Hesburgh (1917 --).

I can't afford it: The Hidden Costs of Not Seeking the Brightest and the Best

We are fortunate to live in a time when cutting edge, high-tech veterinary diagnostic and specialty-based medicine, as well as allied health for animals, is available. Examples of this care include:

- Board certified specialists in *every* field of veterinary medicine, including dentistry and oral surgery.
- MRI and CT scans, ultrasound, endoscopy, rhinoscopy, echocardiogram and other minimally or non-invasive diagnostic procedures.
- Nuclear medicine as a diagnostic tool and radioactive iodine (I-131) for the treatment of hyperthyroidism in cats.
- Physical rehabilitation following injury or surgery.
- Grief therapy - *different from bereavement counseling* - with a therapist specializing in loss, grief, separation, mourning and anticipatory mourning. Anticipatory mourning occurs when a diagnosis of either a serious or known-fatal-outcome is made. Another cause of

anticipatory mourning is the advancing age of companion animals that causes deep worry and concern. A grief therapist who is well versed in veterinary medicine *and* animal behavior can help to recognize and guide the treatment of mourning responses and post traumatic stress disorder in companion animals. Yes, our animal families experience grief and mourning that can sometimes create physical illness and even death. A few highly qualified grief therapists are also capable of helping to manage chronic, catastrophic and terminal illness as well as hospice and comfort care.

- Animal behaviorist consultations.
- Legal counsel from attorneys specializing in animal law.
- Animal health insurance programs.
- Professional bonded and insured nanny services.

If any of these (or others) has been recommended by a veterinarian, a common first reaction is often, "I can't afford it." However, the actual *costs* extend far beyond financial considerations. There are also *costly* powerful emotional and psychological components. Far too many people are not aware that they can actually *save* money, grief and life itself, if they turn to specialized care early.

Scenario One

Your otherwise healthy cat is diagnosed with hyperthyroidism. She is a good candidate for I-131 treatment (destruction of the overactive thyroid gland with radioactive iodine) and the cost is over $1,500. The treatment involves her being away from home for five to seven days while it is performed in a safe facility. I-131 is given by a single subcutaneous (under the skin) injection, requires no anesthesia and produces temporary radioactive body fluids that must be properly handled and disposed. By law, it cannot be done on an out-patient basis.

The cost of this treatment might *seem* like a great deal of money in addition to the added worry about having your feline friend away from home and family. Be assured, it is well worth it and, in the long run, is actually less expensive and more effective than all other treatments including surgery which is no longer considered the standard of care. While there may be a rare cat who is truly too sensitive, anxious, etc. to tolerate being away from home, most do *very* well in treatment. Even those who *seem* too sensitive or anxious to be away from home, often do far better than anticipated by their guardians. There are also cats who are *not* candidates for I-131 treatment because they have co-existing conditions (such as chronic renal disease) that are incompatible with the treatment. Here, even successful treatment of hyperthyroidism is problematic as it exacerbates the kidney condition. At the very least, I recommend a consultation with a Board Certified Veterinary Endocrinologist as soon as the diagnosis of hyperthyroidism is suspected or made and *before* treatment of any kind is undertaken.

If a cat is a good candidate for I-131 treatment and does *not* have kidney disease or any other condition that would preclude treatment with I-131, treatment should not be delayed. There are superb facilities that even offer a *Cat Cam* that allows you to monitor your friend in real time on a computer screen or other *smart* device while she is in treatment.

Why the cost of I-131 treatment is less expensive and a better overall choice than oral medication at home: When oral medication (Tapazole, aka: Methimazole) is the choice, it is given in twice daily doses. It requires *very* frequent monitoring with blood tests and echocardiograms. In addition, Tapazole is often not well tolerated and creates adverse side effects, especially vomiting, which is the most common. Other negative side effects of the Tapazole are less common but more worrisome. These include liver damage, decreased red or white blood cells and platelets. Platelets help blood clot, so loss of platelets can cause bleeding. Loss of white blood cells predisposes cats to infection, and loss of red cells causes anemia that can even be fatal. It is important to be aware that Tapazole is *not* a drug without value. It is often used to stabilize hyperthyroidism prior to I-131 treatment.

Some, but perhaps not all, veterinarians are very well versed in these matters and will be able to tell you if your cat is a good candidate for nuclear medicine. If your primary care vet suggests the use of Tapazole without discussing the possibility of I-131, I recommend that you open the subject with her and arrange for a consultation with a Board Certified Veterinary Endocrinologist *before* undertaking any permanent course of action.

If you live in the tri-state area of New York, New Jersey, Westchester and Connecticut, count yourself lucky. The premier, cutting edge animal endocrine care facility with locations in New York City and Bedford Hills, (about thirty-five miles north of New York City) is available to you and your feline family.

This matchless care is brought to you by Dr. Mark E. Peterson, DVM, Diplomate ACVIM and his associates at Animal Endocrine Clinic (www.animalendocrine.com). Among his many accomplishments, Dr. Peterson was awarded the *2012 Veterinarian of the Year* by the American Veterinary Medical Association.

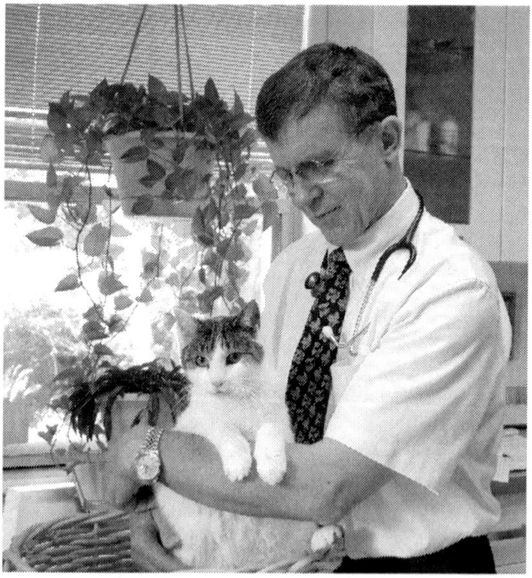

Mark E. Peterson, DVM and Hypurrcat Puff Mama
Photo provided by Animal Endocrine Clinic

People have come from as far away as Virginia to enjoy the benefits of Animal Endocrine Clinic. You will find Dr. Peterson's website is easily the most dynamic and fully informative site you have ever seen. Please spend time reviewing it in full even if you are not in need of endocrine specialty care at the present time. Also keep in mind that dogs have endocrine disease (diabetes may be the most common endocrine disease in both cats and dogs) and cats have endocrine diseases other than hyperthyroidism. Dogs rarely have hyperthyroidism but hypothyroidism (underactive thyroid glands) is not uncommon in dogs.

Mark E. Peterson, DVM, Veterinarian of the Year 2012
Photo provided by Animal Endocrine Clinic

Dr. Peterson has cared for three members of your author's feline family, as well as *many* others I have referred to him over the years. Not every result can be ideal or perfect but, in my personal and professional experience, there have been nothing but *purrfect* outcomes with Hypurrcat. Hypurrcat is the name of the program for I-131 treatment of feline hyperthyroidism at Animal Endocrine Clinic.

Scenario Two

Your cat or dog has had a battery of the usual and customary tests, yet the cause of symptoms remains unclear. Your vet recommends a consultation with a neurologist at a cost of over $160. The neurologist recommends an MRI with a cost of over $2,000. You have no animal health insurance and *bite the bullet* for the procedure and the costs. The MRI reveals no pathology and additional testing or medical management is recommended.

At this point, you are beginning to feel that the expense was "for nothing." You may even suspect that the recommendations were all contrived for profit. Nothing could be further from the truth! It is equally important to rule out the existence of pathology and learn what is *not* a cause of symptoms as well as to discover what *is*. Therefore, it is often advisable and necessary to have an MRI to help make (or rule out) the correct diagnosis.

For example: A single seizure or multiple seizures are not necessarily caused by epilepsy and some seizure disorders do not present with typical seizures at all. They manifest as peculiar and unusual behavior changes. There are numerous other neurological conditions that will present with seizures, including brain tumors. However, not all brain tumors will present with seizures and, some seizure disorders such as *focal* seizures, will present with episodic behavior changes of an unusual nature. Simply treating the seizure is inadequate if the underlying cause remains unknown. Brain tumors occur more often than one might think. In cats, a commonly found tumor is meningioma. Meningioma can only be diagnosed with the use of MRI.

Most meningiomas are not malignant, but they are dramatically life-altering and life-threatening just the same. These tumors (depending on exactly where in the brain they are located) can often be successfully removed by surgery, restoring cats to a rich, full life.

Meningiomas are known to recur and follow-up MRIs are necessary for life. In general, a single surgery can offer up to three or more years of uninterrupted, normal good quality of life. Some meningiomas never recur and others may recur quickly. There are, however, the rare few who may require two or more additional surgeries and or Cyberknife® and yet will continue to do well for long periods of time. One dramatic example of this occurrence involved your author's history-making, fabulous feline friend, Trevor.

Trevor, Seven Year Survivor of Multiple Meningioma
Photo by Barbara Meyers

CyberKnife ®

The CyberKnife® Radiosurgery System uses a high-tech, image-guided and computerized robotic control system to deliver radiation with sub-millimeter accuracy. The CyberKnife® radiation beams are shaped to conform tightly to complex masses and deliver multiple radiation beams from many points outside the body to the targeted tumor. On its own, each beam is relatively weak, but when they converge on the identified mass, they deliver high-energy, pinpointed radiation with astounding power.

Every cat and every situation must be evaluated individually and there are no hard and fast rules to be applied across the board. Brain tumors can present themselves with a dramatic and often sudden change in behavior that is unlike any other behavior change. While all behavior changes are not brain tumors, every behavior change, especially one with rapid onset, must be properly evaluated to determine if there is underlying physical pathology. An MRI, CT scan and other cutting-edge technology can save your cat or dog's life just as it can your own.

Scenario Three

Your dog or cat has a behavior problem ranging from *seemingly* uncontrollable behaviors to aggression. All behavior problems are a serious life-threatening and life-altering condition for people as well as animals.

Many companion animals with undisclosed behavior problems are relinquished to shelters where they languish in poor conditions for months or years, or they are executed because they are considered unadoptable. You may have been encouraged by others (including some professionals with limited skills or biased views) to *"just get rid of him"* by any means possible such as relinquishment to a shelter or pound, or even by ending his life. Only those who hold animal life as cheap and disposable will be free of the anguish that accompanies these choices. Among those who are not in the aforementioned group, these decisions are likely to produce years of regret, guilt, and complicated grief if acted upon.

Looking critically, let us stop and take a moment to address the reality of shelters. Despite what may be their sincere and best efforts, most shelters offer little more than warehousing. Shelters that boast high adoption numbers may not reflect the numbers of animals who are adopted but returned, and there is unlikely to be any long-term follow up to know how successful the adoptions really were. It takes multi-millions of dollars to build and maintain the kind of shelter that is *really* what animals need; one with an enriched, environment that closely replicates a home atmosphere, *not* a *warehouse* or *mini-jail.*

Returning to the scenario, your vet (or someone else) has recommended that you seek the intervention of an animal behaviorist. The costs can range anywhere from three to six-hundred dollars or more depending upon how many animals are involved. There may also be additional costs to implement recommended changes in environment, medication, and other necessary adjustments.

The costs of *not* seeking this kind of care are astronomical on every level. For example, a single incident of inter-dog aggression can result in injuries costing upward of two-thousand dollars in veterinary care. Inter-dog aggression can also result in the death of one or more dogs or cats in the household. Transferred or redirected aggression toward anyone attempting to intervene in an episode of aggression is not uncommon. This can result in serious life-threatening injuries to those who attempt to intervene. In the case of aggression being transferred to an infant or toddler, injuries can be fatal.

Other behavior problems, while, perhaps not as overtly dangerous are nonetheless troublesome and damaging. House soiling and inappropriate litter box use (feline elimination disorder), household destruction resulting from canine separation disorder, or normal though unacceptable, feline use of furniture as scratching posts, all may necessitate the replacement of carpeting, furniture, baseboards, wall boards, electronic equipment and more. Animals engaged in these behaviors are *not* enjoying themselves. They are either behaving normally or are seriously distressed and chronically anxious. They can also injure themselves during the commission of these uncontrolled acts and, therefore, need emergency veterinary care. Even after such injury, the behavior will not stop recurring without professional intervention. There are many more examples of the high cost of underestimating and, therefore, not seeking these life-saving interventions. Do not fail to discuss this with your vet even if he does not bring it up immediately. Explore the possibilities with the professionals who are recommended, interview others than those recommended, and become fully informed so that you can make choices that you and your animal companions can truly live with. Please keep in mind that your primary care veterinarian is not a behavior specialist. He will want to help, but may lack the training and ability despite his knowledge of general animal medicine. Ask for a referral to a behaviorist, *not* a trainer. In the case of cats, there are no *cat trainers*, and therefore, a behaviorist specializing in feline behavior is the answer. If none is offered, seek a behaviorist through other means such as a referral from someone who is familiar with the work of a feline behaviorist or through a computer search. As always, be *very* careful about who you engage to become a part of your care team. A behaviorist may very well have the lives of your beloved animal friend in their hands much the same way as a surgeon does when animal friends are on the operating table. Unwanted behavior ends the lives of healthy animals more so than any illness or injury!

Do not turn to antiquated, unkind and punishing methods that are ineffectual in addition to being harsh and unnecessary. These methods include spraying water in the faces of dogs and cats and throwing a can of coins on the floor to startle a dog who seems to be misbehaving. They do not work and they will further aggravate and distress a cat or dog who is already anxious, confused and upset. In the case of aggressive dogs, these methods may even provoke a full blown attack!

Furthermore, children believe what you *do*, not what you say. They are deeply affected by the choices and attitudes modeled by their parents. Parents who choose harsh methods of dealing with family companion animals are instilling in their children the fear that they, too, are disposable if they should become ill or misbehave.

Allied Veterinary Care Professionals

Veterinarians are not the only professional care-givers involved in our animal companions' lives. The entire animal hospital staff remains of critical importance. Not every technician is a trained, licensed veterinary technician. These people may be interested in and fairly good at their work, but may not be formally educated beyond on-the-job training. People with varying degrees of education staff all aspects of veterinary hospitals. The work performed in hospitals should be assigned to those with appropriate education and experience to insure a positive outcome for all patients. There may be times when an employee is asked to work below the level of their expertise, but the opposite should *never* be so.

I am not suggesting that a non-formally educated staff member is incompetent. However, you must ask questions and feel comfortable with the professionals involved. To achieve an informed level of comfort, you must learn, know and understand the differences among veterinarians, veterinary technicians, veterinary technologists, and veterinary assistants.

The veterinarian is solely responsible for diagnosing, developing a prognosis, treating and prescribing medication and performing surgery. The veterinarian is also ultimately responsible for all patient care and outcomes. Most veterinarians apply for veterinary medical school while obtaining a bachelor degree in a compatible field. If a candidate is accepted into a veterinary medical school, the course of study usually takes another four years, making a total of eight years of training in addition to prior college studies. If the candidate goes on to specialize and become specialty board certified, that choice adds additional years to the overall education. Every state requires a veterinarian to take and pass a licensing exam. Successful candidates are then given a license to practice veterinary medicine. Many veterinarians are licensed to practice in more than one state, and this indicates that they have passed the licensing requirement in each state in which they are licensed to practice.

The veterinary technician is educated to be the veterinarian's nurse, laboratory, radiography and anesthesia technician, surgical nurse and client educator. An anesthesia technician is *not* an anesthesiologist. Veterinary anesthesiologists are highly-trained veterinarians specializing in anesthesia, analgesia, and critical and emergency care (www.acva.org). An anesthesia technician assists the veterinarian or veterinary anesthesiologist before and during surgery.

An entry-level technician is a graduate from a two-year, American Veterinary Medical Association accredited program from a college or university. A veterinary technologist has graduated from a four-year AVMA accredited bachelor degree program.

Veterinary technicians work a full hands-on role in procedures and senior veterinary technicians can go on to supervisory positions in veterinary hospitals, research institutions and other areas of care.

Every state has its own requirements and titles for technicians. They are: Registered Veterinary Technician (RVT), Licensed Veterinary Technician (LVT), and Certified Veterinary Technician (CVT).

Graduates of any American Veterinary Medical Association accredited program may take a national certification exam, the Veterinary Technician National Exam or VTNE. In some states, a state exam and references are also required. Upon passing, the individual becomes certified, registered or licensed in that state.

Once again, it is critical to ask questions of veterinarians and all allied animal care providers without fear. Anyone offended by your questions is probably *not* going to be someone with whom a relationship of true partnership is possible. Asking questions and carefully listening to the answers will not only help you to understand and evaluate all the information you get, it will allow you to begin to forge a partnership between you and the professionals to whom you will entrust your animal family. In addition to asking questions, learn everything you can about the operations of the hospital you are considering.

A well appointed waiting room with a beverage station or other attractions is not enough. While the waiting room described is a nice feature, it is more important to know how well-appointed other areas of the hospital are. A good hospital will be happy to give you a tour of the *entire* hospital upon request. Think very carefully about what you see and smell. For example, are cats in an area separate from dogs? This is very important. Cats require a completely different kind of environment, especially when ill or recovering from illness. The intense barking which is often heard in dog-populated wards can be highly stressful to cats. Many are frightened just by the sight of a dog. For cats, a feline-friendly atmosphere is essential and a feline-only veterinary hospital is even better. The latter may be more difficult to find, but a good veterinary practice that has recognized the importance of a feline-friendly atmosphere can offer many benefits.

Also, what is the size of the kennel your animals will be in? Feline-exclusive or feline friendly hospitals have separate areas for cats and will often provide a size and configuration of kennel that will allow your cat adequate room for a decent sized litter box (not a shallow 8" x 11" tray) and a second level where she can rest. At the very least, cats should be provided with a simple, small hiding area or *safe space* such as a square or cube-shaped cardboard mailing box or little travel carrier which is lined with something soft, washable, disposable, and inviting.

Find out what time the hospital closes each day and who is with the over-night hospitalized patients. Do you *really* want your best friends in a facility where they are completely alone for twelve or more hours? Along the same lines, how frequently are dogs walked to relieve themselves? Do not assume that they will be walked at opening of business. Unless a hospital has staff members exclusively assigned to walking dogs, they may not be accommodated until some time after the hospital opens. Your vet is not your enemy. An open discussion on all matters will ensure that you remain on good terms and that your animal family is getting the best possible care.

If you live in an area that has a full service specialty hospital where the care is cutting edge at all levels, you will have the best range of alternatives. Many people do not have this type of facility available to them. Others simply choose not to take advantage of it. Everyone benefits by asking questions and becoming fully informed in advance. Knowledge is power, and especially so in making informed health care decisions.

Visiting Veterinary Nurse Service

We are all familiar with VNS, the Visiting Nurse Service. Visiting nurses have made an enormous contribution to society through their special expertise and willingness to bring it into the homes of people who need it.

Have you ever wished that this special care were available for your cats and dogs? Many animals are deeply distressed by visits to the veterinarian. Sometimes, visits simply cannot and should not be avoided. The visit can, however, be highly stressful. This is particularly so when sensitive animals have not had the benefit of prior desensitization and conditioning that will prevent or reduce veterinary setting distress. This desensitization and conditioning is best introduced early and directed by a behaviorist. A behaviorist can and should be consulted even if the challenge of veterinary setting distress is pre-existing or long-standing. Complete cure is unlikely but significant improvements that dramatically reduce distress *can* be achieved.

Many chronic illnesses require frequent monitoring with blood chemistry, blood pressure and other basic vital signs and diagnostics. The visit to accomplish this may be postponed or delayed because of the stress to your animal friend and you. If only these needs could be met at home, your dilemma would be solved to a very high degree. In some cases this is a possibility and the solution is worth the extra effort of a search.

Sophisticated veterinary hospitals employ Licensed Veterinary Technicians who may prove a good resource as home-care technicians or who can refer you to colleagues who are. When home visits can be co-joined with the rest of a care plan by the veterinarian or veterinary specialist who is caring for your cat or dog, an ideal partnership is forged. A localized internet search may also be fruitful.

Groomers

Many dogs and some cats require professional grooming. It is as essential to their general well-being as much as it is to their appearance. For example, grooming addresses or corrects matted hair, which, if left untreated, will pull on the skin beneath, causing great discomfort and become the foundation for infection.

Choosing a groomer is a process that should be as carefully evaluated as choosing a veterinarian. There are free-standing (brick and mortar) grooming salons as well as mobile units that come to the home but conduct the grooming in the mobile unit. Others will come to your home and perform the grooming in-home. The latter, *if* they are experienced in feline grooming, can serve cats and small dogs well, but larger dogs do better in a mobile unit where the groomer has everything at his fingertips to accommodate the larger dog. This greater accessibility is especially important for bathing. On the whole, cats do best with in-home-grooming, and all dogs can do very well in a mobile unit. There may be medical reasons for sedating or anesthetizing your animal friend prior to performing the grooming. A common example of *medically necessary* grooming with the aid of sedation or anesthesia, are cats who are badly matted and will not easily acclimate to the process of de-matting and grooming. Under no condition, should sedation or anesthesia be administered by anyone but a veterinarian.

Mobile groomers offer an important benefit in that every animal groomed is the only animal attended to at any given time. This personalized method eliminates the waiting and stress that may be experienced at a free-standing grooming salon.

Your author does not suggest that a free-standing grooming salon staffed by many groomers cannot offer speedy service. Such service, however, is unusual, and unless special arrangements are made, more time will be required for the free-standing groomer than for one in a mobile unit. Moreover, there is usually very little difference in the cost between the two. But even if a mobile groomer is only available to you at a somewhat higher cost, it is well worth the expense.

If you have a breed of dog who is known to require life-long grooming (Poodles, Bijons, Sheepdogs, etc.), it is best to begin introducing them to grooming as soon as they become part of your family.

Grooming should begin at home with a soft brush and, gradually, made into a pleasant and fun experience. The same is true for cats, especially long-haired cats. A visit to a groomer or a mobile-grooming unit should be part of the introduction. The initial visit should not include the actual grooming, but allow your animal companions to see, smell, and hear all that goes on so they are not shocked by the environment when the need for professional grooming arises for the first time.

Lilly, Royal Standard Poodle
Photo by Barbara Meyers

The groomer you choose should be willing to provide a tour of the facility and the opportunity to watch the grooming process. It is crucial to learn exactly *who* does *what* with your companion. Is the entire grooming process handled by one person, or are there people who do the bathing while others do the cut and design, etc.? What are the holding kennels like? How does the facility smell and look? Most importantly, how is your dog or cat when they come home from their grooming experience?

Grooming can and should be a pleasurable experience from which they come home feeling and looking well and happy. Traumatic grooming experiences can be long-lasting and create the foundation for avoidance. The need for grooming should be taken into consideration when you acquire a companion who is likely to need it. Good, professional grooming needs to be done on a regular basis (usually every 4-6 weeks) and can be costly.

For some people, the need for on-going professional grooming may make the choice of certain companions a poor one.

All cats and dogs require regular nail clipping. If nails (in cats, *nails* are referred to as claws) are permitted to go untrimmed, they can grow to a length that can curl and become imbedded in the skin, creating pain, infection and the need, in some cases, for surgical correction. The longer nails are left untrimmed, the longer the vein within them becomes. A long vein is problematic because cutting the claws in this state will cause pain and bleeding, and it will be impossible, at least initially, to cut away enough to ensure comfort and proper mobility. The only way to fully correct a problem so advanced is for a veterinarian to perform claw trimming under anesthesia while properly controlling the bleeding and preventing infection. Even after such a procedure, regular nail trim *must* be done, or the problem will recur. Grooming is not just the way one looks. It is a matter of good health and should be taken seriously.

Companion Animal Nannies

Home care in your absence drastically reduces the amount of stress on animals and allows them to remain in their own familiar environment. In my opinion, the best way to have your animal family cared for is by a professional, bonded and insured animal nanny who will come to your home. There are many other possibilities including care by a novice family member, neighbor, or proclaimed "animal lover." In general, I do *not* consider these sources of care to be safe, and I am not comfortable recommending them. Everyone must and will, ultimately, make their own decisions and choices. Loving or *claiming* to love animals, or having an animal companion does not, in and of itself, qualify someone to perform care-giving functions. Everyone has their own version of exactly what love *is* and what it means to them.

If home animal nanny care is your choice, I urge you to research your options *very* carefully. There are specialists in canine, feline, avian, and exotic animal care. Every species has special needs of their own and should be cared for by someone who is very familiar with those needs and can recognize early signs of illness or other difficulties very swiftly.

Be certain that the nanny with whom you consult during the selection process will be the same person who serves as your nanny on every occasion. Many nanny services are owned and operated by someone who employs a staff of nannies. You and your animal family want and *need* to meet the nanny who will be coming to your home on a consistent basis. Who is she? What are her qualifications and experience? Is she an independent contractor or a direct employee of the nanny service? Ask for written documentation of being bonded and insured as well as being certified in animal emergency care by a recognized authority. She should not be insulted, and you should not fail to ask out of fear of insult. The only insult to be concerned with is the *insult* to your animal friend's well being if left with *Nanny Nastyface*! You cannot ask too many questions or have too much information.

Do not seek a nanny shortly before you plan a vacation or business trip. It is best to find one well in advance. First, interview and find the right nanny candidates. Good nannies will want to meet your animal family to evaluate their needs. You should be wary of any candidate willing to forego this step. When your nanny has been selected, she should begin to visit on a regular basis, first, while you are present and for just an hour or so. This initial introduction should be done at least twice weekly over a period of about a month. Along the way, it can be decided when it is time for you to leave your home and have the nanny and your animal family alone together. During the times alone, go marketing, to lunch, or for a walk, but *do* leave them together without your presence. This time allows for a smooth introduction, the opportunity for your companion animals to become at ease with their nanny, and greater peace of mind when you leave for extended periods of time. After you return from your vacation or business trip, continue to have your nanny visit at least once every four to six weeks to maintain the relationship. These visits also serve the purpose of helping you to become a *regular* or *preferred* client, which will likely boost access to your nanny during emergencies or when you may need to travel with little notice or during high demand times like holidays and summer. Nannies are especially busy during these times, and an established relationship can help ensure that she will be available to you. You must, however, arrange the high volume times as much in advance as possible even when there is an established relationship with your nanny.

Hidden *Nanny Cams* that monitor activities when you are not at home can be used to look in on what is happening. They are not just for children! I would not be without at least one. If you have a big home, more is better. In fact, my preferred and overall choice is a full house monitoring system with videotaping and remote capability to view activities from any laptop computer, *smart* phone or other sophisticated electronic device.

Boarding Facilities

My personal favorite for both dogs and cats (especially cats) is to have in-home care by a professional, licensed, and bonded nanny. There are geographic areas where this choice is not available, and there are people who, no matter what the condition, will not have others in their home in their absence.

Good boarding facilities offer the opportunity to have animal families taken care of at another location when people vacation or are called to business out of town. Be wary of any facility that is not staffed twenty-four hours a day, relying instead on *claims* that high-tech electronic monitoring is safer. Boarding kennels, *doggie day care,* and similar facilities offer group play for dogs. This can be enjoyable and attractive to both you and your dog. Many dogs do very well in group play. However, it is also the environment in which (no matter how careful or good the facility), your dog can contract a variety of contagious diseases. The most common is *Kennel Cough* but there are others. In addition, there is always the risk of being seriously bitten by another dog. At the first sign or report that there has been some conflict (growling or attempt to lunge at or bite) between your dog and another, it is time to permanently remove your dog from that atmosphere. If your dog has sustained an injury (bite wounds, *seemingly* minor or superficial bites, cuts and scratches, lameness, or any other injury), see your veterinarian immediately. Bites create puncture wounds that are often higher in number and location than are readily visible to you. Puncture wounds are particularly dangerous and require careful veterinary evaluation and treatment. Delay in treatment can lead to complications that include fatal sepsis (infection throughout the bloodstream), require amputation, or create difficult-to-repair wounds. If another dog is the target or victim of such behavior from your dog, the same (permanent removal) action is necessary. In either case, the owner or operator of the facility should require that the perpetrator or, in some cases, *both* dogs no longer be accepted at the facility. If the owner or operator of the facility does not insist on this policy, it is your duty and responsibility to take the appropriate action to protect your dog, other dogs and yourself. A consultation with a canine behaviorist should follow as soon thereafter as possible.

Boarding your animal family at a veterinary facility is probably a poor choice. Most hospitals are designed to care for the sick, and are rarely equipped with special boarding facilities. Instead, what is usually, available is a limited area with cages for cats and perhaps a small run for dogs. Your animal family will be spending their days in small, confined spaces within a facility where there are sick animals. Cats and dogs are usually not separated adequately to ensure that cats are in the most stress-free atmosphere.

The exception is the state of the art, full service, twenty-four hour specialty hospital that offers a separate area or building for medical boarding. This facility accommodates those who require special medical care, as well as the kind of attention that every animal away from their family needs. The boarders that can be accommodated include, but are not limited to: diabetics, epileptics, kidney or other organ compromised animals, those with limited mobility or requiring daily medication(s) for any number of chronic conditions.

You do not have to give up vacations, sacrifice the ability to go on a business trip or attend to a sudden family emergency. You do, however, owe it to your animal friends and to yourself to think ahead and have a plan at the ready.

Flowers to the Rescue

Photo by Eileen Rochelle - Canonsville, Maryland

As part of caring for your companion animals, you may be considering Bach and English Flower Essence Remedies. The remedies are a system of thirty-eight different homeopathic, stress-reducing and balancing agents discovered by the British physician, Dr. Edward Bach. They are made from flowers and the flowering buds of trees and are recognized by the Federal Drug Administration (FDA) and listed in the Homeopathic Pharmocopeia of the United States. All the remedies arc free of artificial additives, preserved in an alcohol base (for stability), and reported to be both safe and not affected by any other form of therapy or medication including steroids and chemotherapeutic agents. Bach Flower Remedies are also available in formulas without alcohol and are preferred for animals. They can be taken in combination with other therapies and modalities of all kinds.

The use of flower remedies has grown in popularity but is still not fully enough understood by most. The proper use of these remedies requires extensive knowledge of animal behavior and illness, the human-animal bond, and the remedies themselves.

This requirement is particularly pronounced in cases of complicated behavior problems. Animals are subject to all the emotional, spiritual, psychosocial stress, loss, grief and distress with which their guardians also struggle. In addition, they are subject to the sympathetic resonance of their guardians and circumstances in which they live. Human-Animal Sympathetic Resonance is an emotional phenomenon. The closer or more symbiotic the attachment between person and animal, the more vulnerable and responsive animals will be to the conditions of their guardian family. It is not unusual for animals (companion and others, as well) to reflect or take on the fears, rage, and depression as well as the joy, calm, sense of fun, etc. of their guardian family or other familiars. This can present quite a challenge to them.

Bach and English Flower Remedies and other homeopathic remedies may help animals to meet these and other challenges. All animals, be they bunny or bison, hamster or horse, etc. may benefit from the appropriate use of flower remedies where required. However, no amount of any remedy will change behavior that, though perhaps is unacceptable, is also normal or natural.

Even the best professional flower counselors may not have adequate understanding of animal behavior to select the right remedies and combine them with appropriate supportive behavior or environmental adjustment recommendations to facilitate change. Flower remedies are often thought of as a self-help system, but the best results come from a partnership with a seasoned flower counselor who is certified in the use of the remedies and also a specialist in the area of animal behavior and human-animal relations.

The use of flower remedies is *not* a replacement for proper veterinary care. The remedies do not remove, eliminate, omit or negate veterinary care either allopathic or complimentary. They are best used as part of a comprehensive approach to health and well being. Remedies do not cure or treat, but, instead, act as an adjunct catalyst to the entire treatment plan.

Conditions that *may* respond well to flower remedies include all mild to moderate behavior challenges. It cannot be too strongly emphasized that flower remedies are *entirely* inadequate to treat acute conditions such as canine noise phobia and panic disorders, aggression or chronic anxiety disorders in cats. They *may* be useful for adjusting to a new home or environment, a change in living conditions or the death of another companion animal in the family. Just as we do, animals grieve, and every animal will demonstrate or mask grief in their own particular way. Additionally, flower remedies can be useful in coping with learning situations, recovery from illness or injury, travel and barn stress, all kennel, boarding and care environments where you are not present, management of the emotional impact of chronic or catastrophic illness, terminal illness and end of life. They *must*, however, be part of a larger care plan but are, once again, neither treatment nor therapy. They are certainly *not* a substitute for comprehensive pain control or hospice care.

When properly used for the right conditions, if the remedies do not bring the results desired, do not conclude they are ineffective. There is every reason to expect they can help at least to some degree in mild to moderate situations. Seek professional guidance. Often, an experienced, professional flower therapist is crucial in matching the right remedy with the behavior or condition while also enhancing the care plan with other recommendations.

Chapter Eleven

Loss, Grief and Mourning

"Show me the heart that is not wounded and until it is, though lovely, it remains unfinished."... Barbara Meyers.

During my lifetime of companionship with animals and in my professional role as grief therapist, I have experienced and been privileged to be part of the sacred circle of dying and death and its impact on companion animals, wildlife and the people who care about them.

This privilege is not to be taken lightly. It must be appreciated and honored with care, skill and empathy. It must also produce concrete results while eliminating the ordinary and common *cold comfort* of platitudes, clichés and stereotypical trivialization. When people choose to invite me into their sacred space, they have not only sustained a heart-shattering loss but are likely to have also been the victims of insensitive and painful statements and bad advice from so-called well-meaning friends, family and others. Statements hurled at those wounded and tangled in grief cause great additional and unnecessary pain. They are told, "Get a hold of yourself," "Move on," "It's *only* a dog. You can get another one." *Only* a dog? *Just* an old cat? The *only* thing our beloved animal families represent is the single experience in life that offers what we all need and want - complete acceptance, unconditional love, deep and everlasting friendship and trust.

Grief Therapy

Who may need, want, or benefit from grief therapy?

- Anyone with members of their animal family who have been diagnosed with a chronic or recurrent life-altering or life-threatening illness.
- Anyone whose animal family member has been diagnosed with a critical, catastrophic, or terminal illness.
- Anyone who has an animal family member that has diagnosed with an illness of known-certain fatal outcome or disability from illness or injury.
- Anyone who has an animal family member who is coming to the close of life because of advancing years and decline.
- Anyone who has already sustained the death of an animal family member.
- Others who have become permanently separated from their animal friends due to lifestyle changes or have had the heart-wrenching experience of a lost or missing animal.
- Those who are, themselves, or who know someone else who is seriously or terminally ill and unable to continue to care for their companion animals.

The goal of grief therapy is to help people to discover and uncover their own way through these and other difficult situations and to make informed, loving decisions with which they and their companion animals can both live and die. Another goal is to prepare people to work through the various elements of their personal grief, helping them to move toward a place where they can be comforted by tender memories and, if they so choose, share their lives with other animals free from any sense of disloyalty.

The Classic Stages of Grief and Why They Are Misleading

Most of us are familiar with the various classic, stages or states of grief: denial and isolation, shock and anger, bargaining, depression, and acceptance. These stages were first formulated to describe the dying experience, but were later applied to grief and bereavement. This early model is *not* to be taken literally. It is very general in nature, and though these states or stages may exist, they are not experienced by everyone. Moreover, there are other possible states such as reinvestment. "Closure," an over-used and highly questionable state, can easily and correctly be argued as a non-existent and unattainable goal. Thinking sensibly, one does not *just* close an account of love as though it were an empty bank account.

It is my belief that seeking the culturally popular version of closure is an unreasonable and futile goal. What is more useful and more important is finding truth; not *the* truth or someone else's version of truth, but your own personal truth. Finding your own truth also holds the very strong possibility that you can, over time, *make friends with* both a new wound and the revival of old wounds that surface with a new injury. It is also true that, while often near-to-impossible to envision, you *will* be able to approach a future that can hold comfort, tender memories and the ability to choose to reinvest in love again.

Whatever *name* you give or assign to your feelings, one must know that *any* emotion experienced, is not experienced in any fixed order. You may return to a state already experienced or move among them all without any particular order and in seemingly random and unexpected patterns.

The notion that all you need to do is pass through set stages as if traveling with a roadmap to successful grieving is oversimplified and complicates an already treacherous pathway. I suggest that the entire *stage* theory be completely discarded as a formula or strict recipe for grief recovery.

Denial

Perhaps more so than any other emotional component involved, denial as a part of grieving is often both misunderstood and misdiagnosed.

There is a certain mercy in the sharp blade that carves the heart with fresh, raw grief. It is much like the temporary painless state of a severe burn that severs nerves and disconnects reality providing some time to ready ourselves to cope. Only with time, as the edge of injury wears down, does the pain really begin.

The painless, numb or frozen state I describe is too often misidentified as denial that must be eliminated, removed or even forcibly taken from the newly bereaved. This is frequently attempted by well-intended friends, family, and even professionals such as bereavement counselors, self-help group members and leaders, as well as many others. Clumsy attempts to remove perceived denial is often harsh, offers no benefits, and usually adds to the pain. Because the bereaved are vulnerable, they can easily be made to feel that their behavior is unacceptable, wrong, or inappropriate, and that there is something seriously wrong with them. These conclusions are, of course, completely without validity.

Temporary denial or, more accurately, disbelief is a normal, healthy internal defense mechanism that serves an important function. When anyone attempts to forcibly remove it, they are committing an act of unkind ignorance, especially if something equally or more useful is not offered in its place. After attempts are made, mourners are left with nothing with which to protect themselves, thus, becoming more isolated and alone in their pain.

Disbelief is not a state of delusion or something that needs *fixing*. Left to do its work for the bereaved, it will dissipate over time. The amount of time varies widely. If and when it interferes with the ability of a person to function in reasonable ways it then deserves professional attention. The bereaved should also feel free to consult with a grief therapist at *any* time they choose, and not be confined to seek help only when they are deeply troubled or desperate. Even if they are coping fairly well, a consultation with an expert grief therapist is a gift one can give to themselves to ensure a continued smooth recovery and added strength to manage the unexpected.

If the bereaved *are* deeply troubled at any time, or if there is well-founded doubt about how they are coping, it is advisable to seek the help of a grief therapist. There are also times when those who care about another are so worried about what they observe that they too hastily seek ways to convince the bereaved to "get help." In these situations, if the bereaved reject the well-meant but possibly premature and unwanted urging, the worrier would do better to seek help for themselves so they can better understand what they believe to be a problem in someone else. Learning how to help someone we care about serves a dual purpose. It brings relief from fear and unnecessary worry and also it gives one the tools to manage a foreign and confusing situation. Watching someone you love struggle while being unable or unsuccessful to help is a particularly disturbing form of frustration and grief that is also deserving of attention.

Sudden, Accidental or Violent Death

"He always played safely by himself in the back yard. I never dreamed he would or *could* leap over the fence and onto the street." This is often the opening statement that begins to describe a sudden animal death.

Murder of animals is another unexpected and sudden loss. It occurs more often than is widely known or recognized. Criminals murder animals every year during the commission of crimes. There are also many revenge killings of companion animals by neighbors and other malicious people. Additional animal deaths are perpetrated by the uncontrolled behavior of companion animals who are permitted to roam freely, walk off-lead, and run *wild* in parks and streets without responsible supervision by their guardians. Still more lives are wantonly taken by hunters in pursuit of blood sport.

Shock, guilt, trauma, and post-traumatic stress can follow and linger for years, both to people as well as other companion animals in the household. In cases where animals are murdered during the commission of a crime or are the purposeful and intended victims of revenge killing, some hope lies in changing the laws that govern these criminal behaviors. Crimes against all animals should be prosecuted to the full extent of the law while efforts to change the laws continue to be pursued. Attitudes toward animal injury and death perpetrated with intent must change also. Regarding accidents, however, they *do* happen. That is why they are called, "accidents." Nonetheless, there are many that are preventable. For example, a large number of companion dogs, cats, and passing wildlife drown in swimming pools every year. It is not because animals do not know how to swim. It is because they panic when they cannot find an easy way out.

Skamper-Ramp

Skamper-Ramp easily solves the problem. If you own a pool, it is a *must*. (www.skamper-ramp-store.com). Even if you do not have a companion animal, do you really want to wake up the sight of a dead animal (cat, dog, raccoon, and others) in your pool? It is not only an unpleasant greeting but a health hazard. The Scamper-Ramp prevents death by allowing an animal who has gotten into your pool to climb out by means of an inclined surface from the water to the ground.

Scamper-Ramps in Use
Photos provided by Gamma 2

If you think the fence you have constructed around the pool (perhaps for child-safety) is going to help keep animals out, think again. Animals are easily capable of scaling or getting under any fence and making their way into the pool. I like to see two Scamper-Ramps in every pool and perhaps more in exceptionally large pools. In this case, more is better.

FrogLog

Smaller creatures for whom the Scamper-Ramp is not effective, need a FrogLog. FrogLog is the invention of Maryland wildlife biologist, Rich Mason. His work with the United States Fish and Wildlife service involves wetland and other habitat restoration.

FrogLog saves native wildlife who find their way into pools by providing them with a safe way out. It is estimated that each pool with FrogLogs in it saves seventy-five to one hundred small animals and untold numbers of beneficial insects annually.

When frogs, mice or other small creatures fall or jump into a pool, they instinctively swim toward the pool wall in an attempt to escape. In a FrogLog-equipped pool, upon reaching the wall, they will climb up the little platform onto the mesh ramp, and safely exit the pool.

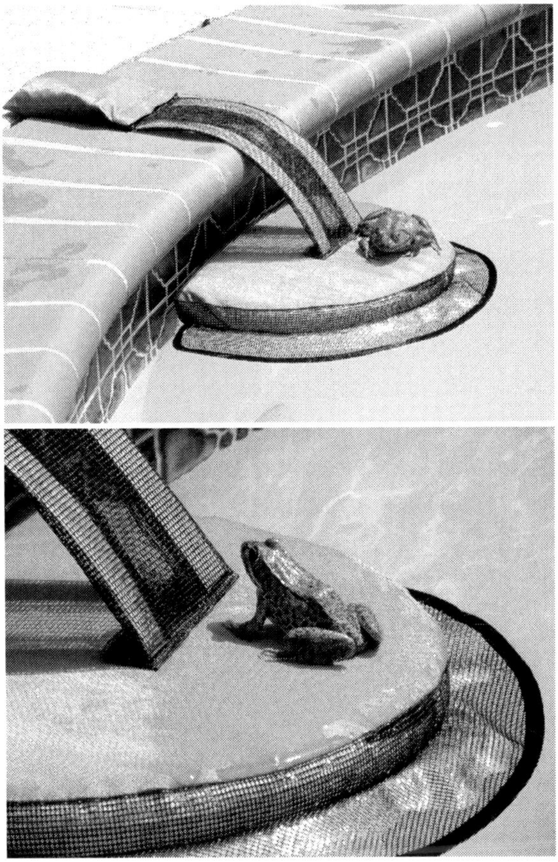

FrogLogs in Use
Photos by Rich Mason

FrogLog is designed to hold the weight of amphibians (frogs, toads and lizards) and other critters (bats, squirrels, chipmunks, ducklings and even some baby or juvenile birds) who are no heavier than the average adult squirrel, which is approximately one to one-and-one-half pound. Without a FrogLog, they will drown and you will find their bodies floating in the water. Unlike squirrels, chipmunks, and other small mammals or birds, amphibians will not drown but if they cannot quickly exit your pool, they will be exposed to toxic levels of chlorine that will kill them because they have permeable skin that easily absorbs toxins. Their dead bodies will greet you and your children when the family goes out to enjoy a swim.

Some people consider these animals to be pests and have little understanding or appreciation of their important role in the ecosystem. Even for those who, sadly, do not value their lives, no one wants to expose themselves or their children to the sight of a floating, dead animal in their pool, pond, fountain, or hot tub. Therefore, every water feature should be protected with at least two, three or more FrogLogs depending on the size of the pool or other water feature. FrogLogs should be an addition to the Skamper-Ramps. You will need both for your pool, and certainly need FrogLogs for other, smaller water features. The benefits are many; you are saving animals' lives, keeping your water clean, and reducing the time and money spent on maintenance.

FrogLog is as forward-thinking as its inventor. Remembering that Mason is a wildlife biologist with special interest in wetland and habitat restoration, the following is yet another example of the magic of animals. Mason said, "It is amazing how quickly the animals respond when a sterilized corn field is returned to its natural state. Within hours, aquatic insects such as diving beetles and water striders appear as if they were waiting. Wetland vegetation naturally appears from dormant seeds in the soil which is incredible since herbicides may be liberally applied to the fields every year. Within days, frogs return. Ducks, herons, and other birds show up in a matter of weeks. The restorative power of the natural world is something to behold. When we respect, care for, and help Mother Nature we can be part of the answer instead of the source of the problem! "

Frog Log (www.froglog.us) is a simple, free-floating, inexpensive device that requires no complicated installation, tools or instructions. It is a brilliant example of Ockham's Razor (the theory of William Ockham 1284-1347) summarized as: "The simplest model, answer, or solution is the most likely to be correct." Discovering the simple answer is often not simple. Mason spent hundreds of hours researching and developing the FrogLog.

When asked what inspired and held him to the work, he simply said, "My passion for the diversity of life on earth is what drives me."

Life Jackets

Foam swim vests and life jackets are widely available from a variety of retailers. They should be used any time your companion dog or cat is around water and especially when they are on a boat. Dogs generally do well and accommodate quickly to life jackets, but cats are not likely to take to it with the same ease. Many cats will become immobilized and even fall over when confined to a coat, sweater or jacket of any kind. If you spend a great deal of time boating and want your cat to travel with you, it is best to introduce her to it early and gradually. Never force a cat to do anything! Do not imagine that "she'll just get used to it." You may need professional help from an experienced feline behaviorist in order to accomplish this without trauma. If you forgo the safety of a life jacket because you have not had success in introducing it yourself and you have also decided not to seek professional help, your cat or dog may pay for it with his life!

Allowing Cats Outside

Another dangerous practice to avoid is allowing cats outdoors. I do not, under any circumstance or for any reason, allow my feline family outdoors. It is a simple equation: "out=death!" It is not a matter of *if*, but only *when*. If you have made a practice of allowing your cats outside and there has never been an incident of them having gone missing for an extended period of time, becoming injured or killed, please do not be convinced that it is the safe, smart, or kind choice of a well-informed and loving guardian. Your experience only means that, up until now, you have gotten away with it. Being outside exposes cats to all kinds of disease, injury, and death and also has a very strong, negative impact on their behavior once they return indoors.

Birds Killed by Free Roaming Cats

In addition to the dangers awaiting cats, according to the National Audubon Society, an estimated 100 million birds fall prey to free-roaming cats every year. Some of the carnage comes from the activity of feral cats and may be unavoidable. The rest comes from companion cats whose families permit or even encourage them to go outside in the interest of a misguided notion of freedom. There is no acceptable reason why cats should be permitted to injure and destroy birds in this manner. If one is so unkind and foolish not to care about birds, there is still good reason to shun the practice; cats are in danger of becoming the victims of their own behavior. If a cat ingests a bird or any other prey that has been intentionally poisoned (far too many *are*), the predator cat risks being poisoned by default.

Purr...fect Fence

For those people who will not change their misguided notion of freedom, the answer for maximum outdoor feline safety is found using the Purr..fect Fence. (www.purrfectfence.com). Purr...fect Fence is a virtually invisible containment system that allows cats safety on their own property but prevents them from leaving.

Free-Standing Purr...fect Fence

All fence photos provided by Purr...fect Fence

Cats at Play in Free-standing Purr...fect Fence

Cats Enjoying Free-Standing Purr...fect Fence

There also is an additional option that provides outward facing arms with each post in the system so that other animals cannot enter. It is not common for most other animals to be able gain access without the second arm option but I recommend that the second arm model be used because it provides an extra measure of safety and peace-of-mind. When properly placed to completely exclude areas that hold bird and squirrel feeders, the

Purr...fect Fence also protects wildlife. Sequestering areas that hold bird and squirrel feeders, protects wildlife only from *your* cats. If cats are allowed out in your neighborhood, I recommend that the Purr...fect Fence be installed in dual sections: one to separate your cats from wildlife feeders and another to protect the feeding area from other cats getting in. Feeders that are unprotected from cats are equivalent to a neon sign reading, *"Free Lunch-All Cats Welcome!"* A sectioned Purr...fence is very easily created and a gate that provides you access to care for the feeders is the final touch.

I installed the Purr...fect fence for my feral cat, Jack, who lives on my enclosed and fully protected deck and garden in Purr...fect safety and happiness.

Jack under Highbush Cranberry in his Purr...fect Fence Garden

Photos by Barbara Meyers

Jack's garden not only has a Purr…fect Fence, it has two heated houses and a heated water bowl for winter. Weather permitting, Jack has easy access (through a door) to a wide area of garden that is below the wildlife-friendly areas where the bird and squirrel feeders are placed. He has no access to that area because of the Purr...fect Fence. Jack loves his garden and, there, he is *King* of his domain. Because of the sectioned Purr...fence, both he and the wildlife who come to grace the garden with their song and beauty are completely safe.

Jack enjoys the company of my indoor feline family with whom he engages in communication and play through sliding glass and screen doors that are never open beyond the screen door. The screen door is protected from being torn by claws with plexiglass installed at the highest level paws can reach.

There is also a Purr...fect Fence for dogs. The canine version can be added to any existing fence that is too low. How low is too low? Too low is a great deal higher than you might think.

K-9 Addition to Existing Metal Fence
Photo by Purr...fect Fence

Dogs with high levels of anxiety, panic, or *any* motivation to scale a fence of considerable height (even up to seven or eight feet) can do so with ease. It makes no difference if the fence is made from wood, cast iron, aluminum, or PVC. When constructing a fencing system, be mindful of the zoning regulations in your area. Many do not permit a fence of any kind to be higher than six feet. If six feet is all you have, the Purr..fect Fence conversion of an existing fence the safest and best answer to this kind of limitation.

Please also be aware that six feet presents no challenge to any cat whether he is in or outdoors. We have all seen or heard about the cat who climbed a tree so high, a professional rescue team with a *cherry picker* was required to rescue him.

Special Note: If motivated enough by a highly-valued target, all companion animals and wildlife will make every attempt to reach the target and are usually successful. When not successful, they are often injured or even killed in the attempt but they *will* do it. Their willingness and abilities must not be underestimated. For this reason, I do not use or recommend any fencing system other than the Purr...fect Fence.

There are always exceptions to the rule, and there *may* be the very unusual dog or cat who will be fully contained with *any* fence. Even with this risky and highly questionable premise, your animal family is not safe from other animals who can meander onto your property. There are also some *specialty* fences that create the illusion of safety. They may very well prevent your dog or cat from leaving the containment area. However, they offer no protection from other animals entering. Additionally, animals (of varying species) can and do scale or dig under your ordinary fence, or otherwise *Houdini* their way beyond any safety perimeter you can buy or create. Thus, your cat or dog is left vulnerable to aggressive dogs and cats who carry a fatal or contagious virus, and any number of other life-threatening dangers. Please do not bet your cat or dog's life on the fence you have or a misguided notion of *freedom*.

How to Obtain these Special Products

With the exception of some specialized products like the Purr...fect Fence, most of the products I recommend by name are available in animal supply stores or online retailers. If you live in New York City or Astoria, Queens you can walk directly in to a branch of *Whiskers* (www.1800whiskers.com)

Whiskers was founded by Randy and Phil Klein in 1988. They have dedicated themselves to the well being of companion animals through their mission to bring the concepts of wellness to companion animals and their guardians.

They carry high-quality, superior and organic food and all manner of things for cats, dogs and small mammals. There is an in-store grooming service at the Astoria location and Whiskers hosts free educational seminars that are open to the entire community. I am pleased to say that several times each year, I present "*Ask the Therapist Day*" at Whiskers in Manhattan.

Visitors can attend a seminar on any one of a variety of subjects chosen for the day. They also have the opportunity to talk (pro bono) with me in the context of a mini-consult to help solve a simple problem or help understand a more complicated one. These complimentary mini-consults are not likely to solve complicated problems, but they illuminate the path to solutions and, more often than one might think, are the key to unraveling a confounding puzzle. A good time is always had by all!

Photo by Randy Klein

Violent Death

Violent death for animals comes in many forms and includes outright murder or death resulting from being caught in a body-gripping kill trap, steel-jawed leg hold trap, and other traps. The deadly body-gripping traps are frequently called *Conibear* traps after Canadian Frank Conibear, who first constructed this instrument of death.

In 2005, Zephyr, the rescued, beloved and gentle American Staffordshire Terrier of Gail Murphy of Sag Harbor, New York, was caught in a fur trapper's Conibear kill trap placed only fifty feet from a hiking trail. The traps are baited with fish or other highly fragrant foods to lure animals into them. They are indiscriminate in nature and unintended victims such as dogs, cats, young deer and many others are trapped and die a miserable death. These animals are referred to as *trash* animals by the fur trapping industry. They are considered trash because their pelts are usually of no value to the trapper or the fur industry. Valiant efforts to free Zephyr were in vain. Zephyr did not willingly give his life for any cause. It was taken from him by greed-soaked, unspeakable brutality, cruelty, and suffering. Zephyr's legacy to others lies in the enactment of Zephyr's Law, banning the use of the Conibear instrument of torture from use on all Southampton land.

Zephyr

Photo provided by Gail Murphy

Zephyr will live on through other unintended victims who may be spared his fate in Southampton. Sadly, the intended victims (usually rabbits, raccoons and fox) as well as *trash* animals and other wildlife will continue to be trapped for their pelts and die horrific deaths in places all over the country and the world.

Accidental Death

It is not uncommon for people to leave their companion dogs or cats in closed vehicles where they die from heatstroke. Dogs (and other animals) become overheated very rapidly. This, combined with their inability to sweat, makes for an inefficient cooling system that cannot self-adjust. Simply leaving a window partially open or parking in the shade is never adequate to prevent the deadly consequences. With the exception of travel to and from a veterinary visit, people are more likely to travel with their dogs than with their cats. Therefore, the incidents of cats dying in this manner is considerably lower. Never leave your dog or cat alone in a car for *any* reason whatsoever!

Vehicular death from being hit by a car occurs because companion animals are regularly permitted outside without supervision or because they have, truly, gotten outside *by accident*. Among these vehicular deaths, there are more than just a few that occur when they are run over by a family member who has not seen their cat or dog as they exit the driveway of their home or they are struck by a passing car in the street. Deaths from riding lawn mowers are another cause.

The "accidental getting out" can be avoided with the construction of a simple airlock at both front and back entrances to the home. Decks and terraces are also places where the airlock concept can and *should* be employed to prevent unintended escapes. It is recognized that there are some homes where the construction of an airlock is not possible because of architecture. In these cases, companion animals must be protected from *escapes* through careful, pre-planned sequestering areas that should be designed specifically for each home as well as the number and species of animals involved. An accomplished behaviorist should be fully familiar with the *how to* and a consultation with such a specialist is advisable. If you already have a behaviorist or *trainer* who has failed to draw the subject of *escape* to your attention or does not have swift and practical solutions to offer if *you* have introduced the subject, you are not with the *right* professional for you.

Airlocks already exist in homes equipped with a mud room. A mud room that is one that is separated from the rest of the house by two additional doors. Mud rooms act as a staging area when one enters with packages or muddy boots. Airlock is synonymous with mud room and, once inside the airlock with the entry door closed behind you, you are in an area with the main entry door to the interior still closed. There you can organize your packages and yourself without the threat of your dog or cat dashing out the primary entry door as you open it to gain access. Even if your companion animals or children come running towards you when you open the second airlock door, they can only go as far as the first airlock door that is now closed behind you and cannot exit to the outside.

Sudden Death

Sudden death can take place at home, in a veterinary setting, or anywhere else. It occurs from sudden cardiac arrest, respiratory failure, massive brain hemorrhage, or break-through of crisis from a previously well controlled, chronic illness. It can also happen as the result of a covert medical condition that gave no advance warnings through symptoms. Poisoning is another common cause of sudden death and can come from a myriad of sources: ingestion of toxic household cleaners, house and garden plants, chocolate, marijuana, alcohol, antifreeze, raisins, grapes, and the sweetener, Xylitol.

Xylitol is known to cause fatal liver failure in dogs and, while it does not seem to be as serious a hazard to cats, it remains advisable to insure that both dogs *and* cats are not fed food with Xylitol in it. This can be a bit tricky. Xylitol often called a "wood sugar," is more precisely a five-carbon sugar alcohol found in fruits, vegetables, and birch. Considered safe for people, it can cause acute hypoglycemia (dangerously low blood sugar) and liver failure in dogs. Xylitol is not always identified by name. It *may* not be listed as "Xylitol" but also appears as "natural sweeteners" and sweetening agents of all kinds in candy, chewing gum, baking powders, cookies and other baked goods, chewable multi-vitamin compounds, food storage containers, mouth washes, fresh-breath products, moisturizing nasal wash, and more. Xylitol is reported to be generally well tolerated by people but it can cause nausea, vomiting, diarrhea, headache, and gastrointestinal upset in some.

Do not feed or allow your animal family access to products that contain or *may* contain Xylitol. If you suspect they have ingested a product with Xylitol or *any* of the aforementioned poisons, run-don't-walk, to the nearest emergency veterinary center.

Anesthesia

John G. Hynes, DVM (www.nycvet.org) said, "There may be some routine surgeries and other procedures, but there is no such thing as routine sedation or anesthesia." Every competent veterinarian should confirm Dr. Hynes' words of wisdom. Hynes is not just a veterinarian with a single sentence of words of wisdom. He is an exceptionally skilled primary care veterinarian who is an active advocate for his patients and *all* other animals. He does not just *talk the talk,* he *walks the walk* daily and does so with unmatched devotion and compassion. John Hynes truly *makes a difference!* Returning to the subject of anesthesia, it is a necessary and critical component in care. Therefore, every precaution to ensure safe anesthesia must be undertaken. It is the reason why pre-anesthesia or sedation blood chemistries and, in some cases, other diagnostics like echocardiogram, chest x-ray, etc. are recommended, required and necessary. Many people feel that these tests represent just another way for their vet to unnecessarily increase their bill, but it is *not* so. These procedures are the protection your companion animals need and should not be denied.

Even with every precaution, complications and death may arise from anesthesia. The potential danger is noted in the disclosure in the authorization for surgery or surgical procedure that you sign. If you have not discussed the potential danger in detail with your vet, do so. No one can predict with absolute certainty that anyone can tolerate or will recover from anesthesia. The risk is always there. Animals usually tolerate sedation and anesthesia well, but it is necessary to fully understand that there is always some degree of risk. There are also risks in *not* doing that which requires anesthesia or sedation. The risk-benefit ratio must be carefully considered. Some conditions (known cardiac, kidney or other organ disease) make it unwise or impossible to risk anesthesia, but your vet will know and advise you on the best choices.

Difficult Choices

Faced with complicated circumstances unrelated to illness, people sometimes choose to end a healthy animal's life. This is known as convenience killing. There may *seem* to have been no other option, choice or *good* choice. In retrospect, this is rarely so but nonetheless, the pain, guilt and grief that results requires care and healing just as with any other loss.

Many veterinarians will say "no" to convenience killing requests and they are to be very much admired. Others believe that if it is going to be done anyway, they would rather do it themselves and do it with as much gentleness as possible. Good arguments abound on both positions. This highly controversial matter must be decided by the ethical and moral standards of each vet and every person who makes the choice to end a healthy animal's life.

Necropsy

Necropsy is often referred to as autopsy, but there is a difference. Autopsy derives from the ancient Greek (*autopsia,* to see for oneself) and is a post-mortem (after death) examination of one human on another. Necropsy is a post-mortem examination by a human on another species.

From time to time, death occurs in such a way as to make it difficult or impossible to know the exact cause. When there is a compelling *need to know*, a post-mortem examination and dissection of the deceased may be desirable. Many people choose to forego learning the exact cause of death because of the invasive nature of necropsy, its emotional implications and the time required to accomplish it.

Veterinarians can perform a limited necropsy in their own operating rooms. But if a detailed exam with toxicology (the study of the presence, nature, effect and detection of poisons and other toxic substances) and tissue slides are needed, it must be done in a major veterinary institution or laboratory. Your veterinarian will be able to arrange it if requested. It comes with additional fees but well worth it when needed.

Grief Support, Self-Help Groups and Hotlines

Support, self-help groups and bereavement hotlines are widely available. They are usually free of charge and can be found with a quick internet search of any city or major veterinary teaching institution.

Every loss is unique to itself, the circumstances, the people, and the animals involved. For this reason, not every loss requires the same kind of grief support or therapy. Some require nothing more than *tincture of time* and the support of an immediate circle of caring people around them.

For people who *just want someone to talk to* and do *not* have critical needs associated with severe, crushing, or extended and undiminished or increasing grief that interferes with their ability to function, a free hotline service may serve them very well. If you choose to explore a hotline, be aware that the person you speak with is highly unlikely to be a formally trained, certified grief therapist or psychotherapist specializing in animal-related loss and grief. The person who takes your call may be a veterinary student, other staff member or volunteer. This is not to say that they cannot be helpful, well-meaning, a good listener, and kind.

Like hotlines, support groups may or may not be useful in the same way. The group dynamic is a very powerful atmosphere, and can be as destructive and counterproductive as helpful. The newly bereaved are usually *not* good candidates for a group atmosphere because they have raw and urgent needs that can easily be lost or overwhelmed by a group. The consequences can leave those who have been slowly growing the courage to speak overlooked in favor of a newly-arrived participant who may be more vocal.

Not all support groups are created equal. Most are "open-ended." An open-ended group is one that usually meets on a monthly or bi-monthly basis and welcomes anyone at any time. The loose structure appears attractive in that no appointment is required, it is generally without cost, and one can come and go as they need or please. The free-form nature of the meetings hold a strong potential to become a superficial, social gathering or *coffee klatch* bound together only by what seems to be a shared experience.

If a group is to be effective, it is my opinion that it should be close-ended. Close-ended groups consist of six to eight people, all of whom have had some individual therapy with the grief therapist leading the group. These are people who may want and are also ready for group interaction. The group should agree upon and commit to a fixed number of weekly meetings that usually do not exceed eight weeks.

A great majority of people who have had the benefit of individual grief therapy find that they have no need for group participation. For those who do, the group can be beneficial when participants are carefully selected and monitored by the same, previously involved therapist who has worked with each group member. This oversight ensures that the group has the best mix of people and goals. Just as all groups are not created equal, neither are all group leaders, therapists, or counselors.

Additionally, it is not uncommon that people who have good, productive relationships with therapists and counselors for many other life issues, find themselves very disappointed when they have experienced or anticipate an animal-related loss. Not every therapist shares in or values the human-animal bond. If they do not share and appreciate the bond, there may be a tendency to underestimate the loss. There may also be false and insensitive interpretations of companion animal-related grief that are too quickly and inaccurately assigned to transference, projection, or *psychobabble*. *Psychobabble* is a term used to denote a pop-culture *buzzword* vocabulary. The term also implies that the speaker of *psychobabble* lacks the experience and understanding necessary for use of proper psychological terminology. This can lead to misdiagnosis and misclassification of natural variations in human psychology as pathological or mentally disordered. These inaccurate conclusions give rise to exaggerated *medicalization* of normal emotional and psychological states or conditions in the bereaved and especially so when the grief is animal-associated.

Grief therapists have or *should* have a unique understanding of their specialty that gives them the opportunity and responsibility to offer something over and above that which can be had with their primary therapist. This can and should be accomplished while not supplanting the good work that can continue to go on between clients and their primary therapists for issues other than grief. It is similar to consulting a neurologist rather than relying on the family physician or internist. If you have a brain tumor or seizures, do you really want it handled by an internist or do you prefer a neurologist? This is not to suggest that you should abandon a good relationship with your internist, but only to highlight that you deserve to have the benefit of a specialist to get you through a challenging time. With your permission, a good grief therapist will want be part of a team so that you can profit from her intervention while preserving your relationship with your primary therapist. The insights of both professionals can make substantial contributions to help ensure the best outcome for you.

Chapter Twelve

A Graceful Exit

"Death ends a life, not a relationship"... Morrie Schwartz from Tuesdays with Morrie by Mitch Albom.

Close of Life: Hospice, Palliative and Comfort Care

As time and illness bring our beloved animal friends toward the close of their lives, how best to care for them can be complicated. The dying are *still* alive! Many are good candidates for home hospice care, and such care should not be overlooked. The daunting questions become, "*Who* is a candidate" and "Exactly *when* should it be employed?" These complex questions cannot be answered within a single guideline. They hinge on individual animals, people and their respective situations. In general, when a companion animal has little or no realistic opportunity for a recovery from illness or seriously debilitating decline, one should begin to look to hospice care.

Because veterinary medicine now offers so much, there is the temptation to begin or continue aggressive or heroic treatment that has little or no chance of changing the outcome. The desire to do so is understandable but *not* advisable. Veterinarians have the ability to deliver this treatment, but also have the responsibility, obligation, and privilege to advocate for their patients' well being. The ethical veterinarian will tell his patients' family that while treatment *can* be given it does not mean it *should* be given. "Just because we can, doesn't mean we should" is a jewel of genuine wisdom.

When aggressive treatment is no longer effective, and there is no realistic chance for extension of a meaningful life, it may still *not* necessarily be the time to die or to be helped to die. It *is* time, however, to change course and offer freedom from stressful and futile treatment. It is also time to begin to replace treatment with pain control and gentle, supportive care to provide for as much comfort and pleasure as possible.

Once more, it is the privilege and obligation of veterinarians to advocate for animals, and they must also do so while *not* telling people what to think and what to do but rather to help find solutions, direction, and offer broad choices about what is available. Some veterinarians are so busy and overwhelmed that they and their staff can become indifferent, rushed, or biased against treating the terminally ill. They may offer little or no information on palliative care, and may even direct or persuade people elect premature euthanasia instead of hospice care. If guardians are not offered and also do not actively seek referral to a specialist in hospice care, they may be left with narrow options or a wait-and-see, do nothing approach. Specialists in companion animal health care include not only specialized veterinarians but also experienced animal-oriented grief therapists well-versed in hospice care.

Dying a *natural* death may be a romantic notion held by some but it fails to address the hard truths. More often than not, natural death is difficult, unkind, filled with pain, and replete with elongated, unnecessary suffering. Many animals need help to leave their broken bodies and they should not be denied this compassionate assistance.

Helping animals to die should also not be presented in cavalier, unacceptable or coercive ways with insensitive comments like: "You should put him out of his misery" or "Just let nature take its course,"

Recognition of the powerful bonds that unite people and their animal families must be validated and respected without compromise at *all* times. This truth holds especially so at end-of-life. People who share exquisitely tender bonds with their companion animals are relieved and happy to learn that their options are more than just either futile treatment and long hospital stays or a swift and premature *pulling the plug* for the terminally ill. Many animals trapped in the cycle of on-going heroic care need not have what is left of their lives occupied with frequent or elongated hospital stays and end in undignified misery. They can go home to enjoy whatever quality time (often longer than one might think) remains and, thereby, allow their guardians a chance to secure their bonds with the gift and pleasure of caring for them and, when finally needed, help them to die with dignity and comfort, surrounded by the people and things they love.

Dr. Alice Villalobos

Dr. Alice Villalobos with Her Olde English Bulldog, Neo
Photo by Joy Kennely

Hospice care for animals is but one of the many specialties of oncologist, Alice Villalobos, DVM, DPNAP. We have Dr. Villalobos to thank for introducing the concept of *Pawspice* to the veterinary profession. *Pawspice* (rhymes with hospice) combines palliative care with a kinder, gentler standard of care for companion animals diagnosed with cancer and other life-limiting disease (www.pawspice.com). Best known as "*Dr. Alice*," she is a long-time respected colleague and leader in this highly specialized area of care. Her credentials, accomplishments, awards for excellence and leadership in veterinary medicine are too numerous to list. They include but are not limited to being the recipient of the Leo Bustad Companion Animal Veterinarian Award and the UC Davis Alumni Achievement Award "*for her pioneering role in bringing oncology services to companion animals*." She is also president of the Society for Veterinary Medical Ethics (www.svme.org) and the past president and editor-in-chief for the American Association of Human-Animal Bond Veterinarians (www.aahabv.org).

Dr. Alice and I share membership in two (SVME and AAH-ABV) of these ground-breaking, innovative organizations that are dedicated to making change in the lives of companion animals, their guardians and the veterinarians who care for them.

Urgent Caution about Hospice Care

Do *not*, under any circumstances, rely on a free-standing hospice facility that, for a fixed or suggested *donation* fee, offers to sell or give you hospice care away from your home, hands, eyes, and heart.

The *only* acceptable hospice care for companion animals is in *your* home. Only in your home can you and your beloved remain together while surrounded by your team of support. The primary team should consist of your veterinarian(s) and a competent grief therapist who has special expertise in companion animal hospice care. These are the foundation of a collaborative, compassionate, and loving contingent that supports you and your beloved as well as the rest of the family including other companion animal family members.

These precautions are further emphasized in light of a very disturbing case in the state of New York in 2010. People for the Ethical Treatment of Animals (www.peta.org) investigated and uncovered a self-proclaimed hospice and rehabilitation center (Angels Gate) in Delhi, New York. The shocking evidence discovered and documented by PETA was turned over to the Delaware County District Attorney's office. After reviewing the case and conducting a search of Angel's Gate, the owner was charged with five counts of animal cruelty, a violation of the state's agriculture and markets law (failure to provide sustenance) and possession of a controlled substance. The Times Union in Albany, New York reported that after discovering an employee of the Delaware County District Attorney's office had worked for Angel's Gate, the case was transferred to the Broome County District Attorney in Binghamton, New York. At the time of this writing, the case is still pending and expected to go to trial. While this example may be the most egregious to date, sadly, it will not remain the only one of its kind if steps are not taken to permanently dismantle it and others of its ilk.

Helping Animals to Leave Their Broken Bodies

Actively helping animals to leave their broken bodies is the loving, responsible choice when it is needed. Once the decision has been made, there are many ways in which to accomplish it. There is no one, right way. Each guardian individual or family, as well as every companion animal must be carefully considered when making the choice. Sometimes, choices become limited because the need to help bring a merciful close of life presents itself following a crushing emergency and the decision requires relatively swift settlement in a hospital setting. Conversely, when close of life is imminent as the result of long, advancing, illness or age, there is more time to plan and arrange it.

Some may feel that the planned end-of-life for a beloved friend is ugly or unseemly, but it is *not*. The views of others should not color your personal decisions. A tender, compassionate and carefully planned end-of-life can offer choices and circumstances of a *good-bye* that can be a comfort and create memories that will honor and help celebrate a precious life and a bond of love.

Along with the general guidelines regarding quality of life, compassion, and the myriad of factors that answer the *when* question, is you author's adage that has tenderly served many over the years: *"Better a day early, than a day late."* This means that it is better to make the decision on a day that may *seem* to be a bit too early, than to postpone it (even one more day) to a day that will live on in memory as certainly having been *too late*. *Too late* involves having pressed the boundary of *when* so far as to have invited suffering and conditions that will make it more difficult to achieve a gentle and smooth exit from a broken body. An example of this is that when the body is very close to death but not yet there, blood pressure falls quite low along with other functions and finding a vein in which to administer the *fluid ticket home* becomes difficult or impossible as veins collapse denying entry. Difficulty in finding access to a vein without pain or distress under those conditions can be very great even for the best veterinarians. Consequently, it may become necessary to end life by means of intra-cardiac or intraperitoneal access. These terms refer to placing the necessary drugs directly into the heart or into the abdominal cavity. These choices are neither attractive nor ideal.

Helping your beloved to die can take place either in a hospital setting or at home. The home setting is not always the best choice in complicated situations but, when carefully arranged, it can prove a great comfort to everyone. There are some veterinarians who offer home end-of-life care only to their established clients. Others specialize in home care and will make it available to all who call upon them when the time comes.

The standard protocol of care is to begin with an intravenous or intramuscular injection of a very strong sedative that creates deep unconsciousness. This injection is followed with a second drug that creates respiratory and cardiac arrest followed swiftly by death that takes place in about thirty seconds. It is considered and accurately described as "quick, peaceful, and without struggle."

Quickly after death takes place, some animals will emit a moaning sound that can raise alarm. It is caused by air exiting from the lungs and *not* a sign of pain, struggle or life. There can also be some twitching in various parts of the body which is the involuntary action of muscles and in no way a sign of life or an incomplete end-of-life.

Upon death, a completely relaxed body may release body fluids from the bladder or colon. This, too, is entirely normal. It is also possible for fluids to be released from the nose. It is usually not immediate but may take place hours later. Knowledge of these natural after-death events prevents disturbing unexpected surprises. If you are taking your friend home from a hospital setting, prior knowledge of the latter (fluids released from nose) is especially important. It also holds similar importance if life comes to a close at home and the beloved will not be transported for burial or cremation immediately... but more about the choices for burial and cremation later.

Animals do not always die with their eyes closed. This is a natural phenomenon of the body. If you are uncomfortable with eyes remaining open or partially open, you may ask your vet to close them or do so yourself. Eyes will not necessarily respond to this adjustment. Closure with surgical glue is *not* recommended. Additionally, once people understand that eyes remaining open is perfectly natural, they rarely make this request.

The reason we see deceased humans at funerals, in film, and elsewhere with their eyes and mouths closed into permanent repose, is that experts in the funeral profession set the features of the dead through the use of *eye caps* placed under the lids. A similar device is used for the mouth. The deceased are arranged with the best possible facial expression and overall body presentation. Funeral care experts also use special cosmetics to make the entire appearance of the dead as natural and pleasing as possible.

This type of preparation is not available for animals but there is much that can be requested and arranged if you are aware of the availability. An important example is that you can ask your vet to express the bladder, clean all body orifices, and gently pack the anus with a bit of cotton to absorb seepage.

If you bring a casket to the hospital or have one prepared at home (in the case of a pre-planned-in-home end-of-life) you can ask your vet to help place him into the casket. The casket can be lined with anything of your choice - a favorite cotton blanket and small pillow is often used but there are many others. The pillow should be only so big as to serve to raise the head enough to be satisfying to the eye. He should be arranged in an overall position that is as pleasing as possible to you. This should be done very soon after death while it is still easy to accomplish. Waiting too long makes an aesthetically pleasing arrangement impossible because the body becomes less flexible with time.

You can *dress* or decorate a casket in personal ways through adornment with natural flowers, religious symbols or elaborate décor. Various objects of love and memory can be placed in the casket alongside the beloved. How it will look and what it will hold is an entirely personal choice.

If cremation is the choice, it is necessary that there be no metal, plastic, or heavy fabric in the casket. These materials create smoke problems in the secondary cremation chamber (the secondary chamber will be explained in detail later) and cause the cremains to turn black as opposed to the usual white to off-white color. You may also request that he not be disturbed or removed from the casket and enter the cremation chamber or grave exactly as he is. In the case of cremation, this can only be done if the casket and its contents do not include the materials described earlier, and if the crematory does not have a policy that insists on the removal of animals from their caskets.

There are a wide variety of beautiful, decorative, heavy-weight, corrugated storage boxes that can also be used as caskets if you plan ahead. They usually work quite well for cats, small mammals, and small dogs weighing less than twenty pounds. Larger dogs require a casket that is stronger and designed to hold their larger size and weight. If you have not planned ahead or had the gift of time with which to plan ahead, many hospitals have caskets on hand at all times. They are made from the same sturdy corrugated cardboard described, are white in color and *not* decorative. They are, however, entirely acceptable and available in the large and extra-large sizes needed for dogs.

You may want a memento other than those you already have at home. You can ask your vet to give you a cutting of hair or take an inked paw print that can be framed. There is also a clay paw print that can be made into a permanent decorative memento. Some clay prints require baking at home and others do not. Many veterinary hospitals have both the inked and clay paw prints available and may even ask you if you want one.

Both prior to and after your friend *changes worlds*, you can spend as much or as little time together as you wish. Many larger high-tech and specialty hospitals offer a *"Serenity"* or *"Comfort Room"* that is separate from the customarily busy areas of the hospital. These rooms are equipped with pleasant furnishings and softer lighting. Some have optional music and look nothing like the typical exam room. Your entire *"Good-bye, dear friend"* can take place in this setting, thus avoiding the more clinical setting of an exam room.

Care of the Body After Changing Worlds

If death takes place in a hospital and you choose not to take her home with you for a time prior to burial or cremation, you should be aware of three major things: exactly how her body will be cared for until transport to the cemetery or crematory, what is involved in the choice between burial and cremation, and the choices among different types and categories of cremation.

Transport to the Cemetery or Crematory

You may choose to have your vet arrange the transport if you do not, personally, take her home, to a cemetery, or crematory.

It is important to understand that transportation from a hospital to a cemetery or crematory may not take place swiftly. If you do not choose your own, the crematory or cemetery your vet has contracted with makes regular pick-ups at every animal hospital on their contracted route. A very busy hospital may have a pick-up twice weekly or more often. Less busy hospitals may not have a pick-up more than every ten days or longer. If you are comfortable with the latter, there is nothing wrong with it. Most people report that they can be comfortable with it because they envision their beloved being handled in a similar fashion to their human family and friends. Without advanced knowledge that this is *not* the case and there is, instead, an icy wait in a freezer with other animals (all in trash bags and not arranged in any special fashion) is customary and usual, people can become very disappointed, shocked and distressed. Most hospitals will handle your friend with as much care as possible but the care will not be on a par to that given to deceased humans.

The same time-line is true for the return of cremains if cremation and return of cremains has been chosen. Cremains can take as much as ten or more days to be returned to you for the same reason - frequency of returns at the hospital. This *turn-around* time can be as little as three to five days or as much as a few weeks. The average time is probably about ten to fourteen days.

Some crematories will mail the cremains directly to you, which is a bit swifter and may bear an additional charge. Many people do not find this acceptable because it lacks a certain personal touch or at least the image of personal touch of transfer from one pair of caring hands to another.

If *you* do not bring or the hospital does not supply a casket, after you leave, he will be tagged for identification and placed in a heavy-weight, black, plastic trash bag and kept in a freezer until transport.

Burial

Burial has a completely different set of requirements. Home burial is illegal in many areas but is it often done just the same. It is not recommended unless it is well thought through, you own the property, and can guarantee that you will never move, sell or lease it to someone else. This is an unrealistic position to take but if you strongly prefer home burial, nothing else will do. You must, therefore, think of what you will do with your companion's resting place and casket should you move. If you want to take her with you, you must make the burial site one that provides for the easiest exhumation.

A burial that allows you to take her or him with you cannot, by its very nature, be *green*. *Green* burial will be explained later. You can choose a casket of any kind.

The casket should be placed in a sealed metal container that will not rust, leak, or disintegrate over time. It should be buried at least four feet deep and the grave must be marked so you know exactly where to unearth if it becomes necessary. Surrounding the casket with a generous amount of sand before replacing the rest with earth will permit you to retrieve the casket with greater ease than if only earth is used.

Green Burial

A truly green burial involves no casket or container of any kind. A biodegradable box or casket *can* be used by those who want it to stay as natural as possible but feel the need for something more than a cotton or gauze wrap. She should be placed in the grave in a very light-weight, open-weave cotton or gauze fabric that will, along with her body, decompose as swiftly as possible, leaving only skeleton that will eventually become fully integrated with the earth. Another option is to plant a hardwood tree, such as a maple, over the site. The roots of the tree will embrace the sacred inhabitant beneath it and, in time, the two will form a complete work of Mother Nature herself.

If you choose burial in a designated animal cemetery, be certain that you have a formal, legal contract signed by the highest authority of the cemetery to ensure your permanent ownership and pre-paid perpetual care of the grave.

Buesking Family Plot
Photo by Toula Buesking, Omaha NE

Avoid any agreement or contract that offers only a yearly maintenance fee as opposed to pre-paid perpetual care. If you choose one that consists of an annual maintenance fee rather than pre-paid perpetual care, the cemetery retains and can exercise the right to reclaim the grave, dispose of the deceased and all markers in any manner they choose and re-sell the plot to someone else should you forget or fail to pay the annual maintenance fee.

Differences Among Various Types of Cremation

There is no universal definition for the vocabulary describing the various types of cremation. Every crematory is likely to have their own definition of what constitutes a private, individual, partitioned, mass, or communal cremation. It is, therefore, vital that you know *what* you are choosing and not assume, for example, that what is being called a *private* cremation means that your animal friend will be the only one in the cremation chamber, thereby preventing any possibility of commingling of cremains with others also in the chamber. It may be that the crematory chosen has defined the term to describe only one animal in the chamber as *individual*. *Private* and *individual* are not synonymous or interchangeable descriptions, especially in this context. Again, I emphasize there is *no universal definition of these terms.* The only way to be certain of the exact practice of the crematory you or your vet has contracted with is to speak with the crematory directly. While surprising to you, it is not at all unusual that your vet may not be fully aware of the differences and may be making incorrect assumptions himself. It is also not only possible, but likely, that your vet has not, personally, been to the crematory or witnessed a cremation there. Ask, learn, and become informed.

Cremations handled by your vet are third party agreements. This is because the primary relationship does not involve you; it exists between the crematory and the owner of the veterinary practice who has contracted with the crematory for their services. Cremation charges are billed to the hospital, the hospital pays the crematory and you are billed (not necessarily at the same rate) for the cremation by the hospital. Remember, if your vet is not the owner of the hospital but an associate employee of the hospital, she has little, if anything at all, to do with the business arrangements between the crematory and the owner of the hospital.

You must know exactly what it is that you want and do *not* want. From there, make every effort to learn how the crematory defines the practices that that will amount to what *you* want. This is a very difficult thing to do when faced with sudden death, extreme distress and heartache. At this point, people are usually filled with pain, and may not be thinking clearly. They may sign releases or agreements that they have not read and really understood both in meaning and implication and are relying on their assumptions. They are also relying on their deservingly trusted vet who may also be unaware of the differences. Some have likened this to having your physician make funeral arrangements for your human family or friends, a practice unheard of and one that would never be found acceptable. Veterinarians, however, are asked to play many different roles. Some roles extend far beyond those of other professions.

Additionally, despite their love for their animal family, many people *prefer* that their veterinarians manage after-death care for them. This care, however, should be fully understood, so that veterinarians can perform the extra service for their clients exactly the way they really want it. In summary, "If I don't know exactly what you want, I cannot give it to you."

As a society, we tend to fail to take advantage of pre-need funeral arrangements for ourselves and more so for our companion animals. Pre-need education and arrangements are easily available from any funeral home or crematory both for people and animals. In fact, funeral homes have an entire department devoted to this field. A pre-need specialist will even come to your home to discuss options with you at no charge. Similar services are available from animal crematories and cemeteries, though it not usual to have someone come to your home. Nonetheless, staff will be happy to discuss pre-need care with you by telephone. A personal visit to the crematory or cemetery is an even better choice. Armed with prior knowledge gained through your telephone discussions or visit to the crematory, if you choose to have your vet make the final arrangements, you will be able to make choices using the crematory's definition that represents what you *really* want. Having established a primary relationship with the crematory or cemetery, you may decide to maintain that relationship and bring your animal friend there, yourself. The choice is yours and your veterinarian will support and honor your wishes, whatever they may be.

Making arrangements at the time of need often leads to impulse-based decisions and reliance on others who, though they may be professionals and well-meaning, have no personal or intimate knowledge of your wishes, the needs of your family as a whole, your financial boundaries, and other details. The desire to *get it over with* can lead people down a road of regrettable decisions that are easily avoided if we take advantage of all there is to know and are prepared.

As a path toward this knowledge, for the purposes of this book, the following definitions are offered. Again, please remember that it is more important to know what you want first and then learn how the crematory of choice defines it.

Private Cremation

Reminder - For purposes of this book, a private cremation is one in which only one animal is in the cremation chamber. This is essential if you want your friend's cremains returned to you. It is the only way to ensure that there will be no commingling with the cremains of other animals.

Commingling of cremains cannot be avoided when more than one animal is in the cremation chamber even if each is in their own cradle, pan, partition or tray. When more than one is in the chamber in his own cradle, pan, partition or tray, this may be referred to as an individual, private, partitioned or sectioned cremation. There is, in fact, no actual wall of partition or separate section between each animal beyond the trays and cradles. Hence, remembering there is no universal definition of these terms, any or all of the terms mentioned *may* be used to define more than one animal in the cremation chamber as opposed to the presumed conclusion that *private* and *individual* both mean and guarantee only one in the chamber. Because crematories do not confine themselves solely to private cremation, it is more efficient and cost effective for them to perform what is called *individual*, *partitioned*, or *sectioned* cremations for people who want cremains returned to them. It is interesting to note that such cremations have never been, are not now and are highly unlikely to ever be chosen or permitted for human cremation. The only exception may be in the case of disaster where there is no possibility for identification of the deceased, requiring that all be buried or cremated together. This is known as mass burial or cremation and often takes place at or near the site of the disaster.

The Cremation Chambers

It is important to understand how cremation is accomplished. Located underneath the floor of the cremation unit, the secondary chamber is only one part of the cremation unit. The secondary chamber is the area where all emissions are eliminated. It is separate from the primary chamber that holds the deceased. The process begins with pre-heating the secondary chamber. Each state has its own requirements for the level of heat in the secondary chamber. In general, it ranges from 1,400-1,800 degrees Fahrenheit.

As the temperature rises, heat is transferred to the primary cremation chamber above. When the level of required heat is fully reached in the secondary chamber, the deceased is placed into the primary cremation chamber and the cremation burner is engaged. The cremation burner is located in the chamber that holds the deceased.

The intense heat that is required for cremation is such that, at some point, the skeletal remains begin to behave a bit like popcorn in that they will move about and transfer to other parts of the chamber. If other animals are present in the chamber, when *pop* and transfer occurs, that is when commingling takes place. When your friend is the only one in the chamber, any skeletal remains that have shifted location are easily collected for removal and returned to you along with those that have not relocated position in the chamber.

Most animal crematories do not confine themselves to *private* (one animal in the chamber) cremation, though they may offer it at a worthwhile additional cost. You may choose to be present throughout the entire process and take your friend's cremains home with you on the same day. If you do not wish to be there, but *do* want a private (no animals in the chamber other than yours) cremation, this can also be arranged.

Mass Cremation

Mass cremation is employed when there is no request for the return of cremains. The process involves cremating together all the animals whose guardians do not wish to have the cremains returned to them, animals who have been executed at pounds and shelters (many thousands in the aggregate) or collected by authorities who find them dead with no identification or possibility of identification. Also included in mass cremation are amputated limbs and aborted fetuses. This is usually known as *disposal.* Most crematories do more disposal cremation than private. It is rare to find a crematory that confines itself exclusively to private cremation because it is simply not profitable enough to invest in the equipment required and perform a dozen or less cremations a week.

There are a good number of people who feel that when life has left the body, care of the body is of little or no importance. They are at ease with having their companions' bodies handled in this manner.

Very few, if any, know that crematories that provide disposal services may not, necessarily, cremate the bodies but may sell them to a rendering plant. There, the bodies are turned into fat and other by-products that are then used in the manufacture of soap, cosmetics, toiletries, kitty litter, fertilizer, and even food for other animals.

Many people have reported to me that although they are comfortable with mass cremation, they are *not at all comfortable* with the thought that they (or someone else) might be washing their face or feeding their garden with their dead companions. They say, "It is horrifying, disgusting, unacceptable and should not be allowed." But it *is* allowed and goes on daily.

Another assumption is that the cremains of animals not returned to anyone are scattered in a designated, idyllic and dignified place. This, too, is not necessarily so. The cremains *may* be so treated but they may also be disposed of as trash and become part of a garbage dump or landfill.

There may be some crematories that do no disposal work and offer only private or mass cremation with dignity. I know, for certain, of only one. It is Companion Animal Cremation Service (CACS) in Mechanicsburg, Pennsylvania. CACS, and the Pennsylvania State Memorial and Cemetery were founded by its president, Rob Lauver, more than twenty-five years ago.

In addition to serving companion animals and their families with unparalleled respect, integrity, and dignity,

Companion Animal Cremation Service offers video-certified, private cremation using a high-tech, double-camera system. Using two cameras provides the proper angles for documentation and assures redundancy should one of the cameras fail.

The cremation, itself, is never recorded or seen. What is recorded is the respectful placement of the deceased into the empty chamber. The camera records the total time it takes to accomplish the cremation, and also records the removal of the cremains. A DVD is given to every individual or family who chooses not to be present.

What remains after cremation is completed is the skeleton. It is very carefully and completely swept from the cremation chamber and placed into a stainless steel pulverizing unit. There, the very dry, brittle, and fragile skeleton is turned into fine sand. If you have seen cremains that appear to be *chunky* or *rocky* it is because they were crushed with less sophisticated equipment incapable of producing fine sand-like cremains. The *chunky* or *rocky* condition of cremains is not unacceptable. However, a fine sand-like texture is ideal and the only one that meets the exceptional standards of CACS.

At CACS, the cremains are then, carefully, placed into a complimentary cedar urn with a brass nameplate and photo frame. The urn is delivered to the family home if cremation was not witnessed, or can be returned to the family at the office of CACS. If the family was present at time of cremation, the cremains will be personally handed to them upon leaving.

CACS offers emergency services twenty-four hours a day, seven days a week and three-hundred-sixty-five days a year. CACS staff (most often Lauver himself) will come for the deceased within four hours of notification, and the cremation will be done within twenty-four hours after arrival at the crematory. A fully disclosed, certified private cremation agreement features, among many other specific details, a clear description and definition of *private* cremation, what charges will be incurred, and there is also a generous list of items for which there is *no charge.*

For those who do *not* want their companions' cremains returned, CACS offers a dignified option that ensures the deceased will not become soap, fertilizer or trash. It is a *memorial cremation*. Lauver defines memorial cremation as one in which no more than ten, ten-pound animals are placed in the chamber at a given time. However, only five-to-seven make up a typical *memorial cremation* at CACS. Remember, the chamber has the capacity to hold *many* more than ten. However, a number greater than ten does not meet the standard of dignity Lauver demands and delivers. The cremains are then placed in an identifiable location with a permanent, written memorial indicating the names of the animals and their families. The memorial site is located at Lauver's cemetery, The Pennsylvania State Memorial and Cemetery.

Pennsylvania State Memorial and Cemetery Entrance
Photo by Rob Lauver

The site holds memorial columns that are three-feet wide by five-feet high. The commingled cremains are placed into the columns. When the columns are full, any additional animals who are memorialized on the columns have their cremains buried directly in front of the columns with the names remaining permanently in place.

Memorial Column
Photo by Rob Lauver

Lauver also offers a *truly green* burial at the beautiful Pennsylvania State Memorial and Cemetery.

Most of us are not fortunate enough to live close to Lauver's unique facilities. But we *can* and *must* make every effort to educate ourselves and each other about all the options available. This will arm you with one of the most powerful decision-making tools - the knowledge and ability to seek out the protections that come from detailed and fully disclosed information with no *hidden agendas* or *fine print*. Prepared and well-armed with this, you will be able to find and demand nothing less than excellence. Knowledge of this kind will also protect you from ever looking back upon your personal heartache with complications of regret, guilt, anger or any sense of failure or betrayal.

Cremation is Not Final

Cremation is not entirely final in that you must think of what will become of your beloved's cremains when your time on earth comes to an end. You may want to have them at home in your chosen place of honor during your entire life, but what will become of them upon your own death?

A wide variety of the most beautiful and unusual decorative boxes that are ideal for use as cremation urns can be found at Little Gorgeous Things (LGT).

(www.littlegorgeousthings.com/trandjebo.html)

Grace – Unique Cremation Urn and Place of Honor

Photo by Barbara Meyers

Not every LGT specialty box has the interior space needed for cremains. If you are interested in unusual cremation urns, call or e-mail LGT for the internal measurements before ordering. Ian will help you to make the choice you that will serve your needs best, offer you others that may not appear on the site and also be certain that each are adequate in size and depth to hold cremains. Little Gorgeous Things is in the HAST time zone of the U.S. so there may be a time difference that is as much as six hours behind yours. Keep this in mind when you call LGT. Specialty boxes of the classic Egyptian type, such as the cartouche, are one of the many unusual boxes and other items found at LGT.

In ancient Egypt, a cartouche was attached to the coffins of queens and kings. Departing briefly from the cartouche, it is interesting to note the difference between a coffin and a casket. While the two words are often used interchangeably, there is difference between them. A coffin is wider at the top and tapers toward the bottom. A casket is rectangular and of the same width from top to bottom. Caskets were not used in ancient Egypt and are still not favored in many parts of Europe or among certain religious groups.

Returning to the subject of cartouches, a cartouche is an oval with a name written into it – a bit like an exotic nameplate.

Cartouche
Photo provided by Little Gorgeous Things

Over time, many non-royals adapted the practice and engaged an artist to create a cartouche for their own coffin or that of a beloved. A cartouche can be very simple and plain or a bejeweled piece of art. It was believed you would not disappear after death if you had your name written down somewhere.

By attaching a cartouche to coffins, people ensured that their names and those of their revered loved ones were written in at least one place. The cremains of your author's cherished Raymond rests in a Little Gorgeous Things cartouche.

Many people find that, after a number of years or even sooner, they wish to scatter the cremains of their companion animal family themselves. It bears no right or wrong and is a personal decision that is entirely up to the individual. If that is not your choice, you must provide detailed instructions as to what your wishes are for the truly final disposition of the cremains. Your decision should be formalized in your will and made well known to all those close to you, especially your executor, who will be duty-bound to carry out your wishes. Do not assume that your executor knows and will follow any informal statements you may have made in conversation during your lifetime. If you want your companions' cremains interred with you in your casket or grave, or commingled with your own cremains, you must state so through a formal, legal document: your will.

More than just a few people have stated that they want to be buried with the cremains of their beloved animal family. If not formally arranged, even the most well-meaning person you *think* knows your wishes and you *assume* will carry them out may not. People tend to reinterpret or *reinvent*, and replace the wishes of others (especially if they consider them to be silly or frivolous) with their own. They easily tell themselves and others, "Oh, she didn't *really* mean that," or "It's *ridiculous*, I'm not going to do *that*," or "He was just joking!" You do not want that *joke* to be on you, do you? You have the power to see to it that it does not happen.

You would be wise to also take the same care in stating what your wishes are regarding your own end of life scenario. This should include preparing a living will, a last will and testament, health care proxy and pre-need arrangements either for burial or cremation.

Other Choices for the Final Disposition of Cremains

If scattering is not appealing to you and you choose cremation for both yourself and your animal family, you can arrange for *all* the cremains (each as needed) to be in a permanent niche in a columbarium. A columbarium is a respectful and often public place for the permanent housing of cremation urns. The term comes from the Latin, *columba*, meaning dove. It originally referred to the compartmentalized housing of doves and pigeons. Columbaria can be either free-standing units, part of a mausoleum, or another building on the site of a cemetery. If a columbarium is your choice, it *can* and *should* be arranged in advance of need.

Mummification and Freeze-Dry Preservation

Mummification

Mummification is the permanent preservation of the deceased through very complicated and careful methods. It can take five-to-eleven months, requires special preparation for shipping to a facility that will accomplish it, and is very expensive. Preparation for mummification is best done swiftly after death and requires refrigeration rather than freezing prior to shipping. Refrigeration is easy with small animals but if you have a twenty-five-or-more pound dog, it can present quite a challenge. In addition, many people recoil from the idea of keeping their beloved in a cooler (on ice but not frozen) or in their home refrigerator, no matter the size of the deceased.

Costs range anywhere from $6,000 to $130,000 depending on the size of the animal involved and the mummiform (the final protective sarcophagus) chosen. All this must be factored into the choice to mummify.

Freeze-Dry Preservation

Freeze-drying is also a method of permanent preservation. It is very different from mummification, has its own methodology that includes immediate freezing after death, takes many months to be completed, and costs from between four and five-hundred dollars for very small animals (up to about three pounds) to expenditures that can only be determined on an individual basis for higher weights.

Both mummification and freeze-dry preservation, like all other choices, can be *good, right* and *dignified*. They all remain a very personal decision. I urge everyone to make their decisions without the bias or influence of others who may not find your choice acceptable to them. The beloved is yours, the bond is yours, and honoring it in the ways that are meaningful to you should not be overshadowed by the cloak of ignorance, failure of others to understand, or the judgment of others.

Burial May Not be Permanent

Laws governing human cemeteries are highly complex, vary from country to country and have different standards for the time when the entire cemetery can be leveled and reused. In general, when a cemetery has been fully occupied (no more plots available for sale) and the last body buried has been there for one-hundred years, the cemetery (after documenting all the necessary requirements and having been approved by the appropriate governing authority,) can be leveled and all the plots made available for sale again. Exceptions are made for those granted historical status, sacred ground, etc.

However, as applied to animal cemeteries, the rules in place do not specifically mimic the hundred year guideline. There is a great deal of flexibility in the rules, especially if you have not arranged for contracted permanent ownership and pre-paid perpetual care of the grave.

How to Cope with People Who Do Not Understand or Honor Your Loss

There is no acceptable reason to tolerate the painful insensitivities of people who inflict additional harm on the bereaved. The wounded and heartbroken need not tolerate the additional burden of apologizing for or defending their pain. It is, however, what many people find themselves doing; tolerating and even justifying the insensitivity or outright cruelty inflicted on them by others. They tell themselves that the people who are mistreating and disrespecting them do not understand because they have no animal companions of their own, or they do not *really* mean their insensitive comments the way they sound.

Nonsense! It is mandatory to have and actively show compassion, empathy, and concern for the bereaved no matter who is dying or has died. Anything less is uncivilized, abusive and should not be tolerated. For instance, one does not need to have a sister to be concerned about someone whose sister is dying or dead. Most people tend to offer as sincere a response as they can when they learn that a friend's sister has died even if they have never met the sister. Some behave this way because they may truly care about their friend, colleague, associate, or any other person they may encounter in this situation. They also do it because it is a demand of civil social interaction.

Sadly, these social norms are not afforded to animals. There are no social prohibitions against speaking about animals without consideration, respect or sensitivity. People can be blunt and rude, laugh or make harsh comments that would never be otherwise spoken even if the comments accurately represented their thinking and attitude. They would resist behaving this way were they not talking about animals.

It is not always necessary to go to war or permanently end relationships with every insensitive, foolish, or outright stupid person who makes inappropriate comments or asks intrusive questions in place of offering a few kind words. However, from time to time, one may find that *is* necessary and appropriate to end a relationship. It is often, but not always, one that has a long history of disappointments and complications, and the final insult or *last straw* comes with abusive behavior surrounding the illness or death of their animal companion. This, like so many other decisions and choices, can only be determined on an individual basis.

People who are a source of added pain must be stopped. It is not as difficult as one may think and it can go something like the following: When confronted with thoughtless remarks, you need only interrupt, disallowing them to go on, and deliver your own version of, "I'm sure you think that what you are saying is harmless and maybe even helpful but it is *not* and I want you to stop." It is crucial that you do not permit the offender to explain, justify, or apologize. If people who behave this way are permitted to offer qualification, they will walk away feeling they have fully justified themselves and *blame the victim... you!* They will recount the event by telling themselves and others that they did nothing wrong and that *you* over reacted and are unreasonable. People do not give up their self-defenses easily and, despite your obvious discomfort, are likely to make additional attempts to justify themselves either immediately or at a later time. It requires that you tell them that the subject is *not* open for discussion, they have to stop, and they must *not* do it again. You can then just walk away or close a phone conversation with, "I'll be on my way, now. Have a good day," and remove yourself from the situation. This should serve to protect you and perhaps even give the other person pause when thinking about making similar insensitive comments to someone else. The most important aspect of this is *not* to allow yourself to be brutalized and *take it*. If you do, it will only add further pain and isolation to your grief.

In addition to the general comments people will make, there is a list of questions they may ask that are inappropriate. Inappropriate questions often come with the death of a human, too, but people tend to be more harsh and thoughtless when talking about animals. They interrogate instead of offering comfort. The interrogation usually begins with the three most frequently asked inappropriate questions: "How hold was he?",

"How or from what did she die?" and "Are you going to get another one?" The first two questions may also be asked if the deceased is human, but would anyone dare ask the third question, a question that suggests to the bereaved that they should just go out and *get another* spouse, partner, child, or friend?

Many individuals and families have more than one companion animal. This group is subject to comments that demean the special relationship shared with each individual member of the multi-companion animal home. They are assaulted with a peculiar and insensitive logic that results in casual comments like, "It's okay; after all, you have others." Would this flawed conclusion be acceptable if you lost a human child or a sibling but still had other living children or siblings? The answer is obvious – Certainly not!

With regard to the age of your beloved at the time of death, does it *really* matter? When is it "okay" for them to die? How much time is enough? The answer to the last questions are, sometimes, yes, it *was* time and it *was* enough. Nonetheless, in the throws of grief, this answer, even if applicable, is not helpful and creates yet another diminution of the bond fractured by death. People in the circle of the bereaved must appreciate that if they do not know what to say or what *not* to say, it is best to say nothing and just *be there* with as few words as possible. Those who have not learned this lesson and persist in insensitivities must be avoided and prevented from re-injuring the bereaved.

I'll Be There in the Mourning

Managing personal loss in the workplace can be a thorny challenge. Once again, if the loss is of an animal companion, it is not likely to be given the respect and privileges (time off, condolence cards and visits, memorial gifts or flowers) it deserves. In preparing yourself for the response of others to the death of your animal friend, knowledge of the policies of the company for which you work, combined with the past behaviors of your colleagues, is helpful. If you do not know, tread carefully. If you have learned that policies are less than favorable, guard against them by choosing very carefully *if,* with whom, and to what extent you will share your loss. I am not an advocate of lying by omission, but there are times when omission or the *embroidery* of the truth is necessary. There is no shame in the truth but it is best to protect yourself from potentially threatening conditions.

Rather than share the details of why you will not attend work, it may be advisable to simply indicate that a family crisis prevents you from coming in for a few days. If questioned about the explicit nature of the crisis, one need only say, “It’s complicated,” and leave it at that. This method will work, but only if you have followed it prior to the death of your friend. If it is introduced after it is well known that a member of your animal family has been ailing or critically ill, it will not suffice and will, instead, create additional problems. It is not possible to prepare for every work-related contingency, but giving this some forethought in a general way will help to keep your path smooth. If you choose to share your loss openly and allow events to unfold naturally, there can also be pleasant surprises awaiting you in the workplace. People who have not been especially warm or nice to work with may hold deeply hidden tender feelings about animals and be unexpectedly sensitive to you. The reverse however, may also be true, and co-workers you might expect to be kind, are not. As you consider the reaction of others to you, also think about your reaction to them. Most of us spend nearly as much time at work as we do at home, and some of us spend more time at work than at home. Very few of us have the luxury of just walking away from a job without great consequence. Given that you will likely continue to work for your company and with people who have either disappointed or failed to come through for you, think before you speak, react explosively or break down in tears. Do what is in your own long-term best interest. You can still stop insensitive people from harming you and do not have to resign in order to achieve the respect and consideration you deserve.

Never Again: When it All Seems too Much

"Never again" are the two words often thought, spoken, screamed in mute pain, and heard from deeply traumatized mourners. They *never again* want to revisit the pain. They feel that *never again* can they face the inevitable or the path that leads to it. This sentiment is not hard to understand, but the reasons behind it may be. For some, there are unresolved grief-related issues that present a set of challenges *not* best served by reinvestment with another companion animal or even an attempt to expand relationships with animals in the community. People who find themselves in this position are better served by the benefits of grief therapy before proceeding any further. The first goal of grief therapy is not, nor *should* it be, that of reinvesting in another companion animal of their own or anyone else's. Rather, it should provide people with compassionate support and concrete skills needed to manage the debilitating effects of grief. Perhaps later, when healing is well stabilized, they can entertain thoughts of inviting animals into their lives again.

For others, deciding not to have another animal companion is a well-thought-out conclusion. It does not originate from unresolved personal issues and is made for practical reasons that are in the best interest of themselves and any potential animal friends in their future. Their hearts are not closed, they are not suffering from post-traumatic distress, and they are very clear about the decision which is a thoughtful *response* rather than an impulsive *reaction*. Animals remain in their lives in healthy ways other than through personal, in-home companionship. They are able to interact with and enjoy the company of animals in other ways.

Some will easily derive pleasure in the company of the animals of friends, family, and neighbors. Others will choose to more fully appreciate species they were previously less familiar with by joining local *birders* and bird-watching groups, become acquainted with nature trails, and wildlife of every variety. These activities are quickly and easily discovered through an internet search at home or using the resources of a local public library.

Very often, they take place right in one's own back yard. Even in the *concrete jungle* of New York City many surprises await in Central Park (www.centralparknyc.org). There, one can discover the park's fascinating history, ecology and design on free volunteer-led, walking tours sponsored by the Central Park Conservancy. On Staten Island, New York, equal delights can be found at Blue Heron Park Nature Center; a favorite of your author (www.nycgovparks.org/parks/blueheronpark/highlights/12089). There, the Park Rangers and naturalists from Friends of Blue Heron Park (www.preserve2.org/blueheron/) will introduce you to Mother Nature's children and give you skills to identify and appreciate them as never before.

Another very good option is to become a member, volunteer or sponsor of animals through organizations such as:

- Animal Legal Defense Fund www.aldf.org
- Defenders of Wildlife www.defenders.org
- Dogs for the Deaf www.dogsforthedeaf.org.
- Farm Sanctuary www.farmsanctuary.org
- In Defense of Animals www.idausa.org
- Panthera www.panthera.org
- People for the Ethical Treatment of Animals www.peta.org

One may also volunteer their professional or hands-on services to various animal advocacy groups, or become an activist in animal legislation either directly or through an established organization such as a local chapter of Vote Humane. (www.votehumane.org). Channeling one's love for animals outside an in-home relationship with them honors the human-animal bond in important and lasting ways. The variety of activities that accomplish this is extensive and, with motivation and a little research, people can find those that suit them best.

Farm Sanctuary

Among the organizations that are both close to my heart and deserving of special attention is Farm Sanctuary. Before proceeding, please know that all the groups and organizations previously mentioned are no less important than Farm Sanctuary. Each plays a distinct and valuable role in their shared concern and advocacy for animals. It is not possible (within the confines of this book) to describe each of them individually. You can, however, become more fully acquainted with all of them through the links provided to their websites.

In 1986, Farm Sanctuary was co-founded by its current president, Gene Baur (www.farmsanctuary.org).

Gene Baur with Theresa
Photo provided by Farm Sanctuary

It began as an all-volunteer group advocating for the prevention of cruelty and encouraging legislative action and reforms to promote respect and compassion for farm animals. Since then, Farm Sanctuary has grown to become a leading farm animal protection organization in the United States with locations in New York and California. Farm Sanctuary remains firmly committed to its mission to end cruelty to farm animals and to promote compassionate living through rescue, education, advocacy, legislation, and the construction of an on-site, fully staffed veterinary hospital at the Watkins Glen location.

Stopping the slaughter of *downed* animals is among the many goals of Farm Sanctuary. Every year, countless numbers of pigs, sheep, and other animals who are too sick, injured, or weak to stand or walk are dragged, beaten, pushed with forklifts or shocked with electric prods to force them onto slaughterhouse kill floors where they are brutally slaughtered for food.

In 2010, the long fight against this cruelty was won for cattle when President Obama announced a new United States Department of Agriculture rule that bans the slaughter of *downed* cattle at any time. The challenge continues to extend the same protection to all species of farms animals too sick or injured to stand or walk to their death.

Hilda

A lamb, later named Hilda, was the first animal rescued by Farm Sanctuary. She had been tossed onto a pile of dead animals and her seemingly lifeless body was covered with flies and maggots. As Baur approached, she raised her head to him. She was alive! There was some hope. As quickly and gently as possible, Baur carried her into his VW wagon and took her to the nearest veterinarian. She had collapsed due to brutal transport conditions and was not otherwise seriously ill or injured. Hilda recovered and spent the next eleven years roaming the green pastures of Farm Sanctuary's New York sanctuary. During her life, she touched the hearts and minds of millions of people. These included legislators and policymakers who introduced federal and state legislation to ban downed animal cruelties, people who learned of Hilda's plight in dozens of national news stories, and visitors of all ages who met Hilda and learned that farm animals feel pain, fear, and sorrow just as we and all animals of other species do.

Hilda peacefully died in her sleep from old age on September 25, 1997. She is buried in a beautiful garden grove on the farm, and there is a memorial plaque that will continue to touch and teach people for years to come. All that Farm Sanctuary does, from shelters and investigative campaigns, to their legal and legislative actions stems from Hilda and animals like her.

In honor of Hilda and to recognize people who have made a major contribution to the ongoing work initiated by her, Farm Sanctuary established the *Friends of Hilda Club*. I am proud to say that I am among the very first members. The "Friends of Hilda Club Certificate of Appreciation" that displays our beloved Hilda and all she represents, remains framed in a permanent place of love and honor on the wall above my desk.

Hilda is a constant reminder to me and everyone who passes through my door of all that has been done and all there still remains to do to ensure that the future embraces a kindness that excludes no one. We can and *should* rejoice in the many victories, but balance them with the ugly and painful reality that for every Hilda, Theresa, Francis, Noel and the many others now safe on Farm Sanctuary, there are millions like them who remain at peril and will suffer without our help.

Friends of Hilda Club Certificate

Photo provided by Barbara Meyers

Volunteering at a Shelter, Pound or Rescue Group

Great caution must be taken when considering volunteering at a shelter, pound or rescue group. These are places that may very well be in need and deserving of volunteers, but working there often comes at a very high price. Harsh reality, ugly truths, chronic grief, and sadness are endemic in all such facilities. Initially, you may not be aware of these things since most facilities emphasize their success and adoption rates, but may not disclose the pain and suffering you will likely encounter. This is so even if you will not be directly involved with the cats and dogs there and are volunteering your professional expertise in fund raising, computer technology, or any other aspect of the business end of the shelter. Your good intentions may only further exacerbate your own pain and distress. Think carefully before you act. Become fully informed before you hurt yourself further. Broken hearts can be very much like broken mirrors - It is sometimes better to leave them broken for a while than to try to fix them and hurt yourself more.

Chapter Thirteen

Animals and the Law

"The assumption that animals are without rights and the illusion that our treatment of them has no moral significance is a positively outrageous example of Western crudity and barbarity. Universal compassion is the only guarantee of morality."... Arthur Schopenhauer (1788-1860).

Lady Justice (Justitia, the Roman Goddess of Justice) is the personification of the moral force that underlies the legal system. She is depicted as a blindfolded, bare-breasted woman carrying a sword and scales. She has appeared without the blindfold but the blindfold with which she is now associated is believed to have begun in the sixteenth century.

The blindfold indicates that justice is meted out objectively, without fear or favor, regardless of identity, power, or weakness; blind justice and blind impartiality. The scales suspended from her left hand symbolize measurement of the strengths of both the support and opposition of a case. The sword is sometimes seen as sheathed but is most often seen as unsheathed and double-edged, symbolizing the power of reason and justice, which may be wielded either for or against any party.

Justice may be blind but she is not deaf! She has begun to hear voices that have risen up for animals. The voice is strong, growing stronger and heard through the spoken and written words of respected legal scholars and attorneys specializing in animal law.

Lady Justice

Animal law is the most rapidly developing, distinct legal discipline. It has its own body of case law and a growing number of practitioners, academics and scholars. In addition, there is an army of law students in a growing number of law schools who are devoting themselves to protecting animals. The Animal Law Review is a student-run law review at Lewis and Clark Law School in Portland, Oregon, and is the nation's first and only law review devoted exclusively to animal issues. The objective of the review is to educate readers about all sides of current animal-related legal issues. It is published bi-annually.

The Animal Law Review was created by the same group of innovative and far-sighted Lewis and Clark law students who founded the very first chapter of the Student Animal Legal Defense Fund in 1992.

Animal Legal Defense Fund (ALDF)

The Animal Legal Defense Fund (www.aldf.org) has made a significant contribution to animals and the field of animal law. Convinced that the field of animal law was a growing and viable field of practice of national significance, they have been proven correct.

Image provided by ALDF

Today, animal law is a flourishing and respected mainstream field of legal expertise. Not only are there numerous attorneys with thriving practices in this area of law but there is also an increasing number of State Bar Associations that have sections and committees devoted to this important area of legal expertise. Courts generally treat animals as simple property. Thus, if an animal is killed or injured, the "owner" of the property can recover only the market value of the property. The market value of companion animals is immeasurably less than their true worth as beloved members of the family.

Steven M. Wise, J.D.

Attorney and legal scholar, Steven M. Wise, J.D., has practiced animal protection law for more than twenty-five years and has taught Animal Rights Law at the Harvard Law School, Vermont Law School and several others. He is the author of numerous scholarly papers on animal rights and has collaborated and communicated with leading scientists in the fields of primatology and animal intelligence and behavior. This exhaustive collaboration and research has given him powerful and compelling bedrock for his position on animal rights. Wise's position is that animals, particularly primates, meet the criteria of legal *personhood* and should therefore be awarded certain rights and protections. His criteria for *personhood* are that the animal must be able to desire to act in an intentional manner to acquire things and also must have a sense of self. He argues that chimpanzees, bonobos, elephants, parrots, dolphins, orangutans and gorillas meet these criteria. While it is more difficult to demonstrate these criteria in other animals, those who really know and appreciate Mother Nature's children need little convincing that they, too, are deserving of *personhood*.

If legal *personhood* is bestowed upon them it will protect them from serious infringements upon their bodily integrity and bodily liberty. Without *personhood* in law, one is invisible to civil law and might as well be dead.

Wise has written several books that speak to this in detail. The books are eloquent, based on scientific research and colored with an empathy and compassion that is as equally convincing as his most complicated legal arguments. One of the books is *Rattling the Cage: Toward Legal Rights for Animals,* Perseus Books, Cambridge MA 2005.

In *Rattling the Cage*, he writes: "For four thousand years, a thick and impenetrable legal wall has separated all human from all nonhuman animals. On one side, even the most trivial interests of a single species – ours – are jealously guarded. We have assigned ourselves alone, among the millions of animal species, the status of 'legal persons.' On the other side of that wall lies the legal refuse of an entire kingdom - not just chimpanzees and bonobos but also gorillas, orangutans, monkeys, dogs, elephants and dolphins. They are legal *things*. Their most basic and fundamental interest – their pains, their lives, their freedoms – are routinely abused. Ancient philosophers claimed that all nonhuman animals had been designed and placed on this earth just for human beings. Although philosophy and science have long since recanted, the law has not."

In my conversations with Wise, he pointed out that *personhood* is a very complex status. It varies greatly: constitutional, federal, state, and much more. Essentially, persons are rights bearers. For example, two of the elements that make up an individual's rights are liberty and equality. Liberty is a non-comparative right. Equality is a comparative right. Dignity is connected to rights of liberty. If you are beginning to have more questions than answers, or are growing a bit confused, imagine the task of not only fully understanding these complexities but being able to argue them appropriately and convincingly! Wise (and other animal law attorneys) have the ability to do it all and they do it every day of their professional lives.

Wise summarized it in a way that is beautifully simple but *not* simplistic. He said, "We must look to the precautionary principle. If we can't or don't know and we wait until we do, it will be too late. We must act *as if* so as to err on the side of caution." This translates to, "If those who conduct hideous and unnecessary experiments on animals claim they can't or don't know the harm and cruelty they are inflicting, don't!"

Wise argued a case in the Supreme Court of Vermont involving a cat. A decision favoring the plaintiffs would have set legal precedent in Vermont and could have persuaded courts nationwide to alter long-standing animal law principles that deem animals as property. It would have allowed for the recovery of non-economic damages for pain and suffering. Wise believed that by taking this case, the court had signaled it might be sympathetic to his arguments and that there was a reasonable chance of winning. However, on May 11th 2009, The Vermont State Supreme Court affirmed the lower court's ruling, rejecting the plaintiff's (the companion cat's guardians) contention that non-economic damages (pain and suffering and emotional distress) should be awarded. The court stated it would not expand the law to provide this recovery.

The matter may seem closed in the state of Vermont but is not closed entirely! We can look forward to and expect that this will be revisited again and again throughout the forty-nine remaining states and again in Vermont as well. Interests strongly opposed to and fearful of this reform may have celebrated the Vermont decision as a victory but it is, without doubt, an illusion and an empty victory. The Vermont decision is a minor skirmish in a larger war that *will* be won. There is also no doubt that there was a time when those who would have it so celebrated that a man like Barack Obama would never be President of the United States. They, too, *were* and *are* wrong.

Scott Beckstead, J.D.

Another voice heard by Lady Justice is that of Scott Beckstead. Beckstead is an attorney specializing in animal law in Oregon. Among his accomplishments, in 2002, Beckstead won the highest award ($136,000) ever given by a jury for the emotional harm inflicted on the plaintiffs caused by the intentional killing of two companion dogs.

The defendant fatally poisoned the dogs of his neighbors with slug bait and antifreeze; a painful and ugly death! Despite the fact that the dogs were and remain legal property, it is a clear indication that the tide is not only changing but rising rapidly. Beckstead said: "The evidence demonstrated that the plaintiffs loved their dogs dearly and considered them part of the family. The jury's verdict reflects the belief among people that losing an animal you love is very different from losing ordinary *property*."

The matter of personhood for animals is, indeed, important but it is not the only path to victory. This is well illustrated by Beckstead's win and, other similar cases in which non-economic damages are being awarded despite the fact that the status of *personhood* has not been granted to animals. In

2009, Beckstead left the private practice of animal law to accept an appointment with the Humane Society of the United States.

Adam Karp, J.D.

Lady Justice also knows the voice of attorney, Adam Karp (www.animal-lawyer.com). Adam Karp exclusively practices animal law throughout the state of Washington.

Karp founded and served as first chair of the Washington State Bar Association's Animal Law Section and is Vice-Chair of the American Bar Association's Animal Law Committee. A long term member of the Animal Legal Defense Fund, he is a contributing editor of the Animal Legal Report produced by Animal Legal Reports Services and is also adjunct professor of animal law at the University of Washington School of Law and Seattle University School of Law.

Adam Karp, J.D.
Photo provided by Adam Karp

Adam Karp protects and defends companion animals and their guardians with diligence and success. There is a particularly compelling case in which he won a default judgment of approximately $46,000 in King County, Washington State. A default judgment is one rendered when the defendant fails to appear. There are many reasons why a defendant will choose this path. One may be that, on the advice of counsel, the defendant has determined that the facts and circumstances would suggest the strong possibility that a jury would award even more. This was demonstrated in the jury award mentioned in the Beckstead victory. The defendant in Karp's case, Wallace Gray, chose not appear in court. The award of nearly $46,000 is the highest known, to date, by a default judgment and included compensation for emotional distress. It is considered significant because it was awarded by a judge rather than a jury. Jurors can (and in many cases, should) take emotional factors into strong consideration and be swayed by them. When a judge makes the award, it is presumed to be one that is made without emotion and based strictly on the merits of the case. I hasten to add that having an attorney like Adam Karp does not hurt!

The case involved a cat who was fatally assaulted by a neighbor's dog. The cat's name was Yofi, which means "wonderful" in Hebrew. Yofi came to her name when she was rescued by a retired schoolteacher, Paula Roemer, who went to Israel for a vacation in 1992. Strolling down a brick pathway in Yaffo, Israel, she came upon a tiny bundle on the steamy, hot bricks. There was a small crowd staring down at the bundle. When Roemer got close enough, she could see that this *bundle* was a tiny, fly-covered kitten near death. Unwilling and unable to turn away from her, she scooped her up and bussed back to Haifa where Yofi was seen by the only veterinarian there. Slowly, Yofi began to recover and thrive. When vacation time was over, plans were made to return home together. This was not easy to accomplish and, at one point, Roemer gave strong consideration to staying in Israel and applying for residence in order not to leave Yofi behind. Fortunately, this did not become necessary and the two went home to live happily together until February 9th 2004. It was then that Yofi's life was taken in a brutal attack by a neighbor's dog. To her horror, Roemer witnessed it but was helpless to intercede in or stop the event. It is important to note that no one is likely to be able to accomplish this task under such intense conditions. A dog (especially a large, powerful one like the Chow in this case) in full attack mode with his considerably smaller victim in his jaws is able to accomplish the killing in seconds.

Karp is a Four-Star General in the army of attorneys devoting their lives to animals, animal law and the defense of the truly innocent. When asked about his wish list, Karp said, “I’d like to see a time when we live in a vegan world.”

Chapter Fourteen

Tributes, Poetry and Remembrance

"Memory is the Treasury of All Things."
... Marcus Tullius Cicero (106 BC-46 BC)

Greyfriars Bobby

Bobby was a Skye Terrier who slept on John Gray's grave every night for fourteen years. William Brody sculptured the original statue from life. It was unveiled without ceremony in 1873 after Bobby's death and is now in the Museum of Edinburgh. Bobby's red granite headstone was erected by the Dog Aid Society of Scotland and unveiled in 1981 by His Royal Highness, The Duke of Gloucester CCVO on May 13th 1981.

John Gray was a gardener who, with his wife, Jess and his son, John arrived in Edinburgh in the early 1800's. Because of the harsh weather, there was no work for gardeners. To avoid the workhouse, he joined the Edinburgh Police Force as Constable #90, Warrant #1487. One of the conditions of service was that he had a watchdog. He obtained a Skye Terrier and appropriately named him *Bobby*, a term used to describe police officers in the United Kingdom.

Total companionship developed between them and continued even after Gray's death on February 8th 1858. Gray's grave was leveled by the hand of time and unmarked by any stone but the sacred spot was not completely disregarded or forgotten. American lovers of Bobby erected a red granite stone to mark Gray's Grave.

Greyfriars Bobby
Photo provided by www.greyfriarsbobby.co.uk

Inscription on Bobby's headstone:
"Greyfriars Bobby
Died January 14· 1872 - Aged 16 years
Let his loyalty and devotion
be a lesson to us all."

For fourteen years, Gray's faithful friend, Bobby, kept constant watch and guard over the grave until his own death in 1872. Bobby lay on the grave leaving only for food. The people of Edinburgh loved and cared for Bobby but his loyalty remained with Gray.

It is reported that a daily gathering of people would stand at the entrance of the graveyard waiting for the one o'clock gun that signaled Bobby leaving the grave for his meal. The site, located on the corner of Candlemakers Row and George IV Bridge, is visited daily and fresh flowers can be see at all times. Bobby's monument is the most photographed monument in Edinburgh.

Shep, our American Version of Bobby

Shep was the companion of a traveling sheep herder who was working in Montana in the 1930's. In 1936, the unnamed shepherd became ill and was brought to St. Claire Hospital in Fort Benton, where he died. A sheepdog followed the herder into town and set up a vigil at the hospital's door. A nun who ran the hospital fed him during the few days before the man died. When the herder's coffin was being shipped east from Fort Benton railway station to the family of the shepherd, the dog followed it there. Attendants later recalled the dog whining as the door slammed shut and the engine slowly pulled away from the station. With determined head down, he trotted down the track after his friend. On that day, the dog who was later named Shep, began a five-and-a-half year vigil that was broken only by his own death.

He waited for and checked every train that stopped from 1936 to 1942 and was a fixture at the station. Neither the heat of summer days nor the bitter Montana winters prevented Shep from meeting every train and eyeing every person who stepped from them.

Shep's fame spread and people came from everywhere to see him. Many photographed the loyal sentry and tried to make friends in hopes of adopting him. But Shep would have no part of it. In the early years, Shep was aloof and stayed away from people. In fact, after checking the train, he often left quickly to get away from those who came to see him. Later, he became quite affectionate and often posed for photos with the many people who got off the train at Fort Benton just to see the famed, Shep.

Shep was not ungrateful for the love and attention he received and eventually learned to return it. But he was, at heart, a one-man dog. Food, shelter and, later, the love provided by the railroad employees and his many admirers sustained him as he waited for the return of his friend. He never gave up hoping and waiting for him.

Shep
Photo provided by the Overholser
Historical Research Center - Fort Benton, MT
www.fortbenton.com/museums/library.html

Shep was already an older dog when he came to the station house. The years and his vigil had taken their toll. Stiff-legged and hard of hearing, he failed to hear the old 235 as it rolled into the station at 10:17 one cold, winter morning. He turned to look when the engine was almost upon him, moved to get out of the way and slipped on the icy rails. The train hit and killed Shep ending his life and his long and faithful vigil.

Shep's funeral was held two days later. He was laid to rest on the bluff overlooking the station and a monument was built near his grave. It was a painted, cut-out of Shep with his name below it. No passenger trains pull into the station now but Shep still keeps his vigil atop the wind-swept bluff overlooking the abandoned depot.

On the fiftieth anniversary of Shep's death, the community of Fort Benton organized to produce a lasting memorial to their famous and beloved dog.

A beautiful site along the levee of the Missouri River was selected for the erection of a heroic-sized bronze sculpture by Bob Scriver. The site, known as Shepherd's Court, quickly became the town's focal point and still is. It is under the care of the River and Plains Society and the Overholser Historical Research Center of Fort Benton, who carefully preserve and protect their precious historical legacy of Shep. The statue of Shep is a fitting tribute to the bonds of friendship and a reminder of the beautiful story of *Shep, Forever Faithful*.

Queenie, the Dog Who Revealed the Magic

In 1936, Brooklyn, New York was home to an underemployed, handsome, young man who, *at first sight,* fell in love with a talented milliner with flowing red hair. They married and on his way home from work on an icy, winter evening, he came upon a thin, abandoned dog and her puppies. The dog was a Pekingese whose tattered coat was the same color as his wife's hair. He gathered the failing, hungry dog and her puppies in his enormous but gentle hands, put them in a carton he got from a nearby grocer and brought them home. The dog and all four puppies thrived on the nourishment, love and warmth lavished upon them by the couple. People around them said they treated the dog like a Queen and so they named her *Queenie*. Queenie's puppies were adopted by friends and Queenie continued to hold court with the couple.

A few years later, they had a child. When the woman went into labor and then to the hospital, Queenie refused to be left behind. During the twenty-seven hours of labor that produced a baby girl, Queenie waited on the entry stairs of the hospital and would not be budged. The expectant father frequently left the interior of the hospital to bring food and water to Queenie, reassure her, and take her for the short walks she went on quite reluctantly. She was safely tethered by her lead as she kept up her vigil, though the lead did not appear to be necessary as Queenie was *not* going anywhere.

After the birth of the baby who also shared the hair color of Queenie and her mother, Queenie agreed to go home with the father to await the later arrival of the baby and mother. Much to the dismay and disapproval of many, Queenie became the immediate crib-mate and constant companion of the baby.

I was that baby. Queenie was my first animal friend, canine sibling and first loss. Through her invisible web of wisdom and love, Queenie introduced and bound me forever to the *Magical Link* that constitutes the unbreakable and enduring bond between us and between others like us throughout the world.

Queenie and Her Family - Me 'n' Queenie, My Father and Maternal Grandmother

Photo provided Barbara Meyers

The Last Will and Testament of an Extremely Distinguished Dog © *Barbara Meyers 1996.*

I, Grand Duke of Old Mill Meyers, familiarly known as Duke, because of the burden of my illness, realize that the end of my life is near. And so, I hereby bury my last will and testament in the heart of my friend. She will not know it is there until some time after I have changed worlds. Then, remembering me in her sadness, she will know I have little in the way of material things to leave. Dogs are much wiser than men. We do not set great value on *things*. I have only my courage and love to bequeath.

What will become of me as I change worlds? Who knows? I like to believe I will be in a place where I will romp in fields with those who have gone before me; where every hour is mealtime and there are fireplaces with logs burning and I'll spend long evenings with the memory of her touch. This is much to expect but peace is certain.

One last request I make. I ask her to have another if she can. It would be a poor tribute to me not to have a dog. I've never had a narrow spirit and have always held that all dogs are good and more than just a few cats are too! I would suggest another German Shepherd but others could be suitable as well. To him I bequeath my collar, lead and my winter parka that was made for me by the tailor on the bay. I leave him my place in the car, that I loved so much, and wish for him long rides with open windows. A few last words of farewell, my dear friend - Whenever you think of me, say to yourself with sadness but also with happiness in your heart at the remembrance of my happy life with you, "He is the one who loved me and whom I loved." No matter how deep my sleep, I shall hear you and our bond will remain forever unbroken.

The Last Will and Testament of an Extremely Distinguished Cat © Barbara Meyers 1996.

I, Mr. Smith Meyers (familiarly known as Smitty) because of the burden of my illness, realize that the end of my life is near. And so I, hereby bury my last will and testament in the heart of my friend. She will not know it is there until some time after I have changed worlds. Then, remembering me in her sadness, she will know of this testament. I ask her, then, to inscribe it as a memorial to me.

I have little in the way of material things to leave. Cats are much wiser than men. We do not set great value upon *things*. I have only my love and magic to bequeath. These I leave to all those who have loved me, and especially to my friend, who I know will mourn me the most. Perhaps it is vain of me to boast when I am so near to the gate through which we must all one day pass but I have always been an extremely special and distinguished cat!

I ask my friend to remember me always but not to grieve for me longer than she really must. During my life, I have given her comfort in time of sorrow and reasons for added joy in her life. Not even in my death would I want to cause her pain though I know it will come to her. Let her remember that no cat was ever happier but I have grown ill and pained. It is time to say "good-bye." It will be a great sadness to leave her but not a sorrow to die. I accept this part of the journey as a natural part of life, not something alien and terrible that destroys life.

What will come to me after death? Who knows? I would like to think that I will be joined by companions I have known in life. I will romp about in mice-filled fields with those who have gone before me. Every hour is mealtime and there will always a little brook with fresh running water. I will spend long evenings in front of fireplaces with logs forever burning and curl up with memories of her touch and the old days. This is much to expect but peace is certain and a long rest for these weakened limbs will be welcome.

One last request I make. I ask her, for the love of me, to have another if she can. It would be a poor tribute to my memory not to have a cat in her life. I have never had a narrow spirit and always held that all cats (and some dogs, too,) are good. Some cats are better than others, of course, like me! And so I suggest another of similar background but others could be suitable, too. No cat can be as distinguished and handsome as I was but she must not ask the impossible. He will do his best and even his inevitable defects will help to keep my memory ever green. To him, I have left my green chaise lounge and my place in the garden window that I loved so much. I wish him long, sunny afternoons of snoozing and bird watching.

A few last words of farewell, dear heart - I have loved you completely and no matter how deep I sleep, I shall hear you. Always remember that Angels are not allowed to show their wings on earth but there is no rule against whiskers!

The Silver Chain

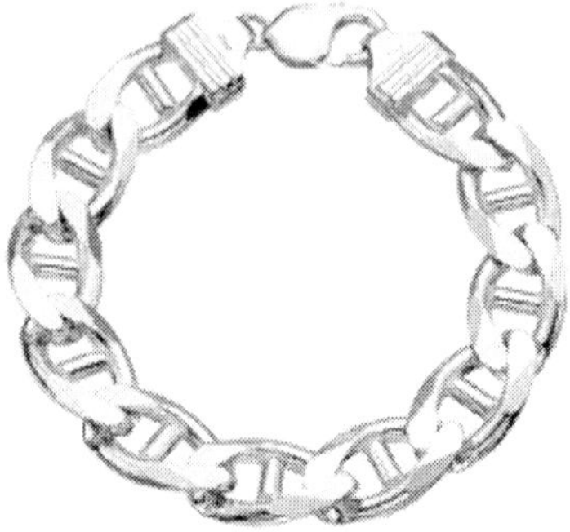

"Remembrance is the silver chain that death tries to break but all in vain. To love and then to part is the greatest sorrow of the heart. Time may fade many things but never the love and never the tender memories." *- By Barbara Meyers*

Stop all the clocks, cut off the telephone, prevent the dogs from barking. Make way for the mourners to come. Let airplanes circle moaning overhead and put crepe bows around the necks of doves. Let the traffic police wear black, cotton gloves. The stars are not wanted now; put out every one. Pack up the moon and dismantle the sun. Pour away the ocean and sweep up the woods. Let me be, at least for a while, inconsolable. *... Funeral Blues by W. H. Auden (1907-1973). - Adapted by Barbara Meyers*

For Jesse, Felis Sylvestris Angelica
A Terrible Thing

Jesse – *Photo by Barbara Meyers*

It's a terrible thing, this silken thread that binds paw to hand, whisker to whisper and heart to heart. It's a terrible thing, this unraveling of its fibers or the sudden severing of its silvery bond. It's a terrible thing, and more terrible still, would be never to have known it at all! - *by Barbara Meyers*

"Near this spot are deposited the remains of one who possessed beauty without vanity, strength without insolence, courage without ferocity and all the virtues of man without his vices. This praise, which would be unmeaning flattery if inscribed over human ashes, but is a just tribute to the memory of Boatswain, a dog who was born at Newfoundland, May, 1803, and died at Newstead Abbey on November 18th 1808."

- Inscription on the monument of Boatswain, Lord Byron's beloved, Newfoundland

"Death leaves a heartache no one can heal, love leaves a memory no one can steal."

-Inscribed on a headstone in Ireland - Anonymous

James Thurber (1894-1961,) American humorist and cartoonist best known for his work in The New Yorker magazine wrote:

"In his grief over the loss of a dog, a little boy stands for the first time on tiptoe, peering into the rueful morrow of manhood. After this most inconsolable of sorrows there is nothing life can do to him that he will not be somehow able to bear."

Make Your Own Tribute

Memorial DVDs can be made from still photos and enhanced with background music, scenery, captions, and special effects. Advanced technology and experts trained in it can be found in many areas. On Staten Island, Transfer City U.S.A. (www.transfercityusa.com) is one such expert facility. Owned and operated by the Plissner family, Transfer City will work together with you to transform what exists in still photos, old VHS tapes or film into a moving work of artistic visual and audio memory. Even some damaged photos can be restored to surprising high quality with many exceeding their original color or contrast. The entire process is overseen by CFEO - *Chief Feline Executive Officer*, Leroy.

Leroy, CFEO, Transfer City U.S.A.
Photo by Cindy Plissner

Bring Me

"Bring me the wounded warriors. They are the wisdom and courage of animal ancestors who hold the magic of centuries. Entwined into my very being, they are my only nobility."
...Barbara Meyers

It is my sincere hope that this book will make a difference for you. If it has, do not simply stop there. Raise your voice to make a difference for those who cannot speak for themselves. Advocate for all creatures great and small. Do not look the other way. Do not leave it to someone else. Practice random acts of kindness. Everyone can do something! It matters and it *will* make a difference. *You* will make a difference. What better can be said of someone than that they made a difference?

Hippocrates of Kos, the Greek father of western medicine, is best known for the oath attributed to him. There is some controversy around its origins but the central theme is clear and sound: *Primum Non Nocere* - First do no harm.

"*In the end, we will remember not the words of our enemies, but the silence of our friends.*"... Martin Luther King, Jr. (1929 – 1968).

If we allow these simple but profound concepts to guide us in all that we do, we will find our way to kindness. Great structures will be erected, technology and medicine will thrive. We will reach into the stratosphere but it will matter little without kindness. A future that does not fully embrace kindness will result in the nuclear winter of our very essence. The rest will stand as an empty monument to a morally corrupt and failed society.

First, do no harm.
Do not be silent. Above all, be kind.

"It is better to be kind than right."
... Barbara Meyers 2012.

~~~
~~~

Afterword

"A photograph taken today is a lifetime of yesterdays preserved in memory for all the tomorrows." ... Author unknown - Adapted by Barbara Meyers

Dear Readers,

As we come to the end of our journey together, I leave you with my thanks for spending time with me, and an *Afterword* about the photographs on both the front and back covers and the backstory on the inspiration for the back cover. They are, for now, the last of the *secrets* of *The Magical Link.*

The cover photos are not *stock* or random representational images of unknown animals. They are my own family. Each brought with them the *magic* of love and transformation. I knew them intimately and the photographs were taken by me. They were *linked* to create and give life to the cover art by Jessica Braun through her own special brand of *magic.* Those seen here are the originals. None were altered at the expense of authenticity.

Duke

Duke was the most dangerous dog I have ever known. He was one hundred thirty-five pounds of unyielding aggressive force. Found wandering and hungry, he was taken in by friends who, after a few days, found themselves immobilized around their kitchen table with Duke refusing to allow them to rise. Able to very slowly reach for a near-by telephone (no cell phones then), they called me for help but did *not* tell me what I would find upon arrival. In hindsight, this was a very serious error but, as it turned out, I came through unscathed. Quickly assessing the situation, I convinced Duke to come with me voluntarily.

Young, healthy, clearly of superior breeding, and with perfect confirmation and disease-free hips and elbows, I would not allow his life to end because of his behavior. At the time (1980), much less was known about medication to assist in the rehabilitation of aggressive dogs. I used all the then-known techniques of special canine education but refused to include harsh methods. It was evident that he had already been intentionally educated in that way and with disastrous results. It also explains why a dog of his quality was found roaming the street. His captors very likely found themselves the victims of their own corrupt and nefarious behavior and just turned him out into the street to fend for himself and be a danger to others. I was warned and aware that I, too, could become his victim. Even a properly muzzled aggressive dog has the ability to fracture a human skull with the force of his head striking against it. Despite and against all odds, I was determined to try to help him. I knew that the advanced state of his learned out-of-control aggression could not be *educated* out of him. I also believed that his behavior *could* be redirected to guarding and protection work but *only* on my word or hand signal. Further, he could, in time, also be a well-socialized and happy dog. And so it was!

In accordance with the law and also to protect us, because he met the criteria, Duke became both my beloved friend and an officially Registered Guard Dog. At no time we were together was he required to act in his official capacity. Perhaps I should not, but I must admit I took great amusement in watching people make way for us when we walked on a busy street together. Though no longer a threat to anyone, his very appearance was heart-stopping.

Magnificent in every way, my great tower of strength, friend, champion and protector was stricken by an especially aggressive cancer and *changed worlds* at only five years of age.

"Stole my heart and left too soon."

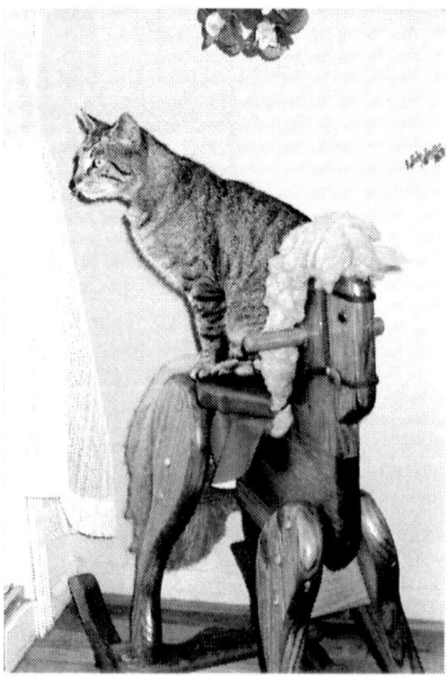

Smitty Bird-Watching From His Rocking Horse

Mr. Smith, affectionately known as *Smitty,* was the quintessential cat; the green-eyed, mackerel-striped tabby with the classic "M" on his forehead. His profile (on the front cover) was taken from a photo of him on his rocking horse. It was not just a fine place for bird-watching; he would engage the rocking feature by shifting his body back and forth while also remaining perfectly balanced. When the *rock* was sufficient, he would settle onto the saddle and enjoy the ride.

He also appears in close up in *The Last Will and Testament of an Extremely Distinguished Cat.*

Mr. Smith, like so many others before and after him, came to my garden as a seriously injured, starving young cat. Not far from death's door, I immediately transported him for veterinary care. He was FIV (Feline Immunodeficiency Virus) positive, had multiple, infected bite wounds (the primary mode of FIV transmission), and had sustained a fractured hip and tail with complicating osteomyelitis (infection and inflammation of the bone and surrounding tissue) in his lower back and tail. He was a tough little boy and, after hospitalization for three weeks and a great deal of home nursing care, made a complete recovery with no need for amputation of his tail.

Because of his FIV status, *Smitty* could not join the rest of the feline family but lived very comfortably and happily in my office and consulting room. It was apparent that he never had a home but was inexplicably an unusually friendly and gentle feral cat. Some have what I call (there is no scientific evidence to confirm it) *the friendly gene* and *Smitty* was one of them. In fact, it has been my great good fortune to know more than just a few feral cats with *the friendly gene.*

Smitty was great fun, very dear and sweet, and everyone loved him. At only two years of age, he died from unexpected consequences of a common, but necessary, surgery. Though in a specialty hospital with an experienced and competent surgeon and critical care team, he could not survive. Sudden death often, quite literally, arrives in a single heartbeat. It is the fault of no one, none of us are immune from it, and the pain is ineffable.

"Pain quiets and softens, but love does not."... Barbara Meyers

Rebecca Drinking From Birdbath

Rebecca came to my garden on a beautiful April evening. One glance told me that she was an exhausted, nursing mother who was also struggling with an upper respiratory infection. She was both hungry and thirsty but too tired to get to the pond so she drank from a bird bath. I quickly prepared a plate of grapes, little peanut butter sandwiches and cat food. With great caution, I brought it to her. Her weary luminous eyes met mine, her outstretched *hands* (paws) caressed mine as she gently took the plate from me, and a bond of trust and love was forged in that moment.

With delicate, nimble *hands* she slowly ate all that was on the plate. As I looked on with a strange amalgam of both elation and worry, I also watched her leave with slow but determined steps. Would she return? Where and how are her kits? What more can I do to help her if she *does* return?

Rebecca returned the next and *every* evening for about two weeks. During that time (after consulting with a colleague who was a licensed wildlife rehabilitator trained and authorized to handle raccoons,) I put antibiotics into her sandwiches and watched her grow strong, healthy, swift, and joyful. And then, on a very bright, moon-lit night, she brought five kits with her!

Two of Rebecca's Kit

Dressed in the classic black *mask* of all raccoons, they were the most adorable, curious, raucous little gang of lovable bandits. Rebecca was a loving and devoted mother who kept them in line but also allowed them to safely tumble from places they were not quite yet able to negotiate. When their antics went too far to be safe, she interceded. With all the strength I could muster, I neither encouraged nor permitted them to bond with me lest they think that people were safe or friendly – they arc not!

What was between me and Rebecca was something that happened deep in our core on that now so-long-ago night and would never be broken.

They came all that summer and were a complete delight. As autumn began to color the trees, I prepared myself for their departure believing that I would not see them again. This was based on several factors that included a very close approximation of when they were born and the general behavior patterns of raccoons.

To my surprise, they continued to come during winter, although a bit less often. Winter behavior begins with well-stocked dens and they spend most of their time there. Raccoons do *not* hibernate as bears do.

The following spring, the now adult kits brought their kits! ...and so it was for many generations. Some, but not all, returned on a regular basis but Rebecca was a constant presence. She lived to be about ten (above the average age for wild raccoons), and died peacefully of natural causes in the garden she loved. Her cremains are buried under a cedar tree I planted in her memory. She and her extended family are buried deep in my heart.

"You make a living by what you get.
You make a life by what you give."
... Winston Churchill (1874-1965)

Eastern Tiger Swallowtail
Drinking Nectar from Butterfly Bush

She did not have or need a name nor did I give her one. It seemed to me that to carry even the weight of a name might be too heavy for this delicate, gossamer-winged Eastern Tiger Swallowtail beauty. Summer brought many beautiful butterflies to my garden where they drank nectar from Butterfly Bush, Joe-Pye Weed, Milkweed and other native plants designed to attract butterflies.

In the summer of 2000, she was the first to come to the garden. I was tending to the pond when she flew in, circled about and went directly to the Butterfly Bush that, I later learned, she favored above the others. I went about my task while noting how very special she was. Eastern Tiger Swallowtail butterflies, especially to the untrained eye, can look much like others of their subfamily. The Eastern Tiger Swallowtails bear many unique shades of color and markings, and she had more than usual. As I pondered this, she lit upon my shoulder and stayed as I stood frozen in time. Initially, I was afraid to move and end what I was sure would be only a moment. Eventually, after far more than a moment, I could no longer hold the pose and decided that my extended treat was over and I would get on with the pond and other gardening. I did so and, still, she did not leave my shoulder.

Butterflies live for only one glorious season and she spent that season with daily visits to the garden, my shoulder, head, hands and once, the tip of my nose! On the last day of her life, she came but did not drink. She lit upon my shoulder as she did on that first day and so many days thereafter. She then went to the crest of my ear and I could feel her wing fluttering against my cheek. From there she made her way to my hands. Without plan or thought, I found my palms joined and open as though to fill them with water. Instead, she filled them with her delicate beauty and died there in her self-selected sanctuary of my grateful hands. I held her for a long time and then returned her to the warm earth beneath the Butterfly Bush. Though I did not know it at the time, she left my cheek with a powdery kiss of color from the bright yellow of her wing.

Butterflies, including many Eastern Tiger Swallowtails, have come since then. Each is a brief precious gift. They are not anonymous, they are not less valuable or beautiful but they are also *not* her.

"May the wings of the butterfly kiss the sun
And find your shoulder to light on,
To bring you luck, happiness and riches
Today, tomorrow and beyond."
.... An Irish Blessing

The Star Thrower (aka *The Starfish Story*) is part of a sixteen-page essay of the same name by Loren Eiseley (1907–1977). It was published in 1969 in *The Unexpected Universe*. *The Star Thrower* is also the title of a 1978 anthology of Eiseley's works (including the essay), which he completed shortly before his death. The original work is told in the voice of a narrator and is quite different in many other ways. There are hundreds of adaptations of Eiseley's beautiful work but, sadly, too few include the attribution he deserves. I would not allow *The Magical Link* to be among them.

The choice to have the back cover revisit the story and the entire theme of *making a difference* was inspired by a man who has made more of a difference for which he can ever be adequately thanked or acknowledged. Affectionately and deservedly, readers, please allow me to introduce you to *Stardoc,* John G. Hynes, DVM.

Stardoc, John G. Hynes

John Hynes has dedicated his life to throwing starfish, *starcats, stardogs* and *starspecies* of all kinds back into the sea of life and hope. As you read this, he may be in an examination or operating room in a local hospital or, with loving compassion, helping one of his patients to gracefully *change worlds* either in the hospital or in their own home. He may be also educating PATH (People Protecting Animals and their Habitats) volunteer veterinarians to serve in Central or South America on special spay/neuter and rabies vaccine programs and deliver other veterinary care to underserved areas. Finding or *making* time for everything in a balanced way, he may also be spending time with his canine family, Sophie and Tobias, and the people who mean the most to him. A public, practical and private voice for all animals, *Stardoc* is also a vegan who quietly lives his philosophy in every way.

"I am only one, but I am one.
I cannot do everything, but I can do something.
And I will not let what I cannot do interfere with what I can do."
... Edward Everett Hale (1822-1909).

~~~
~~~

Author's Annotation

The Last Will and Testament of an Extremely Distinguished Dog
and
The Last Will and Testament of an Extremely Distinguished Cat

In keeping with the highest standard of both personal and literary ethics, and in order to negate even the appearance of impropriety, plagiarism or failure to attribute, the author wishes to disclose and acknowledge the following with thanks to Carlotta, Eugene and Blemie O'Neill

The original work is that of Eugene O'Neill (1988-1953), American playwright and Nobel laureate in literature. *The Last Will and Testament of Silverdene Emblem O'Neill* was written on December 26th 1940. O'Neill wrote the moving elegy in memory of his Dalmatian, *Blemie* to comfort his wife Carlotta, who was devastated by Blemie's death on December 17th 1940. According to Carlotta's diaries, she loved Blemie at first sight while Eugene *liked* him.

Blemie is buried at Tao House in Danville, California, where the O'Neills lived from 1937 to 1944. The inscription on his tombstone is:

Blemie
Silverdene Emblem
Born Sept. 20, 1927 England
Died Dec. 17, 1940 Tao House
Sleep In Peace Faithful Friend

In March of 1986, the firm representing the estate of Eugene O'Neill, Cadwalader, Wickersham and Taft, LLT, NYC, confirmed both verbally and in a written document that the work was in public domain and Barbara Meyers was free to copyright her version of *The last Will and Testament of an Extremely Distinguished Dog*. In addition, she was also free to copyright *The Last Will and Testament of an Extremely Distinguished Cat,* and, for the life of the copyrights granted in 1986, all alterations of or additions to both or either are considered part of the granted copyrights.

Voices of Trust

When I first shared my intention to write The Magical Link, I received an unanticipated and humbling response from colleagues, clients and friends I had the privilege to work with over the years. The following letters and stories are from some of those who placed their trust in me. Also included are letters from Drs. Hynes and Sacerdote, who read the manuscript and wrote from that perspective.

John G. Hynes, DVM

Photo provided by John G. Hynes, DVM

It has been my privilege to review *The Magical Link* for veterinary medical accuracy and count Barbara as a respected colleague and valued friend.

The Magical Link will take you on a journey you will not soon forget. Humans have co-existed with animals since the beginning of civilization. It is only in the recent past that we have truly begun to understand the emotional lives of animals and the complex worlds and societies that each species calls its own.

From dogs and cats to dolphins, elephants, chimpanzees, horses and tigers; Barbara Meyers explores and gives us a fascinating perspective and unique understanding of these magnificent, often misunderstood creatures, and our relationships with them.

The Magical Link is awe-inspiring and guaranteed to change the lives of those who read it.

- *John G. Hynes, DVM*

Alan Sacerdote, M.D.

Photo provided by Woodhull Medical Center

This richly illustrated, highly readable work is both a remarkable reference and a guide for anyone whose sphere of concern includes the wonderful animal beings who are part of our families, our homes and our planet.

It is also a *must* for all health care professionals including physicians, nurses, veterinarians, psychiatrists, therapists of all kinds (psycho, physical, occupational, speech, etc.) and educators at every level of learning from K-12 to post-graduate degree levels. Not to be omitted are law enforcement, care givers of children and adults with special needs, funeral directors and anyone whose knowledge should be broadened so they become more enlightened and effective in their lives and work.

Meyers has written nothing less than a hymn to the cosmic gift that is truly *The Magical Link*. It is also *the missing link* in our society and this book has the power to change that, the lives of the people who read it and the animals and people they come into contact with.

Alan Sacerdote, MD, FACP, MABD - Chief of Endocrinology, Woodhull Medical and Mental Health Center, Clinical Professor of Medicine S.U.N.Y. Downstate Medical Center and N.Y.U. School of Medicine, Professor of Medicine, St. George's University School of Medicine.

Robin Dickson, President and CEO Dogs for the Deaf, Inc.

I first heard Barbara speak at an Assistance Dogs International conference over twenty years ago. She is truly a passionate and compelling speaker and writer whose mission is to assist people with the overwhelming grief associated with the loss of their beloved companion animals, and assistance or other working dogs. She understands the intense bond between people and their animals and the pain that is inevitable when the animals must leave us.

With an empathy and compassion rarely seen, she walks together with people on the uncharted roads of loss and grief, giving them the *roadmap* they need to make it through.

Robin Dickson with DFTD Demonstration Hearing Dog, Bonsai
Photo provided by Dogs for the Deaf

Barbara has served (*pro bono*) on the Advisory Board of Dogs for the Deaf as our grief therapist and crisis interventionist for many years. She has helped the entire program, our staff as well as untold numbers of our recipients through the very difficult times of anticipated loss, illness or injury and death of their Assistance Dogs. She also helps them to manage their disability again until they are ready for a new dog. Without exception, everyone has told us that Barbara was the only *sound* at the end of their dark and silent tunnel.

Mary Grace Tortora, Veterinary Hospital Administrator

My relationship with Barbara Meyers goes back to early in

my career and has continued over the last twenty years. Barbara has served as a behavior consultant and grief therapist. She has also helped my clients to manage chronic illness and better understand the medical as well as emotional aspects of it. She has, personally, rescued vast numbers of cats, kittens, dogs, and wildlife. She has been responsible for their veterinary bills and made them a part of her own animal family, found homes for them, or released wildlife back into their natural surroundings. If wildlife are permanently disabled but otherwise well, she places them in the permanent care of wildlife centers where they enjoy life-long care and protection while also serving as ambassadors for education.

Wild Peacock
Rescued by Barbara Meyers
Photo by Barbara Meyers

Her patience, insight, and knowledge has resulted in the rehabilitation of seemingly *impossibly* complicated and dangerous behavior problems being resolved in many homes and, thereby, truly saving lives and relationships between and among people and their companion animals. Whether it is related to aggression, anxiety, fear or abuse, she has solved them all.

Barbara has helped countless numbers of clients come to terms with their grief over the passing of a companion animal. She has also guided those who needed assistance in the process of deciding when the time is appropriate for home hospice care or a compassionate assisted end of life. But it does not stop there. She stays with people through the entire process of healing the painful loss, afterwards.

Her skills in creating hospice and comfort care are matched only by the unique way in which she weaves a plan that cares for the entire family. Without it being obvious, she is able to quietly lay the foundation for a future that will hold a place for another dog or cat when people are ready. Conversely, if circumstances are such that another companion is not to be in their future, she is easily able to help people gently close that door but not their hearts!

She has always been a leader in the community and no one will ever forget the time and expertise she gave as a volunteer crisis interventionist and grief therapist immediately after, and for many long months following, the September 11th attacks.

She served all individuals, families, groups or organizations as well as the K-9 search and rescue and cadaver teams' dogs and their handlers. These highly sensitive and specially trained dogs love their work and their only reward is a *find.* There were signs of a *find* everywhere at Ground Zero and, what was to become later known as *The Pile,* but there were few if any whole *finds*. The dogs would have, literally, worked themselves (and their handlers) to death had it not been for her intervention in identifying that, at some point, their attempts were not going to produce anything but damaging frustration, exhaustion and their own demise. I am very excited to see *The Magical Link* become a reality and have no doubt it will be a remarkable and inspiring read!

Gene Baur, President and Co-Founder, Farm Sanctuary

Gene and Ramsy
Photo provided by Farm Sanctuary

What began as the rescue of one animal, Hilda, a sheep who was left for dead in a Pennsylvania stockyard, helped fuel a movement and led to the creation of Farm Sanctuary...a place where animals who are raised for food are appreciated, often for the first time, as the emotional, intelligent individuals they are. *The Magical Link* extends this experience of discovery and compassion to companion animals and many more of the creatures with whom we share this planet. We are honored to be counted with Barbara Meyers as an advocate for so many who, while they have *voices*, have no *human-like* voice or vocabulary of their own.

-Gene Baur, President and Co-Founder, Farm Sanctuary, Watkins Glen, NY and Orland, CA and Los Angeles, CA

Dr. Ellen Cahn, Rego Park, NY

I have two senior cats with behavior problems and chronic illness. Barbara has helped me to navigate the rough and complicated waters of knowing when a specialist is needed, making the appropriate referrals to those specialists, learning to ask veterinarians the right questions and implementing their advice in ways that are custom designed for me and my cats.

Dr. Ellen Cahn
Photo provided by Dr. Ellen Cahn

She has a very creative approach that takes into account the needs of both cats and their human family. She has given me behavioral insights that have improved my relations with my cats and their interactions with each other. Her guidance in managing the emotional as well as the medical logistics of chronically ill cats has given me the ability to keep on track with their health care and not permit those needs to overwhelm or displace our bonds of love and joy.

On November 16th 2011, they celebrated their 15th birthday. This is a day that was not expected to be reached and, were it not for Barbara, it would not have been!

She *whispers* so well, she can even do it by phone! She deserves the moniker given to her by so many who call her, *The Cat Whisperer.*"

-Dr. Ellen Cahn – DHL (Doctor of Hebrew Literature) Rego Park, NY

Toula Buesking, Omaha, NE

My sister, Andi, and I have spent our lives in the company of dogs. In 1987 our Olde English Sheepdog, Misty Blue, was suffering from arthritis and other mobility problems.

I learned about Barbara Meyers through the many books we read seeking answers. In each one she had either written a chapter or was quoted and referred to as "renowned for her vast expertise in the fields of grief therapy, animal behavior, management of illness, use of Bach flower remedies for animals, and strong animal advocacy." We had good vets but they were not interested in or able to go beyond straight-out diagnosis and treatment. We all (Misty Blue, Andi and I) needed so much more. I called Barbara and life changed immediately.

What a gift that was! Not only did Barbara guide me to the best health solutions for Misty Blue, she has counseled me in the care of all our dogs with keen insight and wisdom every year since that first call. She gave me life-saving skills and techniques for my diabetic puppy, Mandy and directed me to the best treatment options for the challenges faced with my beloved Twinkle Star and Rufus.

Barbara's boundless generosity and open heart has enabled our professional relationship to blossom into a deep and abiding friendship, which continues to this day. She has always given selflessly of her time and expertise on behalf or our precious canine family and our own health and well-being.

There is a very special connection between us. She seems to be able to *read my mind and heart* and know exactly what I need even when I do not seem know it, myself.

Rufus
Photo by Toula Bueskina

Many years later when Rufus and Mandy died within seven months of each other, Barbara's warmth, understanding and compassion helped me cope with the pain, anguish and indescribable sadness that swept over me. The miles between us disappear because

Barbara's care and concern transcends distance. It is a great comfort knowing that she is just a phone call away. Her friendship has touched my heart and enriched my life in more ways than can be described. Andi and I feel truly blessed that Barbara has graced our lives. For her invaluable expertise, remarkable kindness and love, I am forever grateful.

-Toula Buesking, Master of Fine Arts *(MFA) Omaha, NE.*

Elke Gonzalez, San Antonio, TX

Clara and Elke Gonzalez
Photo provided by Elke Gonzalez

I have been deaf since childhood meningitis. My world was a lonely and frightening place for many years until I became the proud recipient of a hearing dog from Dogs for the Deaf in Oregon. Candy was an Australian Sheep Dog who became my best friend, my ears, my heart, and my life. The world opened for me and then, without warning, I saw my Candy killed before my eyes in a tragic accident that ended her life and mine, too. I was more alone than ever and alone with my grief, too. ...Until Barbara Meyers brought me back from the dead and helped me to recover so well that I was able to open my heart again to Clara; my gift of gold (she was a golden retriever) who was with me for many years. During that time, Barbara came to Texas to speak at a conference and we got to spend two days together – all three of us!

The years brought Clara to the natural end of her life and even though I was still heartbroken, I had Barbara at my side as though she were right here in Texas with me – that's what she can do ! Again, I recovered and still have my, now retired hearing dog, a Pug named Minor. All along the way, Barbara guided me in the care of my dogs and the rest of my life, too.

In the two decades that my life has been blessed with Barbara, my confidence has grown so much that Minor can enjoy a happy retirement and I can take care of him and two rescued cats, Sofie and Kali, just has he, Clara and Candy took care of me.

Yvonne McGrath. Staten Island, NY

Sid
Photo by Jim McGrath

I believe in angels. Every once in a while we are granted an opportunity to meet an angel who makes a difference in our lives. In 1999, my three-year- old bundle of black and white love, a cat named Sid, was so gravely ill that he was not expected to live. We were told we should take him home to die.

Sid was no ordinary cat. He had special qualities and we wanted him to go on living. He was diagnosed with FIP; a deadly a feline virus. Now he needed a miracle, and very quickly. By sheer luck I came across a flyer with Barbara Meyers' name on it. It listed her extensive credentials and expertise in animal behavior, grief therapy, hospice and palliative care, plus referrals. We called and she came to our home the next day. Barbara bonded with Sid and the family like glue on paper. Her skill, expertise, experience and loving care led to a miracle for Sid. She was, and still is, our angel who restored Sid's health so that he and the entire rest of the family are still enjoying each other. That was twelve years ago.

Paul Harvey was the radio commentator who was known for his closing line: "*And here's the rest of the story.*" So, here's the rest of the story: Barbara did not cure FIP. No one can do that. Her veterinary medical knowledge, experience and intuition were screaming, "misdiagnosis." She did not give us false hope but referred us to an expert for a second opinion. Sid did *not* have FIP. He had *exactly* what she suspected, was treated for it, recovered fully, and *that's the rest of the story!* Barbara Meyers definitely makes an impact on animals and their families. God bless her!

Nelly Badia, NYC NY

I first met Barbara at a lecture. When it was over, I spoke with her, personally. I described a urinary tract problem my cat, Aurora (my precious Aurora!) had been struggling with and it was not getting any better with the recommended treatment. Barbara explained the general workings of that part of the body and referred me to a specialist who resolved it all in short order. For the first time, I learned about the kind of *partnership* that people can have with their vets if only they knew about it and could arrange it. It was easy for me because Barbara made it all happen and she was in the partnership with us.

Aurora
Photo by Nelly Badia

Aurora lived a happy, healthy life for another ten years and when it was time, because of that partnership, we helped to close Aurora's life with love and dignity.

When it came to the final moment it was Barbara, who she knew and loved so much, who held her in her arms as she changed worlds. It was also Barbara who introduced me to that beautiful way to describe death...*change worlds*.

I will never forget how she handled all the final arrangements and brought with her, a beautiful casket that she prepared for Auora. The pain of losing Aurora was great but because of the quiet gifts Barbara brings along with her expert knowledge, I was able to grieve and celebrate her life at the same time.

I want to draw a heart as big as the world with 'Barbara' written in the center. The inscription would be: Barbara - Kindness, Generosity, Knowledge, Guidance, Support, Wisdom, Intelligence, Courage, and a Great Sense of Humor, too!

Judy Saltzman-Schwartz, Port Washington, NY

Duncan
Photo by Matt Schwartz

What was supposed to be one of the happiest times of our lives, gradually turned into a stressful and anxiety-ridden situation for me and my husband, Matt. I had it all: a new husband, a new house, twin babies on the way, and the dog I had waited for all my life. Duncan, our Black Lab, had always been affectionate and well behaved. He adored playing with other dogs and thrived on human interaction. Both my husband and I loved him deeply.

Late in my pregnancy when Duncan turned eighteen months old, he started showing obvious signs of aggression. The subtle signs were always there but until Barbara identified and explained them, I shrugged them off, attributed it to his youth, and convinced myself they were isolated incidents. It began with occasional guarding of food and toys, growling when he was tired, demanding attention in *pushy* ways, and it steadily worsened.

By the ninth month of pregnancy, I was resting a lot on the couch and Duncan would lie beside me on the floor. When anyone approached the area, he would jump up and give a warning bark and growl. We thought his protection was loving and endearing. Not so!

After the babies arrived, Duncan would growl at anyone who even moved in his general direction and, quickly thereafter, if anyone simply began to rise from their chair. He also growled at our dog-walker when he attempted to put on the leash or bent towards him to remove it. The last straw came when Duncan bit and injured two other dogs. One of the families reported us to animal control. Duncan now had a *criminal* record and we feared he would be confiscated and executed.

We were afraid to have visitors, nervous to walk around him, feared for the safety of our children, other dogs, and him too. We were told by many (professionals as well as others) to "get rid of him" and some even suggested we "just put him to sleep." Unthinkable!

Through a very lucky course of events, we found Barbara, our savior. The moment she entered our home, Duncan showed immediate respect for her. The more we mapped out a plan for Duncan and our family with Barbara, the higher my spirits and hopes rose. The program was tailored specifically for our family, our schedule and most importantly Duncan's well being. She designed a broad combination of therapies that included our own behavior modification and fun exercises that addressed his specific issues. She made it easy to fit my hectic schedule and the results have been dramatic and priceless. Duncan loved the exercises and his behavior improved rapidly. What I most appreciated, was that Barbara put Duncan's best interests first and treated him with dignity and respect. He was never thought of as "the bad guy."

Duncan is now a happy and healthy thirteen-year-old year old. Barbara literally saved his life and our relationship with him and each other. Our sons adore him and he worships them. Our entire family continues to live as one harmonious *pack*."

Dorothy Hurley, Staten Island, NY

I have known Barbara Meyers for over twelve years and always thought of how we first met as serendipity. My husband and I had just lost our beloved dog, Yeats. I felt as if all the color

Yeats

Photo by John Hurley

had gone out of my life. I was drowning in grief. I went to see a therapist who was recommended to me by a friend. This therapist was unselfish and smart enough to recognize that she was out of her depth in this area of special expertise and was not the therapist I should be seeing. She gave me an article about the loss of companion animals that had a quote in it from Barbara. It also had her contact information.

I will never forget the moment I called Barbara. I got her answering machine and when I tried to leave a message, I could barely speak because I was crying so hard. Barbara somehow deciphered the information and called me back in less than ten minutes. As soon as I heard her calm voice and reassuring words that told me we would get through this together and that she would be with me every step of the way, I knew I was going to be O.K.

She literally saved my life. She has a wisdom about her that gets to the heart of any matter in the kindest way. You just *know* that when you are with her, everything is going to be alright. I am so proud to call this remarkable woman my friend. Yes, we have truly become friends. This is something that breaks all the *rules* of traditional therapy and therapists. It takes a special kind of courage to be a wise and benevolent *rule-breaker* and know exactly if, when how and to do it. Barbara's got that kind of courage. She is simply the absolute best at what she does. There is no one better.

Miriam Harris-Kaplan, NYC

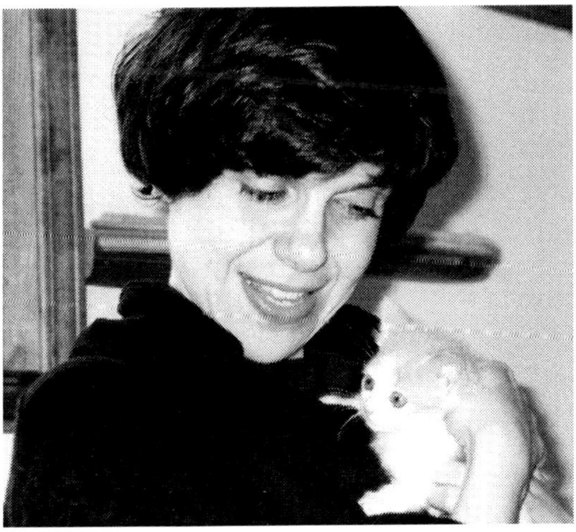

Miriam Visiting Barbara's Kitten, Emily

Photo by Barbara Meyers

In the 1980s, I was a newly minted massage therapist living with roommates. I was at a blessing of the animals and introduced to Barbara Meyers when her delightful toy poodle named Skila, came into my arms as though we were old friends. I suppose, in some way, we must have been because she *knew* that Barbara and I had to meet! Our connection was immediate; we enjoyed a day together and exchanged phone numbers.

A few years later, in 1992, I had my own apartment and was free to adopt the feline companions I was longing for. Enter Sid and Samantha. I wanted to adopt cats who were in their senior years as many people overlook them and they have less chance for happiness in their golden years. Samantha was a wise old soul and Sid was a *trickster*. I realized I needed help in learning to be a good cat mom and, thankfully, I found Barbara's card that I tucked away among my buried treasures.

With wisdom and gentleness she was there every step of the way, from finding the best cat litter to learning to medicate when needed. Only two years later, they died fifteen days apart. Barbara led me through the grief process with insights I had not seen in any other human being. I wept and I mourned. I asked the usual question: "When will I get over this?" Barbara said: "You *won't* get *over* it but you *will* get *though* it and I'll help you to do it. There will always be a hole in your heart but it can be filled with love and tender memories." And that is *exactly* how it was!

When I was ready, I adopted Rhiannon, a sweet little *pussywillow* (Barbara's description of her) and six weeks later, I adopted Teleia, another older cat who was being passed over in a shelter. Teleia moved in and *took over*. She was a bold, brassy, *diva-like* lady who stole everyone's heart except Rhiannon's.

Barbara helped us manage the *sibling rivalry* and acclimate my darling girls to live in peaceful coexistence.

In 1999, I was diagnosed with multiple sclerosis. Barbara was, and still is, a key player in managing my MS and not letting it get in the way of being the best cat mom I could be. Her medical background and skills in understanding both human and animal medicine as well as behavior in both species makes her the "go to" person for all manner of things. Over the years, there have been challenges and losses. I married and my girls introduced my husband to how amazing cats are. A few years later, Rhiannon and Teleia *changed worlds* and we grieved for them, together.

And then we met Nia. She was five at the time and is now eleven. She is a sweet, cuddly, orange tabby girl with special health care needs and a sensitive, shy personality. Barbara has taught me to manage all this with ease. When there was inappropriate litter box behavior, I immediately called her. In a flash, she knew this was not a behavior problem but the signal of illness. She got us to the *right* specialist and nipped a potentially fatal condition in the bud. I shudder to think that someone without Barbara to turn to might have labeled her an inconvenient bad cat and just dropped her off at the pound to be killed. It's done all the time!

We are blessed to have Barbara who knew exactly what was going on, which veterinary specialist to consult with and how to tailor and polish the doctor's advice to work well and easily for both of us. Barbara is well respected in the veterinary profession and really good vets always refer to and partner with her to deliver the best overall, truly coordinated and seamless care. It makes a big difference when done that way. Barbara, with her wisdom and gentleness, has helped me to be a good cat mom and, I dare say, a better person. Nia and I are so lucky have her in our lives. Barbara is *the real deal!*

Gail Murphy Sag Harbor, NY

While trying to console myself after the death of my dog, I found Barbara in one of the many books where she is listed as *the* resource of choice for loss and grief as well as animal behavior.

When I read her quoted philosophy on mourning and loss and saw she was from my home state. I searched for her on the internet and found her website. I spoke with her and within a few days, was on my way to Staten Island. I didn't know *exactly* what to expect but knew I was going to meet with the right person.

I was grief-stricken over the loss of my fourteen-year-old year old dog, Opie, who died on the morning of Christmas Eve in 2008. I was truly alone for the first time in my adult life and could not help agonizing about if I had done the *right thing* at the *right time* by helping him to die. My life was filled with second guessing and *what ifs*. In general, I was numb to life itself.

I recognized that I was mourning and depressed and needed to speak to someone who would not dismiss me (as so many already had) for caring so deeply. My intention was to meet with Barbara for the typical therapist's hour which, by the way, is *not* forty-five minutes with Barbara. It's a *real* sixty minute hour! In what felt like minutes, three hours passed. Barbara helped me gain more perspective on myself, animals, our connection with them, and their personal acts of living, loving and leaving us.

She gave me "tools," which is the very modest way she refers her amazing wisdom and uncommon empathy and compassion, with which to settle my thoughts about a loving and dignified euthanasia and its place for peace.

My chronic grieving extended back to 2005 and I also recounted to Barbara the violent death of my dog, Zephyr. While on a winter walk in a nature preserve on Long Island, he was lured into trap baited with a bucket of fish. The loud, gunshot-like sound of the trap echoed in the bucket while the trigger released the metal jaws around his skull and throat. He strangled to death while I helplessly struggled to save him.

The shock and disbelief of such a horrific and cruel device of torture was something I did not know about. It is hidden from most of us because the public is not aware of the extent to which they are used by trappers who want only the pelts of their victims.

It inspired me to embark on a battle with local and state legislators. Legal success did not bring Zephyr back or change the terrible way he died, but we certainly made a small difference for the safety of other animals and people. That incident changed my life forever.

Even with the success of *Zephyr's Law*, I remained in a place of frozen heart-break. Without Barbara, I would still be there. I have *her* to thank for helping me embrace the loss of my dear friends and to hold on to the memories that keep me strong and on the path to peace. I am a better person with more character for having been challenged with this tragedy and found my way out through Barbara.

I also felt that I could never have another animal in my home or life and did not know how I could live with that. She told me something that changed my life even further. She said, "I know you can't see it now but I promise that even if it's true, there are still ways to share your life with animals in a meaningful way. You can be a *happy* part of their lives and make a big difference by becoming skilled at canine education and helping dogs to be well behaved and well socialized members of their families. The dogs and people you teach to live in harmony will be dogs saved from pounds, shelters, execution, and *traps* of all kinds."

Today, I am accredited canine educator who is fulfilled by my work and the wonderful dogs and people who are part of my life. I have chosen not to have a dog of my own but only because I am away from home so much of the time.

Justin Braun, Putnam Valley NY

Barbara is one of the single most compassionate and kind people I have ever known. I credit her with saving the life of my beloved cat, Isabelle. Isabelle found me in 2003 when I was living in Williamsburg, Brooklyn. About the same time hurricane Isabelle blew through, a little white cat began frequenting my block. It was plain to see that she was homeless. I rescued her and made a place for her in my home and in my heart. I was told by my vet, a well thought-of doctor in Brooklyn, that Isabelle was FIV (Feline Immunodeficiency Virus) positive and she had a life expectancy of about five years. Quickly, Isabelle and I grew very close and she proved to be one of the great loves of my life. She was a constant light of companionship for me during some of my darkest moments as a bachelor, a law student, and a part-time musician/sound engineer. As a tough street cat, she took little guff, but she slept alongside me, came when I called her name, and provided affection on lonely days and moments of joy, the same.

Isabelle
Photo by Justin Braun

By 2010, I was married and my life was quite different, but Isabelle was still very much with me, despite my vet's original dire forecast. In February of that year, I grew concerned when she began vomiting, which prompted me to take her to the vet. Unrelated to the vomiting, an x-ray revealed a tumor in her chest. We were told that Isabelle had cancer and all we could do was *take her home to die* because there was no treatment and no hope of recovery. My worst fears for my beloved companion seemed to be coming true. Luckily, my wife and I had already been working closely with Barbara regarding some, now-solved, behavior problems with our two dogs. As soon as we told Barbara of Isabelle's impending death, she sprang into action. She felt that the diagnosis and recommendation to "do nothing," was highly questionable at best. She urged us, in the strongest possible way, to get a second opinion. Barbara arranged for Isabelle to be seen by renowned specialists and helped coordinate her care. A more detailed diagnosis and treatment approach was made. The tumor was fully operable and, with surgery, she was able to make a full recovery. Barbara remained involved during the entire process, explaining the procedures, consulting with Isabelle's specialists, helping us to make informed decisions, and keeping us "sane" throughout the ordeal. Needless to say, if we did not have Barbara in our lives, my wife and I would have accepted our original vet's recommendation and Isabelle's cancer, left untreated, would have surely spread throughout her body. I am so thankful we had Barbara in our corner!

Whether she is rescuing a mother and her kittens trapped under an overturned boat in a marina, finding solutions to behavior problems, assisting the grief-stricken in coping with devastating loss, or teaching, lecturing and writing, her desire to make the world a better, safer place for animals is matched only by her talent and ability to do exactly that. For three decades, she has saved thousands from unnecessary suffering. Isabelle is one of them. All I can say is thank you, Barbara, for insuring that Isabelle, who continues to thrive as of this writing, still shines her light in our lives.

Helen Sauter, Staten Island NY

Others will site her formal credentials, accomplishments and the many ways she has consistently given to her community and the world for decades. I will tell of her in a single word: Kindness. She lives, teaches and is kindness personified. Often quoted saying, "It's better to be kind than right," she is both! Though never outright militant, Barbara is a fierce advocate for a cruelty-free lifestyle and feral cats. She has rescued innumerable and inspired others to do the same. She is *The Cat Whisperer*, godmother, and "attorney" to all animals.

A

B

C

R

S

T

U

V

W

About The Author

Barbara Meyers is a Certified Grief Therapist, Human-Animal Bond Consultant, Animal Behaviorist, Certified Bach Flower Therapist, and Animal Advocate in private practice on Staten Island, New York. Among her numerous awards for excellence and contributions to her profession, she was nominated as "*The Most Inspirational Woman of 2012*."

She has been certified in Thanatology (the academic study and practical knowledge of dying, death, grief, and mourning) in association with her study with Dr. J. William Worden at the Harvard University Child Bereavement Study and is a Symposia Lecturer at New York-Presbyterian Medical Center (The University Hospitals of Columbia and Cornell) and Associate Faculty Member (on sabbatical) in Death Studies/Seminar on Death at Columbia University in New York City.

Her ethology (animal behavior) skills have been honed with the Center for Applied Animal Behavior in Berkeley, California and with Dr. Eric Klinghammer of Wolf Park, Indiana. Because of her exceptional skills in feline behavior, she has been given the moniker, *The Cat Whisperer.* Her *whispers,* however, are equally well heard by dogs and other animals.

Certified in the use of Bach and other Flower Essence therapy, she is considered an outstanding expert on the use of these remedies in animals and developed the first protocol for the use of the remedies in animals. She has special interest and expertise in pain recognition and management, hospice and close-of-life care for animals and support for their human families.

She is the author and or the subject of numerous articles in trade and professional publications, magazines, and newspapers. In addition to *The Magical Link: Love, Mystery and Other Secrets About the Bond Between People and Animals*, she has co-authored three books on the subject of animal-related loss and grief.

An active member of many professional and animal advocacy organizations, her appearances include but are not limited to: National Geographic, CBS Nightly News, The Society of Medical Jurisprudence, The Delta Society, The Human-Animal Bond Association of Canada, Humane Society of the United States, Association for Death Education and Counseling, New York State Association of Veterinary Technicians, Columbia-Presbyterian Medical Center Student Nurses, Lutheran Hospital Hospice, The American Holistic Veterinary Medical Association, Assistance Dogs International, Staten Island University Hospital South Beach Psychiatric Center, and Blue Heron Nature Center.

She is a past United States Representative to the East African Wildlife Society and has spent extended periods of time in *the bush* of Kenya and Tanzania. She has also participated in a Magellenic Penguin banding expedition in Punta Tombo, Chubut, Argentina for the University of Washington.

Following September 11th 2001, she volunteered for and carried out (on a pro bono basis) crisis intervention for New York's *Bravest* and *Finest* as well as for the entire community of Staten Island, Richmond County Ambulance Service, the Canine Search and Rescue, Recovery and Cadaver Dog Teams at

Ground Zero, the Home Port, and "The Pile" on Staten Island. She serves (pro bono) on the Advisory Boards of Dogs for the Deaf in Oregon, the Pennsylvania State Memorial Park and Cemetery in Pennsylvania, and the Council on Animal Assisted Therapy in New York City (1984 -1994).

She is an active member of The American Association of Human-Animal Bond Veterinarians, The Humane Society Veterinary Medical Association, The Society for Veterinary Medical Ethics, Vote Humane, People for the Ethical Treatment of Animals, Defenders of Wildlife, In Defense of Animals, Humane Society of the United States, The Farm Sanctuary, and The Animal Legal Defense Fund.

Barbara Meyers lives on Staten Island with her family of rescued, special-needs, fabulous felines.

The *other* side of her practice is: www.centerforlossandgrief.com